Ships Without A Shore

Ships Without ^A Shore

America's Undernurtured Children

Anne R. Pierce

Transaction Publishers
New Brunswick (U.S.A.) and London (U.K.)

First paperback edition 2009

Copyright © 2008 by Transaction Publishers, New Brunswick, New Jersey.

All rights reserved under International and Pan-American Copyright Conventions. No part of this book may be reproduced or transmitted in any form or by any means, electronic or mechanical, including photocopy, recording, or any information storage and retrieval system, without prior permission in writing from the publisher. All inquiries should be addressed to Transaction Publishers, Rutgers—The State University of New Jersey, 35 Berrue Circle, Piscataway, New Jersey 08854-8042. www.transactionpub.com

This book is printed on acid-free paper that meets the American National Standard for Permanence of Paper for Printed Library Materials.

Library of Congress Catalog Number: 2007043183
ISBN: 978-1-4128-0716-6 (cloth); 978-1-4128-1090-6 (paper)
Printed in the United States of America

Library of Congress Cataloging-in-Publication Data

Pierce, Anne R.
  Ships without a shore : America's undernurtured children / Anne R. Pierce.
    p. cm.
  Includes bibliographical references and index.
  ISBN 978-1-4128-0716-6
    1. Child rearing—United States. 2. Parent and child—United States.
      3. Child development—United States. I. Title.

HQ769.P575 2008
305.2310973—dc22   2007043183

Contents

Introduction

Growing up in America today is so different from growing up in America yesterday that children might as well be growing up on a different planet. From day care for babies, to the exhausting array of "activities" for children, to the expectation that teenagers "build resumes," to the storm of lurid and violent "shows" now deemed appropriate for the young, the landscape of childhood has changed as drastically and rapidly as the landscape of technology. As a new mother, I was astonished that childhood had been so thoroughly redefined, with so little opposition. Although I have an educational background in history, politics, and philosophy, motherhood provided me with a new kind of education, and what I learned unnerved me. The intimidating momentum of "progress" seemed to silence those *who wondered whether all this change was good.* This unsettling observation, which would not leave me alone, led to the writing of this book.

Current views regarding what is appropriate and beneficial for children have reinforced themselves at breakneck speed and with remarkably little resistance. Novel ideas have been embraced with little discussion and in the absence of a forthright consideration of just what human nature permits and what children, by nature, need. Indeed, modern childrearing practices materialized before their potential consequences were really thought about. The children among us who are overwhelmed by stress or plagued by emptiness, who are unable to concentrate or pay attention, who are obsessed with video games and media-induced trends, who lack a conscience and exude apathy, now give us much to think about. My sense of urgency regarding this subject stems from my apprehension that we are on a fast train to somewhere and that "somewhere" is not good. Could it be that America's thrust forward leaves children without a solid foundation upon which to grow?

Throughout most of history, the belief that human nature had certain impermeable characteristics reinforced the idea that we are all born with certain requirements. In this country, the Judeo-Christian ethic combined with the belief in individual responsibility and the oft-observed American desire to "do good," allowed us to accept the idea that children have fundamental needs, which their parents are required to meet: Children *needed* the reliable and continual presence of their parents. They *needed* moral guidance and age-appropriate limits. They *needed* adults who would nourish their intellect and protect their innocence. What was once considered necessary is today considered optional. The recent view of human nature as transient and malleable allows us to view as unessential to the child that which, in all probability, remains essential. Within a framework that sees traditions as choices to be embraced or abandoned at our discretion, and that sees self-fulfillment as a primary determinant in those choices, the fundamentals of the well-wrought childhood are easily forgotten.

We modern adults have latched onto opinions about childrearing that, although perhaps "advantageous" to ourselves, are potentially harmful to children. Steeped in an intellectual permissiveness, which allows us to believe something *is* true because our modern outlook tells us that it *should be*, we have convinced ourselves of these suppositions: that parental substitutes are as good as parents themselves at "caring for" children; that the concepts of nurture and of the maternal are archaic, sexist, even irrelevant; that boys and girls are (or should be) the same except for their bodily components; that young children can benefit as much from a situation where peers are the dominant influence as they could were that influence to stand in the form of a loving, involved adult; that children are "just fine" in single parent families, especially if that family is headed by a woman; that more lessons, sports, and structured "activities" are better than less and that the earlier children embark upon them the better; that it is more important to be a "critical thinker" than a seeker of goodness and truth; and, that identification with the cultural group and political cause are more important than the individual sense of right and wrong. In other words, worldliness is more important than believing in something, while innocence is less important than sophisticated attitudes and competitive skills.

Underlying all of these assumptions lays the belief that young children are resilient and capable of bouncing back from all sorts of stress. Unfortunately, stress is no longer a term that applies primarily to adults. Whether stress comes in the form of a strange care giver or an exhausting "activity," in the form of frightening themes on television, or in the form of "information" (given even to pre-kindergarten children) about the iniquities of the Western world and the need to "save the planet" from environmental doom, the belief is that children can take it. In this assumption, there is a de-valuing of the "child's view" of the world and a diminution of the protective role of parent toward child.

I have been disturbed by the impersonal, often institutional quality of childrearing and by the way in which "socialization" supplants the soaking up of love. Here, in this wealthy, privileged country, are children so over-scheduled that they hardly know what it is to daydream, so institutionalized that they rarely know the contentment of surrendering to the arms of someone they can depend upon absolutely—for whom nothing is more important than giving them the love they need. Here are children as hardened to the feelings of others as the adults in their lives have been to theirs. Here are children whose inarticulate and unfocused thinking and utterances reflect the inarticulate and unfocused manner in which they have been raised. *Love and stability* are the fundamentals of early childhood that institutions and activities cannot provide. They are the conditions that would enable our struggling children to "thrive."

Given that the nature versus nurture debate is once again raging in some parts of academia, some might question how I can argue simultaneously for more parental involvement (for nurture) and for less controlling behavior by parents (for allowing children's nature to unfold). For reasons that will become increasingly apparent, and that I will support throughout this book, the nature/nurture argument, insofar as it is supposed to lead to an either-or conclusion, should be over. Given the advances in brain research and in anthropological techniques, it is simply impossible to deny the influence of genetics and of natural foundations for behavior. Given the abundance of evidence, confirmed by recent research in psychology, psychiatry, neurobiology, and sociology, that parents and communities (especially parents) have *dramatic* effects upon the emotional and developmental outcomes of children, it is simply implausible to deny the influence of the environment. I agree wholeheartedly with Michael Rutter that "nature and nurture do not operate independently of each other" and that "the time has come for an explicit research focus on the forms of interplay between genes and the environment."[1] Our society has been hostage to the nature/nurture argument for too long. As Thomas Gamble and Edward Zigler observe, there is "captivating simplicity" in "the extremes of current developmental thought." Left "unexamined," they all too often lead to "premature conclusions about the likely effects of variations in the early caretaking environment."[2]

The "it's all nature" argument leads to the neglect of our children, to a laissez-faire approach to parenting and to the absurd idea that what parents do, or fail to do, doesn't matter. The "it's all nurture" argument leads to grand designs for social engineering, to the over-institutionalization of children, and to schemes for their programming. It leads to the idea that parents are inventors of children, that they can make children into what they would like them to be, if only they orchestrate the very structure and content of their existence. But our children are not us, nor are they our dreams for the future, nor should they be. Nature and nurture are combined threads in the child-parent relationship.

That emptiness which stems from an inadequate or results-driven "home-life" is reinforced by our collective failure to give our children moral standards to live up to and an American tradition to believe in. Relativism as a philosophy has permeated the nation's soul, leaving its indelible mark on the children we raise. If there really is no high or low, better or worse, beyond each person's definition of these things, if moral questions are not only indeterminate but also pointless, then there really is no such thing as virtue. If there is no virtue, nothing is corrupting. If nothing is corrupting, it follows that we no longer value a child's innocence.

The devaluing of innocence has taken its toll on our children and our society. It helps to explain our willingness to expose children to un-nurturing environments, depraved influences, education into cynicism, and adult stresses at such an early age. It, for example, explains our willingness to expose children to all the wrongs that can be found in the American tradition before we have given them a chance to understand or appreciate it. It explains why tiny toddlers trudge from soccer games, to math tutorials, to gymnastics classes. It permits a culture of teenage resume building that defines adolescence as the high-pressured means to the college end. It provides the excuse when six and seven year olds view PG-13 movies which, forty years ago, would have been "inappropriate" for adults.

When it comes to the subject of raising children, doubting the opinion of the times has meant being subjected to ridicule and branded a reactionary or, simply, being denied a public voice. For example, reports that day care is OK and that working full time does not adversely affect a young child have been loudly proclaimed in the media and in bold print. Reports that day care is not OK and that young children suffer without prevalent maternal care generally have been acknowledged only in brave little journals. This is so in spite of the conclusive evidence (almost all hidden from our view) that day care, especially full-time day care, is generally detrimental to children's emotional and intellectual growth and to their development of a conscience. The connection between the formation of a loving maternal bond and the development of a strong and moral sense of self is not just an abstract theory—it is a connection that is repeatedly confirmed and increasingly agreed upon by objective researchers. The dominant, popular, convenient view of childhood has provided the excuse for suppressing this knowledge and discouraging free expression.

In this free country of ours, I have seen parents and teachers afraid to speak their minds, reluctant even to think unfashionable thoughts. Suggestions that young children need more love and stability than modern society provides are too often made in seclusion, with a trusted friend who would not betray one's belief that nothing could be more important than raising a child well. For the past thirty years, interesting and well-adjusted women who have chosen to postpone or disrupt their careers for their babies have existed in the shadows of our bustling society. Certainly, they have not "appeared" in the media. Like the studies showing the damaging effects of modern choices upon modern children, these women have been invisible.

Recently, there have been isolated and cautious murmurs of dissent. Bright mothers who choose to be with their young children have started to come out of the woodwork. Some teachers are including in discussions of different "learning styles" discussions of differences between students who have received enough parental love and guidance, and students who have not. Those arguing for a reassessment of day care are, once in a while, found on the public platform. However, the timeless findings of D.W. Winnicott, Selma Fraiberg, John Bowlby and others that remind us that the mother has a uniquely essential effect upon the child's emerging sense of self and security are still largely absent from our discussions. Moreover, the media ignores or misinterprets the breaking research on brain growth, on hormonal responses, and on early childhood development—which tells us that young children reap much greater benefits on a one-to-one basis than in a group situation. The press and the "experts" selected by the press ignore those studies that come to the very simple conclusion that the mother-infant attachment and time spent with parents affect and alter a child's growth.

This partiality is troubling. We parents must ask if to be strong is to receive only the messages and information we supposedly *want* to hear; or is it, rather, to demand access to the truth and to insist upon thinking deeply about choices that affect those we love? *Do we want to be ingratiated or would we prefer to be informed?*

The choices we have made need to be examined with regard to their effect upon a child's inner being (call it what you will), with regard to their effect upon a child's actions toward other children, and with regard to their effect upon our country's future moral and social fabric. If large numbers of children are being negatively affected by our choices, then we had better do what we can to reverse the trend. We must take an honest look at the evidence on alcohol abuse, sexual debasement, and teenage pathologies and despair. We should consider the antisocial tendencies and learning problems that are more common and that teachers are seeing at a younger age. Reason, common sense, reputable research intelligently interpreted, and a concern for the good are the appropriate response to superficial and unfeeling interpretations of childhood.

Understanding and challenging the theories and agendas behind modern American childrearing trends is a pressing endeavor. In attempting to do this, I aim to give voice to the many intelligent and estimable educators, child-development experts, researchers, and social commentators who have been ignored because their message was hard to bear. Equally important, is attention to that inner tug of love and conscience that many of us have been programmed to ignore. My own inner tug tells me that the money and effort spent on social-political problems is for naught if children are neither well enough brought up nor well enough loved. For, if the heart and mind are not in good order, pleasant surroundings, well-meaning "professionals," and a political system full of "opportunities" are of limited use.

The literature on this subject is cross-disciplinary and knows no boundaries. The study of children and their parents and of children and the society in which they are raised is the study of the most fundamental and elemental relationships known to humankind. It is at once sociological, political-philosophical, anthropological, psychological, and biological. It draws upon research into hormones, the brain, and behavior, upon psychiatric evaluation and observation, upon scientific inquiry and educational practice, and upon religious/philosophical beliefs and family stories. I have tried, in evaluating the material, to use both common sense and standards of scholarship. In the first chapter, I draw upon those observations I made when my children were young as a bridge to a broader discussion. My focus is both on the societal changes that were altering childhood and motherhood and on the restrictions and parameters that were being placed on *discussions regarding* childhood and motherhood. In Chapter 2, I dig into the flood of research documenting the dangers and disadvantages of "deprivation" in infancy and the early years. The volume and breadth of the research on "insecure attachment" and on institutional rearing is so great that this chapter is filled from start to finish with references to research; I hope this will encourage societal acknowledgement of findings too conclusive to ignore. In Chapter 3, I look at the moral-philosophical underpinnings of current assumptions about the family and of social practices that reflect those assumptions. In Chapter 4, I explore recent educational priorities and the over-institutionalization and hyper-structuring of children and teenagers. Our busy lives allow too little time to question whether all this busyness is necessary and whether the content of our children's education is good.

This book, then, is for the children whom we have placed on the road of lost innocence, unrequited needs, and frantic lives. It is based upon my heartfelt sorrow and upon the research that confirmed my worst fears. It is the story of children so programmed that free play is foreign to them; of neighborhoods like ghost towns and day care centers like Orwellian schemes. It is the story of children in need of love when those who love them are elsewhere; of a baby whose cry is lost in the din of other cries, and so, ignored; of a toddler and a care giver whose every act reminds him that she prefers other children—her own. It is the story of a sensitive and contemplative girl whose capacity for thought dwindles because there is no time for introspection in her hectic life; of a bright and creative boy whose need for intellectual stimulation is filled within the restricted framework of "quality time," not on a continual basis, but in bursts and spurts. It is the story of a pre-teen who has been exposed to so much sexuality and violence on television that ugly thoughts race through his mind when he receives his first kiss; of children who need something to believe in but who are "informed" at a very early age that all virtues are merely opinions and that all things traditional are suspect.

Today, we see parents who have little idea of what really goes on in their children's days, who have entrusted the rearing of their children to near-strangers, and children too young to tell their parents when something dreadful or upsetting occurs. We see children for whom time is not something open ended and full of possibilities but rather something chopped up—into TV and computer time, "activities" time, athletic "training" and academic "enrichment" time, etc. Time, as life, is something to be coped with. We see children exposed to adult situations and ideas way before they are ready to be exposed to them. Modern American children are expected to adjust to as adults would and to understand as adults would the vicissitudes and tribulations of public as opposed to private life. For them, childhood is fast becoming a distant memory.

Notes

1.   Michael Rutter, "Nature-Nurture Integration: The Example of Antisocial Behavior," *American Psychologist* 52:4, 1997, 390.
2.   Thomas J. Gamble and Edward Zigler, "Effects of Infant Day Care: Another Look at the Evidence," American Journal of Orthopsychiatry 56:1, January, 1986, 28.

1

Liberation, Illusion, and the Pressure to Conform

"What do you make so fair and bright?"

I make the cloak of Sorrow:
O, lovely to see in all men's sight
Shall be the cloak of Sorrow
In all men's sight."

"What do you build with sails for flight?"

"I build a boat for Sorrow,
O, swift on the seas all day and night
Saileth the rover Sorrow,
All day and night."

"What do you weave with wool so white?"

"I weave the shoes of Sorrow,
Soundless shall be the footfall light
In all men's ears of Sorrow,
Sudden and light." —W.B. Yeats

We modern Americans tend, at times, to doubt the obvious and believe the absurd. Our recent opinions about early childhood are indicative of this tendency. We doubt that a young child is better off brought up by loving parents than by hired help. We doubt that a baby will reap greater benefits on a one-to-one basis than in a loud, turbulent group situation. Postulating that the sexes are the same except for their physical make-up and "social conditioning," we assert that children can do without one of their parents. (Being so alike, they are interchangeable.) This supposition allows us to deny the very existence of maternal feelings and of a child's need for maternal nurturing; we doubt that the mother has a uniquely essential effect upon the child. We dismiss the idea that children learn to be dependable by being able to depend upon someone, kind by being

1

treated kindly, loving by being with those who love them. We forget that babies need a reliable and secure base if they are to dare to be explorers. We refuse to believe that the fear, anxiety, and anger babies display when separated from loved ones is something natural, instinctual, and indicative of real needs. We achieve this feat of recreating human nature by embracing popular theories and giving in to popular images.

Children, on the other hand, intuitively rely upon the obvious and are suspicious of the absurd. Young boys and girls know they need their mommies and see them as irreplaceable; they feel that the family would be incomplete without Daddy; they believe boys and girls, daddies and mommies, are different no matter how often they are informed otherwise; they sense that their world would fall apart if they did not receive enough love; they believe in right and wrong, long for moral information and age-appropriate limits, and rely upon their parents to do what is right.

It is unlikely that children's developmental needs should miraculously and conveniently change just when adult career patterns and life styles required them to change. It is more likely that the watershed change in how we think about child development came about, not because the "baby boom" generation had better insights into children than all the preceding ones, but because the old ideas would have interfered with our objectives.

We need a better understanding of the presuppositions that influence us as we influence our children. We must ask whether any of these suppositions are false or harmful. Unearthing the problems simmering beneath the attractive bustle of modern American life need not mean returning to our old ways nor discarding women's advances. It *will* make our decisions more complicated because those decisions will be better informed. It will give our forward moving lives a truthful as opposed to illusory foundation. Knowing not just where we are going but why we are going there is ever more essential when we are advancing so quickly and when the pace of our lives leaves so little time for reflection.

Reflection and adequate information will make our choices about whether and how much to work when our children are very young more meaningful, regardless of the choices we make. (I am speaking here of those women who have the choice, not of those who are hard pressed financially.) The choice itself was hard fought for and rightfully won. There were reasons for the women's liberation movement; had there been equal opportunity and equal pay in the workforce and adequate outlets for creative and intellectual expression in private life, the movement would not have occurred in the first place. The choice is one more link in the chain of freedom, a logical result of the belief that we are all endowed with the "inalienable" right to life, liberty, and the pursuit of happiness. It is that very freedom, that confronted me and other mothers as both an opportunity and a dilemma, that calls for us to pause. For, choices are not really choices if they are instinctual and automatic rather than thoughtful and informed. Francine du Plessix Gray refers to "the irony and the anxiety of true freedom." [1] Our freedom allows us to improve our lot and our children's; it also allows us to make egregious mistakes. Women's freedom is essential to the human condition, but the quality of that freedom depends upon the free exchange of ideas and upon facing the realities surrounding us.

Lest some argue that this caveat is unliberated, I would point out that it is precisely an opposing idea, recently resurgent among some brain and behavioral researchers, that because women and men are biologically *programmed* by evolutionary forces, they cannot escape the unreflective *instinct* of biology. While this point was used in the past to argue that women "belonged" in the kitchen, it is currently being used by Steven Pinker, Judith Rich Harris, and others to argue that what parents do does not much matter.[2] We and our children, the argument goes, are our genes—an evolved *product* of nature. In response, I would refer (in an admittedly simplistic way) to free will, to that part of all of us that transcends mere impulse to strive for more, that comes up with an original idea, that overcomes seemingly insurmountable obstacles, that defies popular thinking. Moreover, the evidence is overwhelming that we are influenced by our environment and *can influence it*. From the effects on children of abuse, to the effects on children of neglect, to the effects on children of loss, to the effects on children of an inspiring teacher, or of a loving or a cruel parent, this should be simply obvious. The research on parental influence is too dominant to deny. As David L. Olds of the University of Colorado, Lois Sadler of Yale University, and Harriet Kitzman of the University of Rochester put it in a joint article:

> In hundreds of studies, there is overwhelming consistency in the relationship between features of early parental care and child intellectual, behavioral, and emotional outcomes. (see, for example, Bornstein, 1995[3]) Sensitive, responsive care in the early months of the child's life is especially important. When parents tune into their infants' communicative signals, interpret them accurately, and respond in ways that meet their infants' needs, children are more likely to respond in synchronous ways, display signs of secure infant attachment, and exhibit better behavioral and emotional adjustment later in life. [4]

As we shall see, diverse areas of research in the sciences and social sciences have come to the same conclusion.

This is not to say that we should ignore biology or nature. For, the evidence is also overwhelming that we are influenced by our genetic, biological make-up—by nature. Advances in neuroscience and brain imaging, studies of the animal kingdom and the Human Genome Project make this, too, simply impossible to deny. We will see that included in those findings is the universal emotional and physiological basis of the mother-child bond. To declare that women's maternal inclinations and children's natural longing for maternal love are forbidden subjects is to step away from freedom of inquiry, not toward it. It is ironic that no sooner did we have a choice regarding children and home and the relative emphasis we would place upon them, then there was a pervasive effort to make it appear that there was only *one* choice for self-respecting, respectable women: to move back into the workforce (full time) as soon as possible after our babies were born. Anyone who doubts that this is true did not give birth in the 1980s or 1990s.

Like no generation before, we parents of the baby boom generation and of following generations have been "liberated" from the past. Unfettered by traditional ideas, we have marched steadily forward to the drumbeat of progress. We have viewed the upending of tradition as inevitable, given. Our assumption that the progressive path is the only way to a desirable future has allowed us to ignore the dramatic consequences of our new modes and orders for our children. If the path we have chosen is simply the only forward-reaching path, and if we assume that it is good to reach forward, what use is there in examining the relationship of means to ends? If our trend is inexorable, why provide cause for doubt? Why, indeed, analyze the consequences of our decisions if the decisions are desirable and if the philosophy of our age submits the satisfaction of desires as its closest approximation to the idea of "the good" (all other attempts to define goodness being too "judgmental")?

We come to understand that our liberation should not be examined, except insofar as that examination furthers that end. Such a process of liberation, however, means servitude to the status quo. *For, if liberation from the past means the inability to question the present, it means the decline of the thinking individual. It portends the deliberate suppression of one's better knowledge, one's heartfelt instincts, and one's moral sense for the sake of a higher social order. It can mean that collectivist experiments in social engineering, rather than being seen as just that, experiments, are seen instead as goals.* The experimental is then not permitted to manifest undesirable outcomes. It becomes the role of the progressive media to reinforce the illusion that the experimental approach to childrearing is tried and proven.

Thus, we are provided with an arrogance and permitted to assume that all of millennia was wrong and we are right. We are unable to learn from the past because we have dismissed it as irrelevant. Things in almost all other places and times thought to be extreme—we accept as the norm. Things in all almost all other places and times thought to be normal—we believe to be extreme. Through this inversion of extremes, we come to believe that a mother is extreme if she dedicates herself to raising her children when they are young, that it is "normal" for children to grow up without a father, and that babies are just fine spending their entire day in group situations with professionals who do not love them. Anyone insisting that children need more than one parent, more nurturing, more consistent guidance, and more love than a professional can give is reactionary.

Through the zealous support of the media for this point of view and its barely concealed contempt for those who find difficulties with it, we have received the message that we are not to think too deeply about these things. Lest we give in to nasty little suspicions and doubts regarding the relative well-being of young children brought up under the guise of parental love and those brought up under the guise of paid employees, statisticians painting a rosy, antiseptic picture, and celebrities giving a simplistic, harmonious portrayal of modern families are there to assuage our fears. In the glossy magazine articles and on the bright television screen we are fed a steady diet of easy images which help us to control those emotions and those thoughts which will not be quiet—which cause us to sense that, when mother and child lead predominantly separate lives or when father is absent, life simply refuses to feel harmonious, one's mind refusing to recognize such a life as "balanced."

Two respected psychologists whom I interviewed reported that a sizeable percentage of the women who came to them were seeking help in taming the deep emotions that childbirth had unleashed. They wanted to rid themselves of the "repressive guilt" they felt in dropping their babies off at the day care center and heading to work. Said one, "They have been made to feel guilty about their guilt. They have been told they shouldn't have it." Dr. Jack Westman, professor of psychiatry at the University of Wisconsin Medical School, reported that clinicians are seeing some parents who place their children in day care because of peer pressure.[5] Robert Rector of the Heritage Foundation reported that mothers frequently complain to him of the "intense pressure" that results from the "devaluation" of mothering. These mothers feel that they are under a "cultural assault" which tells them that childrearing is menial and demeaning whereas their experience is that it is worthwhile and essential.[6] In *Children First,* Penelope Leach describes the situation well:

> Every mother wants her baby to have the best and will deprive herself to buy it, but she dare not *give* him herself, the freebie that is best of all, because she fears that she might then be tied to the infant, by his needs and her own feelings, more closely and for longer than she can manage or society will permit. . . . Society suggests that mothers withhold themselves, stay separate, stay in control. Those social attitudes and recommended practices commit many parents to postpartum weeks of unnecessary stress and exhaustion, depression and despair. [7]

Adds Leach, "People are expected to feel strongly about their children, but not to act upon those feelings. Everybody sympathizes with the pain mothers suffer (only mothers; fathers are seldom mentioned) when they leave their babies to return to work, but there is little sympathy for those who avoid that pain by staying close."[8]

The media creates a smooth surface for us, a false harmony, and thereby makes us feel inadequate when our emotions refuse to cooperate with modern ideals. There is the image and there is the reality and we have been under tremendous pressure to make the one conform to the other. There is no doubt that the pressure to conform has been enormous.

Long before most women worked, the non-working mother ceased to exist on TV. In her place were sexy, attractive women with gorgeous figures, designer suits, low cut but tasteful silk blouses, a detached attitude, a passion for work and for getting ahead, and a disarmingly confident view of themselves. Men were shown to admire these women's confidence, to lust for their affections. Life was glamorous and adventurous, and the stuff of life definitely did not exist at home. An American Jewish Committee study documented the trend in 1983. In the AJC's study of twenty-seven situation comedies, the researchers were "startled" to find the "virtual inexistence of the traditional two-parent family" in which one spouse stayed home with the children. Since then, the trend has accelerated, it being impossible to find on television a parent who stays willingly home with his or her young children, and nearly impossible to find a two-parent family.

Insofar as the stay-at-home mom has existed on the screen or in print, it has usually been within the context of a clear didactic message: Staying at home leaves a woman undeveloped, enervated, dissatisfied, and depressed; in short, she is a complaining drudge whose only hope for happiness lies in getting a job and earning a good income. Long before most women worked, innumerable movies such as "It's My Turn" and "Kramer vs. Kramer" bore precisely this message. The happy ending, if there was one, depended upon the woman's freedom from children and home.

"Stay-at-home moms" have existed in one entertainment area: the talk-show, wherein pseudo-psychiatrists and "experts" have helped women overcome their "dependency" upon men and encouraged them to "take care of themselves," thereby moving them swiftly and efficiently into the workplace. Sacrificing for their children, they have been told, is the road to poor "self-esteem" and precludes any meaningful fulfillment. Feelings that going to work is itself a sacrifice when one loves one's baby so much that one thrills in the sight of them and cares about them so that entrusting their upbringing to others brings fearful reflexes of doubt, have only been addressed insofar as they have been assuaged.

TV executives were quick to recognize the ratings potential of the liberated woman. Office politics were potentially hot and steamy, and office women were easier to dress in alluring attire than women at home. In addition, companies buying advertising in magazines and television foresaw the earnings opportunities created by the two-income household. With women possessing tremendously increased spending power, the profit potential for consumer and fashion industries was enormous. Thus, the sexy career women on the screen and in the pages bolstered the earnings of the corporate sponsors by inspiring women to buy the accouterments of success so dazzlingly displayed therein. In other words, the products and the kind of woman who would buy the products were "sold" at the same time. In his advertising text entitled *The Responsive Chord*, Tony Schwartz coaches, "The critical task is to design our package of stimuli so that it resonates with information already stored within an individual and thereby induces the desired learning or behavioral effects." [9]

Only those lucky enough to have the combination of brains, sex-appeal, and a free conscience regarding their children which allowed them to focus on men and business adventures were set up as role models. Take a telling moment on "Dallas" when Pam discussed the possibility of a career with Bobby and Bobby told Pam, his sexy wife, that he wanted a wife with a career. Their preschool age child was never mentioned in this exchange. What we took away from this was that Pam would be more appealing to Bobby if she worked and that being appealing was paramount. We also received the message that Pam and Bobby's child was irrelevant to the discussion.

In television, the experiencing of life means the experiencing of the big drama. Indeed, family is seen as a closedness to experience, the nurturing role within the family as the most confining of all. What is important is the thrill of the moment: the passionate kiss, the big promotion, and the defeat of the bad guy whether through courtroom, boardroom, or bedroom tactics. The little things in life and the quiet moments of life are demoted. After all, how exciting is it to "watch" a woman and her daughter walking hand in hand through a garden, stopping to admire a flower? How interesting, to the television viewer, is a child cuddled up with a blanket, reading *Humpty Dumpty*? How long would we "tune in" to a show depicting a father helping his son dig a hole in the dirt or children sitting under a tree daydreaming? How long will a camera linger on the soft caress of a mother's hands along her child's neck and shoulders? These moments, of course, are not meant for "viewing" and certainly would do nothing for "ratings." They are private, personal experiences, which bear little relationship to the kinds of "experiences" of TV characters and movie stars. That is precisely the point. Some of the best things in life are not meant for viewing and would be diminished if they were viewed. The media, therefore, trivialize and omit those parts of life which are not dramatic enough for the "viewer."

Even "wholesome, family-oriented shows" have lured us into buying easy images. Take, for example, "The Cosby Show," which smoothed over the rough edges of modern life. Two parents with demanding jobs, one a doctor, the other a lawyer, faced the task of bringing up five children from preschool to college age. Miraculously, their lack of time never presented a problem. The Huxtables apparently lacked a housekeeper, a laundress, a chauffeur, or a cook. Logically, then, their evening and weekend hours would not only have been divided between children but also devoted to preparing dinner for seven, washing laundry for seven, grocery shopping for seven, scheduling play dates and arranging for back-up after-school care for the young ones, helping with homework, driving children to activities and sports events, and, in general, preparing for the next school day. In the face of what likely would have been a quite frantic family life in which the parents had little time for each other and almost no time for one-on-one interaction with the children, the parents and children were well-adjusted and calm.

The issues that all families face when they choose to become a family of two full-time working parents simply never arose. The children never longed for more time with their parents and the parents never longed for more time with their children. Missing in this family portrait was the sign of any toll taken on parents or children as a result of time spent apart. What we had was a sauntering pleasantness that didn't make sense given the circumstances. Why didn't the parents, exhausted from days at the office and desirous of making up for lost time with their children, resort to microwave dinners? If the children had school assignments, social arrangements, and/or extra-curricular activities, how did they have so much evening time to interact with parents? How did the evening allow for so much relaxed conversation? Why didn't the parents, during their bedtime conversations with each other, ever worry that the demands of each day did not allow for the "quality time" they had been led to believe in? The answer, of course, is that television was facilitating our entrance into a new age wherein every parent could be guilt-free. The uncomplicated existence of families such as the Huxtables served the idea that parents' long hours away from children did not affect the child nor create anxiety in the parents.

At least "The Cosby Show" did treat children as if children matter. By the time of "The Cosby Show," most television shows were treating children *as incidental to more exciting or important happenings.* In "Married with Children," for example, jokes about all varieties of sex were the continual focus. Subjects included prostitution, group sex, porn magazines, and even blow-up sex dolls. In the TV series, "Heartbeat," "Marilyn" was revealed to us as a warm and humorous person and a skilled and admirable professional. In the final episode, she and her daughter came together for the daughter's wedding after a nine-year estrangement. The implicit message was that Marilyn's liberation from tradition was *more* important than her relationship with her daughter. In a typical episode of "Once and Again," Lily and her boyfriend Rick (to whom she had been unfaithful by having sex with her ex-husband) complained in front of the children that children pose a problem when it comes to illicit lovers being able to enjoy sex.

Since the 1980s, when television *has* focused upon children, it has more often than not *used* them as conduits for sensationalism. With "shock-value" becoming an ever more difficult thing for TV producers to achieve, horrible things done to and done by children sometimes fit the bill. Typical horror movies shown on TV, *Nightmare on Elm Street* and *Friday the 13th*, depict "Freddie" and "Jason" assaulting young victims in grotesque and sadistic ways. Innumerable "crime dramas" portray in graphic detail the sexual and physical abuse of children. Attractive adolescent girls that have turned to prostitution are a favorite crime drama sensation. "Law & Order Special Victims Unit" series included plots such as: a female drugging her own underage sister to be raped by herself and boyfriend while they videotaped the event; a teenaged boy who takes erotic pictures of himself, posting them for money on his own internet site; a wife who lures virgin girls into a trap to be raped by her husband. CSI and Bones frequently rely upon the theme of "young victims" of sexual and violent crime.

"News" programs sensationalize children as well. Most of us have come across one investigative show or another on internet-related pedophilia, and have recoiled at the realization that, in "exposing" predators, the show also "exposes" (often visually and provocatively) too much of the children. In a formal complaint to the Canadian Broadcast Council, a woman decried the teaser used for a January 15, 1999, BCTV, 6 P.M. newscast story regarding the British Columbia court decision that declared child pornography legal.[10] The teaser showed a young girl in fishnet stockings, a young girl showing her underwear, and the bare legs of another young girl in a ballerina pose. Such teasers are common in both "hard" and "soft" news. It is telling that the victims of child abduction or abuse that the news focuses on are usually pretty or handsome.

Certainly, television uses adult liberation as the excuse to disregard the innocence of the young and adolescent viewer. (See Chapter 4 for a detailed discussion of media influence and media worship.) An October, 1997 study of six (primetime) tabloid news programs, such as "Inside Edition" and "Hard Copy," found that stories about crime, sex, drugs, and alcohol drive the shows—especially crime and sex.[11] Consider also the American Family Association's 1999 descriptions of "typical" episodes of these popular shows:

> On Melrose Place, "Amanda has sex with Craig because she found her husband Peter kissing Taylor (Kyle's wife.) Michael doesn't believe Megan (his wife) when she insists her arrest for prostitution was set-up. (She used to be a hooker.) On "Friends," "As usual, this episode focuses on illicit sex, including jokes about promiscuity and masturbation. Joey has casual sex with Kate, his co-star in a stage play, and he's surprised when Kate doesn't plan to break up with her regular lover." On "Relativity," the stories of three sisters and their sex lives "continues." "Isabelle has left her live-in lover Leo, Jennifer is crushed when her married college prof says he has to end their sex trysts. And Karen leaves her husband because he's a hindrance to her affair with Doug."[12]

Note that this is "popular" culture and that it is popular with children. When my children were in elementary school, fourth and fifth grade teachers informed me that their students' "favorite shows" were "Relativity" and "Friends." As my children moved into middle and high school, teachers reported that girls favored "Sex in the City," the archetypal show of "modern culture," that glorifies the one-night stand and apotheosizes women who place sex and self above loving relationships and genuine caring.

Of further note is that the entertainment industry *wants* such shows to be popular with children. In the large scale National Television Violence Study released in 1997, violence was found to be substantially more prevalent in children's programming than in other types of programming (Kaiser).[13] A 2000 Federal Trade Commission report found that, in all three segments of the entertainment industry, profit and opportunism determine how and to whom to market their ware. FTC Chairman Robert Pitofsky reported, "Companies in the entertainment industry routinely undercut their own rating restrictions by target marketing violent films, records, and video games to young audiences."[14] Even shows targeted to preschoolers are *intentionally* laced with violence and sexual innuendo.

Television, the computer, the news, and entertainment industries, and all our forms of instant "communication" project and promote the quick, stimulating image. The images are a mile a minute—sensational, designed to trigger sensory impulses, and hyperactive. As John Thornton Caldwell points out, starting in the 1980s, "television moved from a framework that approached broadcasting primarily as a word-based rhetoric and transmission, with all the issues that such terms suggest, to a visually based mythology, framework and aesthetic based on an extreme self-consciousness of style"[15] Many shows made their presentational demeanor "excessive" while advertising "packed into tiny temporal slugs of thirty and sixty seconds" exploited "the discursive and emotive power of hyperactive and excessive visual style." Viewers were flooded with edgy, fast-paced shows sporting anti-characters with anti-morals—whose hip urban look and self-centered priorities were echoed and reinforced in commercials.[16]

The "liberation" of women from the maternal and of families from traditional morality was tailor-made for the increasingly intense ratings drives of the major networks and the increasingly sensational, drama-seeking format of popular shows, movies, and magazines. Affairs and liaisons were in. Courtroom drama was in. Rocking in a rocking chair was out. Righteous indignation, studied sexiness, and an "attitude" combined with an irresistible, powerful "look" was in; complexity, reticence, and introspection were out. Sexual prowess was in; subtlety was out. Definition was the name of the game. And the question facing most women was, How are you defined? We received the message that women who nurture their young children lose the opportunity to define themselves; that intelligence, strength, and style are incompatible with involved motherhood.

It *is* true that mothers must "look out for themselves" if they are to avoid the gradual sapping away of energy and strength, which can come from being too exclusively focused upon the needs and the advancement of others. (Books such as *The Courage to be Yourself* and *In the Meantime* are reminders of this.) It is also true that older children miss opportunities for creativity and self-reliance if parents focus disproportionately on *their children's* accomplishments. (See Chapter 4 for a discussion of this.) Living vicariously through our children, allowing our ego to depend on the image of our children as successful, leads inevitably to feelings of emptiness in our children and in ourselves; *placing form over substance never works out in the end.* We have been wrongly led to believe, however, that women who have put their careers on hold have necessarily put their substantive side aside. *Contrary to stylized images, mothers who have abiding, deep relationships with their children find meaning in the relationship and create opportunities for meaning through the relationship.*

The smart, confident, and stylish stay-at-home mother has not only been under-represented in the media, she has been non-existent. Imagine seeing a bright, conversant, attractive woman who—for love of her baby, for the inability to leave her upbringing to anyone else, and for the experiencing of the sweetness of her childhood—chooses to stay home with her while she is young. She is proud of that choice and happy with it, even going so far as to give sensible reasons for it. She has interests and manages to pursue them even though she is a mother! She sees her child's early years as an interlude requiring a shift in priorities, not as an obliteration of her professional or creative goals. Then imagine that woman as a dominant feature in a popular TV show or magazine. It is simply unheard of, unseen. As Christine Davidson puts it in *Staying Home Instead,*

> The women's movement of the 1960s was about women having the freedom to make choices and to feel confident and well adjusted, whatever those choices were. But, somewhere along the line, this idea got distorted so that thirty years later there is apparently only one choice for any self-respecting, well-educated interesting woman: to work outside the home. Current distortions of feminism dictate that this is the only place where 'real work' is done. Apparently, this 'real work' should continue indefinitely, even after babies are born because quickly returning to work after giving birth proves how really liberated, tough, and enlightened a woman is.[17]

Davidson asserts, "Contemporary culture communicates a message that few of us miss: It's not all right for an intelligent woman to stay home." [18]

I would take this assertion a step further: By omitting them from its portrayal of reality, contemporary culture communicates a message that the intelligent woman *does not* stay at home. The images surround us, convincing us to choose the prestige of the workplace over the emotional rewards of motherhood. As Dr. Mohammadreza Hojat of Jefferson Medical College observes, such decisions are often based "on an unspoken assumption that material gain is more important than human outcomes, that job prestige is more rewarding than maternal satisfaction, that professional growth should take precedence over family responsibilities, that immediate gratification through the uncertain short-term benefits of employment deserves priority over delayed gratification with certain long-term benefits from human outcomes."[19]

The forces that have lured us into buying these messages are powerful. We have been honed to be finely tuned efficiency experts capable of combining full-time work and motherhood with a tough spirit and a can-do attitude. As Davidson points out, our training left us "cruelly unprepared" for the "soft, inefficient feelings" our babies would bring out in us. We were prepared for the sensations of awe, joy, and emotional exhaustion which a baby engenders only insofar as we were prepared to get those sensations under wraps so that we could move smoothly and quickly back into the workplace. Davidson reports of her own experience, "No one prepared me for the work and exhaustion involved in having a baby, but they said even less about the magic of it all."[20]

The experience of childbirth is, naturally, an overwhelming one, an upheaval in our lives. Bringing a baby into the world is a captivating event with dramatic implications. As Barbara Defoe Whitehead puts it, "across time and across cultures, it is nearly universally understood as a radical and transformative experience."[21] The need to be with baby is felt by us not only as responsible adults who have brought a child into the world and must now take care of it, but also as participants in a poignant adventure. We feel ardently the possibilities with which we are confronted. We know that we are embarking upon an uncharted course. The process of pouring love into the baby while soaking up the baby's warmth and neediness is as wondrous as it is exhausting. It is simply natural for mother and baby to thrive upon and revel in each other, and what is wrong with that? The mother is alive with intense emotion. The baby intensely seeks all the love, comfort, and stimulation the mother has to give. If the mother permits herself, she will discover the unleashing of possibilities within herself that she never knew existed. Mothers have been taught, however, not to allow those powerful sensations to occur. Both women and men have been taught not to allow parenthood to transform them. Observes Dr. Jack Westman, "The fact that parenthood is developmental phase with growth potential for adults often is overlooked. . . . A constituency for representing the developmental needs of children could draw support from parents who want to grow with their children. Then the focus would not only be on a child's need to be with the parent but also on a parent's need to be with the child."[22]

Many of today's parents have become uneasy with the self-fulfillment ethos and resentful of the social pressures which, as Defoe Whitehead puts it, prevent them from "reveling in the event of parenthood." This reassessment of the relationship between work and family is, so far, a quiet, private matter that gets little coverage in the media and no public political support. Those who are employed when they become pregnant are given the impression that quitting work for their baby would be damaging not only to their incomes but also to their status in society and their self-worth. As Dr. Westman observes, "Influencing their decisions are the expectation that they will return to the work force as soon as possible as if childbirth were merely an illness and physical recovery were all that mattered."[23] The emphasis upon the marketplace still overshadows any focus upon the irresistible tug of love and warmth within the family.

We still witness the abstraction of life wherein both parents and children are told not to feel what they, by nature, do feel. Their fundamental orientation toward each, their inevitable attachment to each other are demeaned, mollified, and mitigated so that the broader social and economic agenda may be achieved. Human nature is a funny thing, however. It cannot simply be wished away.

The longing to co-exist with our children is real. The desire to be the predominant influence in their lives exists. The feeling that we *should* be the predominant influence exists. And this will be so regardless of how often we are told to deny it. It is true that guilt is a wasted emotion when it causes us to dwell upon a past about which we can do nothing, but guilt can be a powerful and helpful impetus toward improving upon the present. It can point us down beneath the surface of our lives, forcing us to acknowledge the discrepancy between our actions and our conscience.

The best thinkers regarding childhood, the ones whose research has stood the test of time, have upheld closeness with mother as the greatest gift that any child can receive and as an irreplaceable feature of civilized society. The time-honored research of D.W. Winnicott and John Bowlby, for example, confirms the importance of the ongoing mother-child relationship and upsets the notion that a baby can receive quality care without also receiving it in large quantities. For the general "being-there" of a loved one is required if the infant is really to become attached to her; if he really is to trust in her, and if he really is to "internalize" the experience of constant love. Both Winnicott and Bowlby insisted that it was through their needs being consistently met and through their experiencing of mother as a secure base that infants are able to develop a sense that they can positively affect their own experiences. Given these conditions, they gradually incorporate the image of security which mother provides within themselves and use that image as a source of confidence and strength. Moreover, having spent their days with the one they can rely upon to love and protect them, they come to empathize with others and to behave reliably.

Against the backdrop of their mother's presence, moreover, they are able to "try out" aggressive or anti-social behavior, finding it less rewarding than the closeness they feel with her. Bowlby and Winnicott both recognized mothers' special relationship with their offspring as not only "natural" throughout the animal kingdom and in the history of humankind but also as essential to healthy human growth and to a healthy human society. Stated Bowlby:

> Attachment behavior occurs in the young of almost all species of mammal, and in a number of species it persists throughout adult life. Although there are many differences of detail between species, maintenance of proximity by an immature animal to a preferred adult, almost always mother, is the rule. . . . In such a situation mother can be regarded as providing her child with a secure base from which to explore and to which he can return, especially should he become tired or frightened. . . . Anyone who has no such base is rootless. . . . The records, indeed, make it apparent that ignorance of the natural history of attachment behavior, coupled with a misguided enthusiasm that small children should quickly become independent and "mature" has resulted in practices that expose children and their parents, to a great deal of unnecessary anxiety and distress.[24]

Observed Winnicott:

> At one time what is central and necessary is the loving presence of the internal image; at another time, its prohibitive aspects and support of internal controls; at yet another time, its praising aspects and aid in the regulation of self-esteem. . . . The image . . . becomes an important internal regulator of longing and rage, gives the freedom to be autonomous while closeness is retained, and later is also a regulator of self-esteem. It is the product of the total experience of the infant organism in the earliest months and years, which includes cognitive as well as emotional development, and it later becomes a major tool of those aspects of the person's functioning that we ascribe to ego.[25]

(See Chapter 2 for a thorough discussion of Winnicott and Bowlby and of what babies need to "thrive.")

One of the primary rationalizations for discarding this way of thinking has been the assertion (often articulated or demonstrated in the media) that many mothers are not such good parents. This assertion, while true, blatantly disregards the thorough studies and the age-old understanding that a mother does not have to be perfect to be preferred and that the bonding and the unfolding relationship with her is important to the child's healthy development even if she is not an ideal role model. Winnicott initiated the term "good-enough mother." The important thing, he found, was the being-there of the mother. The good-enough mother responds to the infant's signals continually, allowing him to "internalize" the image of her and to use that image in the formation of a sense of self. The mother need not be wonderful but she needs to be responsive, and her love needs to shine through those qualities and actions which are themselves imperfect. In other words, the mother simply needs to do what comes naturally to most mothers.

We must ask why the work of Winnicott and the many reputed researchers who built upon his findings has been omitted from public, non-academic discussions of modern childrearing practices while the work of much less respected and thorough researchers whose "findings" fit certain objectives has been so visible. Why, for example, is Selma Fraiberg's classic documentation of the "diseases of non-attachment" so blatantly disregarded?[26] Why is Michael Rutter's meticulous catalogue of findings on the connection between attachment and social and emotional adjustment ignored?[27] Why does the psychological, psychiatric, molecular, biological, sociological, anthropological, and neurological research *now confirming the longitudinal benefits of nurturing and attachment* rarely, if ever, make it to the public forum? (See Chapter 2 for this research.) Reason and common sense are ever more important when the "information" with which we are provided is insubstantial.

Feminism deserves much credit for paving the way for women in government, business, higher education, and the workplace in general. It is a hallmark of our society that we now have women in high positions in all of these areas. I believe that feminism would do more for women and would greatly enhance its own reputation if it also acknowledged the essentiality of the mother-child relationship. The truth about "women's history" reveals the need to provide more opportunities for women and more respect for women's intellectual strengths and capabilities, *and* the need to respect motherhood as a glue that holds society together. History tells us that women have been a civilizing force upon society itself. Feminism, as it is currently defined, views accomplishment narrowly, as achievement in the workplace. An alternative feminism would define accomplishment broadly, in terms of women's vast possibilities as human beings whether in the workplace, at home, or in their fundamental contributions to society.

Efforts to discount the unique aspects and the invaluable function of the mother-child relationship have been based upon the selective use of historical materials and unscholarly research methods. Researchers claiming to be scholars use the rare exception in nature as their basis for understanding nature. Observes Thomas Fleming, "anecdotal information is stretched, and a few anomalous cases are inflated to the point that they are equal to the whole vast history of the human race."[28] The Iroquois, for example, are a favorite "starting point" for feminist theories. Iroquois matrons were more involved in political policy and decision making than most other women throughout history.[29] But the men were not sensitive and caring husbands and fathers, as researchers such as Karen Sacks imply, but rather, as Fleming points out, were military imperialists who were usually not with their wives and children but at war.[30] Moreover, the Iroquois pattern did not typify the pattern among Indians of Eastern America nor of other "cultures."

Many feminist researchers do concede the universal presence of sex roles but focus on the supposed historical exceptions to these roles so that they can argue that the belief in such a thing as the fundamental mother-child relationship is based upon "cultural conditioning." Yet, any unbiased cross-cultural study makes this argument impossible. For, in almost all cultures, women have been considered indispensable to a child's upbringing. They have been not only the primary nurturers but also the primary educators. Even the tribes to which feminists point as evidence of women breaking away from nurturing or feminine characteristics, only broke away insofar as such activity did not interfere with the raising of their children. Women of one such tribe, the Hopi, were less nurturant, but only, as Steven Goldberg points out in an article entitled "Utopian Yearning Versus Scientific Curiosity," when the tribe was under extreme external pressure and facing the threat of internal dissolution.[31] Too often, research into "women's history" ignores the large body of reputable cross-cultural studies, which show the special role of mothers in rearing and educating children to be prevalent across time and across place.[32]

Arguments such as that by Phillippe Aries that the concept of motherhood was "invented" and imposed upon women, distort history by ignoring this reality. For Aries, childhood (and hence motherhood) is a social invention rooted in the post feudal bourgeoisie who distinguished themselves from the lower classes by freeing their children, especially the boys, from adult's work and instead emphasizing the child's preparation for adult life. This, according to Aries, was distinct from the "miniature adultism" of the feudal ages wherein children between the ages of three and five became "participating members" of adult society.[33] As Valerie Polakow observes in *The Erosion of Childhood,* the theory of "miniature adultism" is based largely upon the art and iconography of the period which depicted children as small adults. Polakow pleas for an understanding of the medieval child that reaches beyond the surface of these images. She refers to an excellent essay by Peter Fuller which disputes the theory of miniature adultism.

Rather than seeing medieval iconography as representative of the child's true being, Fuller describes it as *misrepresentative.* Fuller explains that mainstream portraiture of the time was a formal depiction projected onto the child from the outside, representative of what the child could become, not of what the child actually was. He notes that in artists' portraits of their own children, the images do convey an awareness of a relatively distinct-from-adult existence and that these depictions contradict the notion of miniature adultism.[34] Thus, Polakow insists, we are deceived if we rely upon the "future-oriented lens" of the medieval adult in attempting to understand the medieval child. Indeed, she pleads that we acknowledge features of childhood and motherhood that span cultures and historical periods: "What if attachment and love, formed during these early hours and weeks after natural birth, are the very basis of human culture? . . . What if the blood tie, too, is a universal root of human culture in which social relationships are grounded?"[35] "One might ask whether any theory can adequately explain such complex and non-operationally defined experiences as love, attachment, bonding, clinging and warmth? Perhaps we need to view these theories as metaphor—as metaphor which becomes defunct when it no longer captures the images of lived-experience—and motherhood."[36]

The theory of childhood as social invention is used to justify massive social engineering projects most of which have as their end "liberating" the mother from the concept of childhood which "oppresses" her by portraying children as dependent, vulnerable and in need of her! In an extreme case, Shalumit Firestone's *The Dialectic of Sex* attempted to destroy the "myth of childhood" so that "cybernetic socialism" could take place. In this sub-human realm, the mother-child attachment becomes unnecessary and unacceptable. Motherhood is supplanted by a community of adults whom the child will choose to relate to; genetic relationships will have nothing to do with a child's residence. After a few generations of "household living," the oppression of women will finally be overcome as children will be artificially produced or adopted, and evenly distributed among households, thereby solving the problem of "physical dependency."[37] I would like to believe that the de-humanizing effects of Firestone's prescriptions for progress are self-evident. Firestone's ideas serve, however, as a warning against other social engineers who, although more subtle and agreeable on the surface, underneath it all seek similar control over the mother-child relationship.

In *Towards a Feminist Theory of the State,* Catherine MacKinnon subscribes to the "constructivist" view of sexual identity arguing that the very idea of gender, of male and female, was "culturally constructed" as a "heteronormative" ideal. According to MacKinnon, "Women and men are divided by gender, made into the sexes as we know them, by the social requirements of its dominant form, heterosexuality, which institutionalizes male sexual dominance and female sexual submission."[38] The idea of the maternal, in her view, is nothing more than a manifestation of that submission, nothing more than "cultural production." MacKinnon takes the idea that all people, regardless of sexual orientation and regardless of how they define a family, should have equal rights and protection under the law and discards it for a new theory which insists that "heteronormative, andocentric, Euro-centric" biases will only be overcome when "gender-free" ideas are given legal and political *supremacy.* Having no foundation in "nature" (there being no such thing), and being nothing more than a social construct, the idea of gender must be destroyed. Democratic reform is not enough to achieve the radically new society she envisions; it is inadequate for obliterating the idea of the normal. By placing everything maternal and feminine under the umbrella of "social invention," such thinkers put themselves at liberty to "invent" *their own social order*, which disavows nature and denies the mother-child bond.

Theories, such as that by Lawrence Stone who claims that children were historically mistreated until the Enlightenment, are used toward the same end as the theory of motherhood and childhood as social invention. The inherent idea is that we should not feel badly about leaving our children's upbringing to others. At least we're not "abusing" them! In

Corruption in Paradise: The Child in Western Literature, Reinhard Kuhn refutes this notion by demonstrating: a) that parents felt a deep affection for their children in pre-industrialized Europe and b) that a door was shut on children in *modern* literature, reflecting a change in our priorities.[39] In *Past, Present and Personal: The Family and the Life Course in Historical Perspective*, John Demos provides convincing evidence that it is in modern times, not in the past, that child abuse has become a serious problem.[40] Moreover, recent historical investigations have discredited the view that early American life was based on extreme individualism that emphasized economic profit over the family. As Allan Carlson puts it, "The new interpretation sees American society, before mass industrialization in the late nineteenth century as strongly familial in nature. The economy was home centered, and most productive activity—from furniture making to the raising and preparation of food—were family based. —At the community level, kinship, ethnic, and religious bonds held America together. These Americans, in historian Barry Levy's words, were committed to the creation of families and to the rearing of children as 'tender plants growing in the truth'[41] . . . Even after industrialization and the rise of large cities, the new historians have shown how Americans sought to preserve the family-centeredness of their society."[42]

It *is* true that, in preindustrial times, children spent an inordinate amount of time on chores done side by side with parents. America in the 1940s and 50s was unparalleled for the extent to which "conveniences" allowed families, especially mothers and their children, just to "be" together. Previous generations would, perhaps, be shocked that we gave up the luxury of relaxed togetherness so willingly.

Articles which try to deny the absolutely central and dominant historical role of the family in "bringing up" children are so flawed as to hardly deserve a hearing (and yet they do receive a hearing in most of our major universities and colleges). It is in modern times that the role of the family is less central and less dominant. Eighty years ago, Charlotte Perkins Gillman discerned a "long term economic trend" toward the steady surrender by the household of its economic functions to the marketplace. In the centuries before the industrial age, the family existed as an independent economic unit, with parents and children working together at "chores" and with parents, rather than schools, educating the children. Although there were times when governments and wars intruded upon the family, across cultures and across time, the family was the predominant social, economic, and educational unit. The massively disruptive Industrial Revolution was, of course, a time when all too many children were essentially surrendered by vulnerable parents to emerging industries in search of cheap labor. Since then, the surrendering of family functions has been more subtle and less glaring but, perhaps, just as significant. Notes Fleming, "The gradual withering of family functions encompasses nearly every phase of human existence: child-rearing and education, economic activities, health and welfare, self-defense, and recreation. A general list of such categories inevitably sounds like a string of ministerial portfolios or cabinet departments, not without reason, since the state ultimately has assumed the functions of the family."[43]

Movement from the farm and from the family owned business into the factory and the corporation also meant the movement of men out of the home, and the isolation of women both from their husbands and from the family enterprises that they, along with their husbands, had previously worked to support. According to figures cited by C.W. Mills in 1951, at the beginning of the nineteenth century nearly 80 percent of the American population was self-employed. By 1940, barely 20 percent of the population was self-employed. As Lloyd E. Sandelands points out, this and the rise of a money economy changed women's status. "And with money to equate goods and services came a multiplication of the things men could do to make a profit. —With greater means of income and less dependence on their wives to earn it, men took on greater power in the relationship with women. Women needed men in a new way. Social power and prestige concentrated in the men's realm of commerce, leaving women to feel left out, left behind, second-class citizens." [44] In this climate, women continued to raise the young, but many began to associate the home with isolation and lack of opportunity.

It is thus recently, not "historically," that women have surrendered their central role within the central family. Women were generally the predominant influences in their children's lives. The devotion of mothers toward children is, quite simply, one of the constants of history. Throughout time and across the world, men have been less nurturant, more sexually active, more aggressive, and somewhat less capable of expressing emotional empathy than women. Women are, throughout time and across the world, more "maternal" than men!

Any honest look at human nature and at the natural world confirms the male tendency toward more aggression and the female tendency toward more nurturant behavior. Throughout the animal kingdom these tendencies manifest themselves over and over again. It is almost always the female who nurtures the young. Harlow's famous experiments showed that monkeys craved their mothers' warmth and affection and that the attachment between mother and baby monkeys was essential for the baby's development. Gerianne Alexander, a Texas A&M psychologist at College Station, conducted research on toy preferences in monkeys. She found that, just like human boys and girls, male monkeys prefer to play with toy cars, while female monkeys prefer to play with dolls. "Vervet monkeys, like human beings, show sex differences in toy preferences," she wrote in the journal *Evolution and Human Behavior*.[45] She speculated that females in both species have evolved toy preferences that equip them to care for infants, while males have evolved toy preferences that require throwing and moving, skills useful in hunting and attracting a mate. Similar behavior has been documented in virtually all species of mammals.

As just one example: female kangaroos nurture the young while the males hunt for food and, during mating season, fight with each other, sometimes to the death. Mother kangaroos keep their female offspring with them even longer than they keep the male offspring so that the males may learn fighting skills from their fathers while the females are learning nurturing skills from their mothers. When watching extended film coverage of a kangaroo "family," I couldn't help feeling sorry for the males. They led such an isolated existence compared to the females. When they were together they were usually competing. The females spent a lot of time cuddling and, it really appeared, frolicking and enjoying each other's company. If the mother loses her offspring, her cries can be heard for days. Before we assume that it is always the male who has the advantage, we might want to look at the animal kingdom. The ability to be really close with others can be a wonderful "advantage."

Recent scientific research indicates that there is, indeed, a difference between women and men, girls and boys, and that women are generally better nurturers. Scientists, under tremendous pressure not to say so, have found that human females are best equipped for the task of childrearing, and children from birth specifically seek nurture and guidance from their mothers. As researchers such as Dr. Sheri Berenbaum, psychologist June Reinisch, and UCLA scientist Dr. Laura Allen have found, men and women are innately different. One of many differences is women's heightened sensitivity to babies' signals and needs. Said Dr. Allen in an interview with John Stossel, one of the rare media persons to broach this subject: "As I began to look at the human brain and more, I kept finding differences, and about seven or eight out of 10 structures that we actually measured to be different between men and women. . . . Testosterone kind of rides a roller coaster until birth. We know that the first rise of testosterone causes the rise of male sex organs. We don't know what the second rise in testosterone does. I suspect it causes our brains to be different."[46] (Dr. Allen was warned by colleagues that such research was not a good idea because it was politically provocative. Scientists are sometimes refused grants until their research promises to lead in more socially acceptable directions.)

Even so, the evidence is insurmountable. Science writer and Pulitzer Prize winner Deborah Blum, in a book entitled *Sex on the Brain*, finds the biological differences between men and women impossible to discount. Being very careful to forbid us from using these differences as "excuses" for exaggerating their significance and from ignoring our basic human similarities, she nevertheless documents large bodies of research showing men and women to be different. The general, albeit slight, male advantage in math and the general female advantage in reading comprehension, writing, and oral expression, for example, are recurring findings across wide and varied sources of research. The female tendency toward nurturing is equally well documented, both in the animal world and in the human. Blum observes, "We come from a species—a series of species, really—with a long history of females as mothers, nurturers, and supporters. There's a graceful, evolutionary kind of logic to the way a mother cradles her child, and, maybe, an equal logic to the distance a father leaves between baby and heart."[47] The calming influence of mother's voice, for example, and her unique ability to capture the baby's attention are broadly documented. Blum finds that "the comfort that mother gives child appears basic, biological, and continuous with (perhaps part of) the same developmental process that goes on in the womb."[48] I agree with Blum, however, that such findings should never be construed "to deny love between father and child." In either case, she emphasizes, "we're talking about a parent carrying a child, holding a baby close, and providing security and shelter."

Recent studies confirm that testosterone and other hormones influence behavior and personality. Research shows, for example, that a genetic defect that causes female babies to be accidentally exposed to the male hormone androgen affects those girls as they grow up. They feel themselves to be "different" than other girls and tend to pursue more "masculine" games and interests. Men with Kleinfeltyer's Syndrome, possessing an extra X chromosome, have a diminished sex drive and are less assertive and less aggressive. In addition, studies show that the Y hormone in men affects their brains and their behavior. Men, for example, tend to have better "spatial, quantitative and visual skills" while women have better proximal senses and more awareness of the nuances of others' and their children's behavior. In *The Female Brain*, neuroscientist Louann Brizendine describes the similarly powerful effect hormones have on females. Hormone changes that accompany the menstrual cycle make women more emotional. Hormonal changes that accompany motherhood make women more adept at some tasks and less adept at others. As Dr. Mohammadreza Hojat of the Jefferson Medical College puts it:

> At the present stage of our knowledge, no technology exists for reversing or altering the nature or the process of these developments which ultimately determine the gender's anatomy or hormonal balance. Behavioral tendencies such as aggressiveness among males and caring among females have been linked to neurobiophysical and hormonal development. These neurobiophysical and hormonal differences determine the human-specific behaviors and many of the characteristics associated with each gender, including aspects of motherhood.[49]

Researchers have built upon the work of University of Chicago neurobiologist Jerre Levy who, in the 1970s, found that the female right cerebral hemisphere has different functions than the male right cerebral hemisphere, the former being more attuned to emotion and to the reading of facial expression. Using MRI analysis, a research team from the University of Alberta found that women's and men's brains work so differently, that they use different areas of the brain even when working on the same task.[50] Richard Haier, neuroscientist at the University of Carolina in Irvine, reports a striking difference in the male and female brain, noting that men and women apparently achieve similar IQ results with different brain regions. He writes in the journal *NeuroImage*, "Human evolution has created two different types of brains designed for equally intelligent behaviour."[51] He found that men have more than six times the amount of grey matter, which is used for information processing and that women have ten times the amount of white matter, which controls networking abilities. He suggests that this may help to explain why men tend to excel in skills requiring more local processing while women tend to excel at integrating and assimilating information.

Breaking findings in neurobiology do not show differences between males and females in general levels of intelligence. The differences lie, rather, in the ways they learn and in the kinds of learning that generally come more easily to them than others. Girl babies, for example, vocalize more frequently than boys. Boy babies bang things more frequently than girls! Girls are more likely to show an understanding of subtleties in language, boys to show an understanding of how "things" (such as trucks, gadgets, and motors) work. Young girls tend to be somewhat better than young boys at sitting and completing a task; young boys to be slightly better at solving quantitative problems. Teenage boys and men tend to be more "physical" and more aggressively sexual than teenage girls and women. Psychiatrist and neuroscientist Mona Lisa Schulz, writes in *Awakening Intuition*, "Women, on the whole have greater access to the right brain and a greater ability to move back and forth between the two hemispheres simultaneously. Men, as a general rule, are apt to use one hemisphere or the other but not both at once: they tend to stay more in the left hemisphere."[52] An open look at the research makes it clear that to say that the exploration of male/female differences is really an exploration of male superiority is to ignore the real findings.

Harvard biologist and psychologist Joan Borysenko sees such findings as these as no threat to female advances as long as they are properly interpreted. She sees women's "relationality" as a great gift and as an intellectual as well as emotional attribute. "Women are relational stars. We love company and conversation. We empathize with others and internalize their experience as our own. . . . As a result, deep and meaningful interaction follows."[53] Even so many researchers, such as Kate Millet and Germain Greer, have spent their careers trying to prove that evidence of male/female hormonal and neuro-biological differences are "biased" or "ambiguous." The fact that evidence of such differences is, now, overwhelming hasn't stopped them. As psychologist Joseph Adelson puts it, "A certain frivolousness in dealing even with simple facts is now so commonplace as to be nearly normative."[54]

Such frivolousness permeates our mass culture. I found it interesting that the discussion of the differences in the kinds of movies men and women prefer in the popular movie, "Sleepless in Seattle" seemed surprising and brave at the time. Many couples seemed to breathe a sigh of relief that at least one "difference" was, apparently, acceptable—jokes about action movies versus "chick movies" became commonplace. These evolved into jokes about men's preference for action-oriented, sports-oriented TV. But the discussion of differences has stayed, for the most part, on the surface—on this very careful plain. Delving any deeper might lead to muddy waters.

Modern ideologues are allowed the contradiction of denying femininity in nature while blaming men and their "masculine tendencies" for women's historical mistreatment because they attribute the masculine impulse to culture, not nature. It is difficult to see, however, how "culture" can explain this. For, how can we be merely products of something we ourselves have created? At some point, one has to acknowledge the significance of the creation of culture in the first place. One has to explain why almost all cultures, even those created in isolation from other cultures, have basic similarities. On the other hand, we have to acknowledge the obvious fact of cultural differences and achievements. (To put it on an individual level: Where does an original idea come from?) At the same time, we have to acknowledge the impact of environmental factors on human behavior and emotions. In an important article in *The American Psychologist*, Michael Rutter lays out evidence that "environmentability and heritability are both strong." States Rutter, "Although some genetic and environmental influences have effects on behavior that are relatively direct, in many instances, the consequences depend on a more complex interplay between nature and nurture."[55] Nature *and* culture *and* originality are all factors of human existence. It is just as absurd to deny the very existence of male-female differences as it is to claim that we are all locked in biological prisons, unable to take a free step.

It would be equally absurd to say that aggression is more important than caring. If it was, as so many claim, some sort of masculine tendency toward domination which allowed women to be treated as second-class citizens, then why would society as a whole benefit from making the sexes uniformly masculine? More aggression is certainly the last thing our violent society needs and, yet, that is the tacit message of shows and articles which glamorize women who are as tough as men are or tougher and which make stars out of the worst possible men: violent, crude, selfish, childish, and irresponsible. If today's society needs anything, it is more civilized behavior. If today's children need anything, it is more caring and more shelter from an aggressive world. Women have been taught to fit into a male world by becoming more masculine, indeed, by denying the existence of femininity and the value of nurturing. This might turn out to have been the most self-effacing thing of all.

Femininity in no way precludes brains, accomplishments, and vigor. It is demeaning to imply that they are mutually exclusive. Equal treatment in the work place, equal opportunity, and equal pay are essential and worthwhile causes. We must continue to work toward these goals where they are not met. But they need not be pursued at the expense of femininity. To assume that the work force and femininity are incompatible is to insist that women stand on men's ground, behaving as men would. Although behaving like a man had short-term advantages in the workplace and was, perhaps, necessary in order for women to gain their place therein, in the long run we do an injustice to ourselves if we do not insist upon our acceptance in the work force *as women*. To be feminine is not to think less hard nor to work less hard, but it is to approach the world with a unique set of strengths and assets—assets from which the workplace and the political realm can benefit.

Nor does involved, being-there motherhood preclude brains, accomplishments, and vigor. As multi-faceted persons, we can have different chapters in our lives. In other words, we can be both career women and involved mothers of young children, but not necessarily at the same time. With the dramatically increased numbers of families postponing parenting until their late twenties and thirties, and with the decreased number of years in which families actually have preschool age children due to smaller family sizes, it is easier than ever before to have those different chapters in our adult lives. Many women have ten years in a career before they have their first child. If they have two children born two years apart, the total number of years spent with them before they are off to kindergarten would be six, a relatively small number. True, it is often difficult to return to an interrupted career or job, but few women who do interrupt their careers or jobs for the sake of their children live to regret it. Moreover, many discover new possibilities for part-time or at-home work.

A Chicago based group called FEMALE (formerly employed mothers at loose ends) recognizes the importance of both career and motherhood and provides support for women who put their career on hold in order to raise young children. The group acknowledges the "time bind" which is the result of trying to manage a demanding career and the needs of young children at the same time. Cincinnati FEMALE co-leader Diane Vorbroker, for example, explains that when she worked, she arrived home just in time to tuck her young son into bed. She detested the pressure and the hustle-bustle and knew that she was "missing too much." She decided to give at-home motherhood a try.[56] Such women are not "masochists" as Susan Faludi, author of *Backlash*, led us to believe but are proud of their multi-dimensional accomplishments. We certainly would not want to go back to the days when men contributed so little to the nurturing of their offspring (many still do) but, if we really are strong women, we cannot simply discount something which evolutionary and genetic science, the observations of astute chroniclers of the mother/child relationship, and our gut-level feelings all indicate: that attachment between mother and baby is both natural and essential for the baby's optimal development. Babies simply thrive upon the showering down of maternal attention and love, but society suggests that mothers get their maternal, i.e. their feminine, tendencies under wraps (see Chapter 2).

Contrary to expectations, it is often not the staying at home with children she adores that makes a woman uncomfortable but the androgynous/masculine ideal, which compels her to apologize for it. Penelope Leach describes one such uncomfortable woman:

> That woman, implicitly charged with betraying her sexual relationship by putting her maternal relationship first, is a paradigm for millions of mothers who wonder if they betray their sex when they put their children ahead of what they perceive as feminist ideals. But to betray their sex, women have to behave in a way that makes females less than males. Being a mother is not less than male but uniquely, splendidly female and therefore something men cannot be, and find it difficult to understand.[57]

The message we receive is that maternal caring and love is good insofar as it is not allowed to supersede love for ourselves. Furthermore, caring for ourselves is defined as follows: We care about our gainful employment in the workplace and expect to achieve fulfillment therein. This message turns out for all too many women to be a distortion, an ideal which maternal love and our deeper nature will not permit. There is a difference between allowing motherhood to "move" us and allowing motherhood to subsume us. Feminism was right to call for a less subsuming vision of motherhood, one that recognized women's need for interests and challenges apart from childrearing. But this vision itself becomes a form of oppression if it requires the detachment between mother and child. For, the attachment between mother and child is naturally intense and grows ever more so the more the attachment is permitted to develop.

Moreover, the nature of the human beast is such that the giving and receiving of love will usually be more fulfilling than making money. Caring about others and reaping the inevitable rewards is often the most fulfilling thing of all and need not be self-effacing. In *The Eclipse of Reason*, written in the 1940s, Max Horkheimer explained that individual freedom and social identity naturally converge. "The absolutely isolated individual has always been an illusion. The most esteemed personal qualities, such as independence, will to freedom, sympathy, and the sense of justice are social as well as individual virtues. The fully developed individual is the consummation of a fully developed society. The emancipation of the individual is not an emancipation from society, but the deliverance of society from atomization, an atomization that may reach its peak in periods of collectivization and mass culture."[58]

While we have been taught that taking care of children is destructive of our identity, most modern women (who are "free to choose" to do so and who have had a broader range of experiences than mothers in the past) find that it adds depth to their personalities, passion to their hearts, and meaning to their days. This is in no way to say that women should "give up" their identity and interests for the sake of it, but rather, to say that motherhood is an important part of that identity—one that does not invalidate the other important experiences in a woman's life.

Because labor and the work environment are not examined in the particular but are, rather, glamorized in the abstract, the truth about labor can be distorted in the same way that the truth about the lives of working women is distorted. Labor is expected to provide those good feelings which family and friends used to provide. The question of how employers are to provide for employees' emotional well-being when the deepest human need is to love and be loved is not addressed. Asks Leach, "What sad and subtle subtext tells them (parents) that money earned away and spent on their children is more important than time spent at home with their children?"[59] In deprecating the joy that comes from giving to and loving others and in disparaging concerns and interests which do not reap economic rewards or contribute to "progress," we have come perilously close to proclaiming impassioned love for one's children a myth imposed upon women by men. Warns Dr. Westman:

> There is an impoverishment of the sense of community and of personal intimacy, as materialism and competitiveness are over-emphasized. Parenthetically, the rewarding, of materialistically oriented activities and achievements in many day-care programs today may propagate this dehumanizing emphasis. . . . The emphasis of the market place in our society is on being admired and implicitly being loved. Often absent is an awareness that the essential ingredient of being loved is the capacity to love others. More critical is the lack of awareness that in order to love as an adult one must have experienced being loved as a child.[60]

We have been led to see such a viewpoint as Westman's as part of some extremist plot to hold women back. And yet, as we shall see, study after reputable study have led to the same conclusion. As we shall also see, study after reputable study have been conveniently withheld from the public view. Reports that children are just fine in day care centers and with care givers and reports that emphasize the need for more day care centers and more nanny services are still far more voluble than reports that emphasize the need for more love and stability in children's lives. This is so in spite of the innumerable estimable studies (see Chapter 2) which reveal the ways in which the development of a child suffers when their need for a steady intake of love and guidance from their mother does not occur.

The inadequacy, indeed the propagandistic nature of modern depictions of childrearing must be addressed. Feminists were right in seeing previous depictions of motherhood as inadequate and demeaning. Mothers were often depicted without complexity and without interests and talents aside from their children. They supposedly accepted housework as their burden and expected little contribution to house and home life from their husbands. Recent depictions, however, are no less simplistic. For the smart, progressive, and beautiful women portrayed in the media, combining demanding full-time careers with motherhood is never a problem, either for themselves or for their young children. When we are taught to continue on with life as normal when life feels anything but normal, we are taught to betray our beliefs and set ourselves down the road of self-deceit and self-doubt. What begins as self-fulfillment often ends up feeling more like exhaustion and confusion. "Parenting" is not incidental; it is monumental and feels that way.

Picture the paralegal mother I interviewed. Although her day ends at 5:30, at 4:00 she starts to worry about and miss her toddler to the point that she has difficulty concentrating. Finally able to leave, she picks up her child from the "learning center" and, on a typical day, heads for the grocery store. This is the last place that either of them wants to be at the end of their long day but there is nothing in the house for dinner. Her child cries and demands to be taken home. When they arrive home, she longs to take her child into a chair with a good book, but dinner must be made. While he clings to her skirt, she puts a quick dinner together. The toddler seems too tired or distracted to eat. He picks at a few morsels and starts to whine. The parents realize he needs to go to bed but are torn between their desire to spend some time with him, to have some input upon his day, and the realization that his day starts early the next day. At 6:45 the next morning, this mother wakens her child from a deep sleep, bathes him, puts a video on for him while she dresses and showers herself, gives him a muffin to eat in the car, and takes him, sad-faced and tired, back to the learning center.

She knows that his sad face will distract her. She reminds herself of the many articles she has read about how good it is to work full time and how beneficial "early learning programs" are to children. She thinks of the laundry she will have to do tonight and wonders when she will find time to do it. No matter how many self-help books she reads she cannot shake the feeling that, both at work and at home, she has too much to do in too little time, leaving her feeling incapable of doing anything really well. What a contrast she is to the sitcom character whose confidence is unfailing and for whom "making up for lost time with children" is never an issue.

The images surround us, pressuring us to achieve what is not and cannot be. Lest anyone doubt that the media has painted too facile and convenient an image, let us examine more real life experiences of mothers, their children, and the effect of "child care" upon their lives. Granted, many of the women I know tend to be relatively "well-off" and therefore able to afford the help which provides them with some flexibility if they choose to stay at home. By the same token, however, the working women I know have available the same flexibility and the best child care that money can buy. Even with these "best-case" scenarios as my vantage point, the media images quickly reveal themselves as inexcusably inattentive to the truth. At the same time, the images reveal themselves as having a powerful effect upon what is true. In other words, some women find the images irresistible and conform to them in order to achieve the undeniable "rush" which comes from identifying with those on-the-go powerhouses seeking an adventure a minute.

*   *   *

Down the street from my old house was a woman who was pregnant with her first child at the same time that I was pregnant with mine. Although she had an attractive offer for part-time work with a small company, she chose to remain in her full time position with a big company due to their enhanced benefits package. The large company gave her a generous maternity leave of eight months. She was warm and attentive to her daughter during that time. The day she returned to work, however, she hardened herself toward those things which previously made her soft. Upon entering day care, her baby went into what might best be called panic and depression, which she manifested by screaming shrilly when being dropped off at the center and by crying, sometimes uncontrollably, night after night all night long. The baby had stopped sleeping. (In "Infant Sleep Disorders and Attachment," P. McNamara, J. Belsky, and P. Fearon document their finding that night wakings and "clinically significant sleep problems" are "significantly associated" with poor infant-mother attachment status.)[61] I was horrified to hear this and assumed that the mother, having a sympathetic nature, would look for an alternative form of care for her child, or perhaps, reconsider her part-time offer. This mother, however, had read a book about just such problems. The book counseled parents that such an initial reaction to day care was normal and that the child "would get over it"; not to feel guilty about it, but to view it as a "developmental phase" in the child's life. In fact, the book advised parents not to ease their children gradually into day care but to break them into the new routine fully so that the transition, although traumatic, could be "gotten over with" as quickly as possible. The writer of this facile book had fallen prey to the modern trend of judging means according to their contribution to a broad social end. *If close analysis of the means are not permitted, the ends are allowed to become more extreme as well.* Soon, we find ourselves making leaps of faith to goals which are themselves inscrutable. We choose goals ardently but not thoughtfully. (Similar books by Sandra Scarr recommend that women return to work as soon as possible—"when the child can't complain very much" and that they not worry about their baby's crying upon entering day care since the child won't "remember" the experience later.)[62]

I was amazed that this mother bought into this theory, deciding that she and her baby would tough it out. She who, while on maternity leave, thought it "wrong to let a baby cry" nevertheless became willing to endure night after sleepless night of her baby's crying. As all intelligent analysts of babies' signals have understood, an essential component in the development of a sense of self and a sense of caring for others is having a loved one respond to those signals reliably and continually. This baby gave her mother the strongest signal a baby can give, but her mother was taught to ignore it. The message her mother received was that women should not reduce their workload for their babies; it is a sign of progress that their career continue to move forward unabated. The consequences of this decision are less important than the forward-looking character of the decision itself.

She who, during maternity leave, had found herself stretched in caring for her one baby was willing to place her child in a situation where one adult had under their auspices five babies. During her year at home, she had expressed amazement at how much work babies were and how much care and attention they required. She had joked that parents of twins and triplets deserved the status of sainthood. If parents of triplets were taxed to their limit, barely able to cater to their babies' physical and emotional needs, how could a care giver who lacked the impulse and incentive of love be expected to do as well or better?

A few years later, I had a conversation with this woman which again struck me as sad and odd. She told me what a difficulty it was for her when her children were sick. The day care, of course, did not encourage the spread of germs. She had found a solution in a "wonderful" hospital day care program for the sick children of working parents. No longer did the parent "have to take time off from work for a sick child." I wondered about the effect of this "transition" upon the child. I worried that a hospital would seem a strange and frightening place to a child who did not feel well. Getting used to new care providers and new surroundings was hard enough when one felt well. Even less so than for an adult, would a strange bed in a strange place be an adequate substitute for the comfort of home. Had she interviewed the staff nurses? Apparently, she had not. Convenience now seemed the overriding factor in her childcare decisions. I recalled reading a newspaper article praising local hospitals for providing this "solution" to the needs of working parents.

*   *   *

I befriended a couple that prided themselves in finding in-home care, rather than institutional care, for their children. They praised their sitter to me, reporting that their children "just loved her." Imagine my shock then, when under the aegis of this beloved woman, the three-year-old wandered unattended down the street and knocked on my door. He seemed, simply, to want to talk. When I inquired about this, the neighbors informed me that he had been doing such wandering for quite some time. When I reported this unsafe situation to the parents, their response was to muse over how difficult it was to find good help. After about a year, the sitter quit. The children, I learned, were sad and missed the care giver deeply. Finally, after many temporary situations, a new care giver was found. Where the previous care giver had been too lax and inattentive, this new woman was her true opposite—protective to the point of oppressive. The aforementioned child, now tightly monitored and controlled, was, literally, not permitted to take an independent step outside. Unless he was holding the sitter's hand, he had to stay still. She barraged this child with incessant words of caution: "You might get hurt, you might fall down, you might get dirty." Rarely did she permit him to visit his friends since it might make him "too excited for his nap." In general, even as he turned five, she discouraged him from entering any situation which she could not control. He was not, for example, permitted to have a friend over on a whim. Everything in his life was sanitized, organized, and barred from disruption.

As logic would have it, this boy's personality changed. He became less adventurous and more passive. It was clear that his care giver was removing the spontaneity of play from his life. Apart from that issue, I wondered how the schizophrenic nature of his upbringing would affect him. What would it do to a child's view of the world to have an overprotective care provider replace one who was not protective enough? I thought of the millions of children whose view of the world was continually disrupted by the changes in those bringing them up. His parents informed me that, even though it had been "hard" for the family to lose the previous person, it "had turned out for the best." They had found someone "conscientious," whom they could trust. The parents, I realized, did not know *how* her conscientiousness manifested itself while they were at work. They interpreted his increasingly inhibited personality as a "shy stage" and did not attribute it to the daily influence of a certain personality upon his.

The deliberate suppression of ones' better knowledge is all too apparent not only in the rationalizations many make if the child care they have chosen does not turn out as well as they had expected, but also in the process by which many choose child care in the first place. On the basis of one or two interviews with a stranger or strangers (sometimes by phone, as in the case of hiring au pairs) and a handful of recommendations made by other strangers, parents reassure themselves that their children are in good hands. The endless stories indicating the futility of such wishful thinking would be ludicrous were they not tragic.

*   *   *

I know a successful business woman who took the task of hiring an au pair very seriously. She thought about it long and hard and, unlike many parents, went through many different agencies and was unwilling to hire someone based on phone interviews and recommendations alone. She insisted upon an in-home interview and found a girl with all the qualities she required, "a sweet disposition and lots of common sense." She reported that her baby seemed happy with this woman. One day, she decided upon a surprise visit home during her lunch break. She found her infant in the crib sleeping and the au pair nowhere to be found. It turned out that she had taken the car for a "quick trip" to the grocery store while the baby napped.

*   *   *

I know of a family who, also, went beyond the norm in the stringency of their nanny-hiring process. They finally settled upon a college student taking a year off from school. She was a cheerful, energetic girl who seemed to love children. One day, this family took a drive down the highway to the next town. On the outskirts, in a section deemed unsafe, was a bar with a big neon sign luring customers with the promise of inexpensive beer and daytime hours. The little girl, three years old, exclaimed, "Oh look, Mommy, that's where we go for lunch to meet _____'s friends."

She likes that place a lot." The mother discovered, one year too late, that what the care giver "liked a lot" and what she wanted for her child were two different things. As a two-year-old her child had, of course, been too young to understand or report to her mother that she and her babysitter were frequenting bars at lunchtime. The choice between raising one's baby oneself and allowing another to raise them is all too often the choice between the known and the unknown.

*   *   *

I know of another family that found a babysitter through an ad in a newspaper. She seemed to have all the right credentials. She attended an expensive college and came from a quiet New England town. Although they did not get to know her before leaving her with their children, she seemed a safe bet. One day, she went out with friends, leaving her car and car keys behind. The family had a school function to attend that night but discovered that the car battery was dead. In a rush, they decided to borrow the babysitter's car. As the children bounced into the car, they pulled a wad of magazines out from under the front seat. The magazines were pornographic .The parents, appalled, could not help but look further. In the glove compartment, they found drug paraphernalia and "sexual aids." This nice girl from a nice family was not what she seemed.

*   *   *

So too, I know, a loving family who hired a "grandmotherly, nurturing type" to live with them and take care of their infant. The woman seemed awfully tired when the parents came home from work but they attributed it to her old age. Finally, they decided to let her go, so un-energetic had she become. A couple weeks later, they discovered that all their hard liquor bottles were nearly empty. They called the woman's son who eventually confessed to them that his mother was a long-time alcoholic. Their baby had been in her care for six months.

*   *   *

I know a family who pride themselves in safety-consciousness. They invest hard-earned money in handcrafted play equipment designed according to exacting safety standards and expensive cars with the best safety reputations. They have scrutinized preschool safety procedures and have tried to instill into their children a respect for safety rules. Imagine their dismay when a friend reported to them regarding their trusted babysitter's behavior at the grocery store: The sitter left the two-year-old unattended in the cart while she wandered down an adjacent aisle. Equally shocking, she drove off without putting the child into her car seat. She simply loaded her into the back seat and drove away. This sitter had been well instructed regarding sensible precautions. Apparently, however, she either viewed these precautions as unnecessary or as inconvenient.

Parents overestimate the extent to which a hired person will mimic their methods of childrearing and underestimate the extent to which care givers will stay true to themselves. It is simply unlikely that a care giver can be "trained" at the age of twenty or older to do things much differently than she already does them. The way she was raised is part of her and *will* come out. Her fundamental beliefs regarding right and wrong are formed. And it is all too easy for her to nod her head vacantly as she is advised of the "values" her employers expect of her. She is who she is, and parents cannot hope to change that with advice and instructions. To believe so is to adopt wishful thinking as an approach to parenting.

If the care giver does perfunctorily follow the guidelines the parents have laid out, the children will sense any half-heartedness. Children are masters of subtlety and nuance and usually know the difference between sincerity and pretense. Thus, children are faced with a dilemma: Who has the right ideas? The woman who is the dominant influence in their days in terms of time and energy spent, or their parents? The children might choose the care giver's ideas. For, again, children are quick to spy hypocrisy. If their parents are so sure that A is true, why would they hire a care giver who believes B? Even more important, children always know the difference between someone who loves them and someone who is merely "taking care" of them, no matter how "loving" the care might be.

It *is* true that some babysitters are with certain children for such a long time that they really come to love them; that many babysitters are so kind and sensible that their manner and practice with young children is beyond reproach. For these very reasons, the children come to love the babysitter. This is the optimal scenario, and one that can work well for working parents. Finding someone who really cares eases the strain for working mothers and their children. The problem is that this bond with the child rarely seems to prevent the sitter from quitting at some future point. And, it is the rare exception who remains "part of the family" after she quits. Often, there is resentment on the part of the parents when she leaves. Often, she is "burned out" from the job and seeks a complete escape. For whatever reasons, chances are that the children will not see her again. For children who have spent more time with this woman than with their own parents, her sudden departure is like a death. Suddenly, they are expected to do without a person they trusted in, bonded with, and loved.

We expect children to "bounce back" from this trauma so long as we find a sitter equally gifted to replace the previous one. This ignores the fact that children from whom a beloved adult disappears are in mourning; they cannot recover as quickly as we would like. A friend of mine never forgave his parents for firing his nanny after they caught her stealing. He had spent most of his time with her and, even at forty years old, had not forgotten the overpowering sense of loss and helplessness when his beloved companion was "let go." Before we overestimate the toughness of our children, we should look back to the vulnerable feelings of our own childhood.

My own first experiences in hiring babysitters left me dazed and disillusioned. When my first baby was six months old, I hired a series of college women to look after him two to three afternoons a week while I completed work on my doctoral dissertation. Although I was in the house most of the time, I did run occasional errands and went to lunch with friends. Looking back upon it, I realize that I talked myself into trusting people that I really didn't trust, and that I explained away certain actions of theirs which gave me pause. I reminded myself of the many articles reporting that most mothers of young children worked full time and that many children were without their mothers all day. In comparison, two or three afternoons a week seemed something not to think about too much. To some extent, I made myself believe that I had found a suitable sitter because I needed to have found one. My confidence should have been shaken by the fact that about half of the many women I screened over the phone hung up without saying goodbye the instant they discovered I would be in the home most of the time! I soon learned how misleading interviews could be.

The second girl I hired (because the first girl had, I had realized, an eating disorder which impaired her energy and judgment) took me for quite a ride. She convinced me to give her a loan for a car and, it soon became apparent, did not intend to pay me back in increments as she had promised. I began to catch her in little lies. (She would give false excuses for being late or absent and misleading statements about how much of her babysitting time she spent chatting on the phone or watching TV.) I am ashamed to admit that I did not immediately fire her for her dishonesty. The knowledge that it would be difficult to find a replacement combined with my rationalization that the amount I used a babysitter was so far below the social norm gave me an excuse to act slowly. But most of all,

I did not want to admit to myself that I had hired a dishonest person to look after my child.

The woman I hired to replace this woman did particularly well in my in-home interview. She was well-mannered, well-dressed, seemed sensible, had all the right answers to my questions, and a list of references. I "trained" her for a week, simply by making her a part of my days with my baby. I mistakenly assumed that my way of doing things would rub off on her. She seemed congenial and eager to please. The first day I left her on her own was the day I fired her. I retreated to my second floor study, keeping the door ajar. She and my baby played for about half an hour. I was surprised to hear more "no's" than I would have expected based on our time together. After their playtime, I began to hear the squeak of my baby's walker. She had placed him there while she made herself a cup of tea. I heard him flying from one end of the kitchen to the other. Half an hour went by and I knew he must be getting tired. He put his all into racing across the floor in his walker, but didn't know how to stop when exhausted. That was a role I fulfilled—giving him the rest he needed when he needed it. Instead of taking him out of the walker, she handed him toys and started to clean the kitchen. She cleaned it slowly, for an hour. Still, he raced around in his walker, panting, unable to slow down. He started to chatter to himself in an agitated, frightened tone. Frozen in surprise, I fully expected her to recognize his state of exhaustion and to pick him up. She picked up a magazine instead and sat down. He raced around while she read. She made herself another cup of tea and congratulated him for going so fast.

I wanted to rush down, but a side of me wanted to see how long she would avoid assisting my child. I had spent a week with this woman. I had paid the agency a finder's fee. I had told the other applicants I wasn't interested. Surely, she would pick him up soon. The third hour he was in that walker, he began to emit a low-pitched moan. I believe he was too tired to cry, or too confused. He had always loved his walker and viewed his ten-minute stretches in it as a great adventure. At three hours exactly, ready to burst, I went down and fired this babysitter. My baby was flushed. His eyes looked wild. When I picked him up, spent, he fell immediately to sleep in my arms. When I asked what she possibly could have been thinking, she seemed genuinely surprised, remarking that he seemed to be having a good time. She assumed that "if he had wanted to get out he would have cried." I realized how little she knew about my child and how little I knew about her.

That night, I was disgusted with myself for not firing her immediately, and for not coming to his rescue sooner. I thought about how glad I was to have been home and how little I would have known of my baby's day if I had not been. When I arrived home, would he have smiled beautifully, relieved to see me? Or would he have let go the cry he would not let go of before? How would I have interpreted that smile or that cry? That he had had a good day, that he was sorry to see her go? And how would she have reported on his day? I felt sure that she would have been as impressive as she had been in her interview.

I had instructed this woman not to turn on the TV and she hadn't. I had asked her to clear the dishwasher and she had. I had asked her to avoid long phone conversations and she had. Indeed, she had rushed a friend off the phone. But I hadn't thought to forbid her from putting my baby in his walker for three hours straight. I thought that went without saying. It made me think about how many specific situations arise in a day spent with a child, each calling for a specific response. (I did finally find a wonderful babysitter, whom I came to trust so fully that I eventually rented an office where, three afternoons a week, I worked on this book.)

A child's day is comprised of countless unpredictable occurrences, feelings, and opportunities all of which are responded to by the adults in their lives in a certain way. These adult reactions give a child a sense of what is appropriate, of how loved she is, of what her boundaries are, and of what possibilities her freedom allows her. The notion of quality time, still an acceptable notion in public discourse and still touted in women's magazines, ignores the fact that every moment in a child's life is potentially significant. Even when a child roams around in his backyard, the willingness of the adult to give the child the space to do so says something. It says to the child: I recognize the importance of play, your need to explore and the relevance of your thoughts. As Amitai Etzioni puts it in an article for the *Utne Reader*:

> The notion of quality time is a lame excuse for parental absence; it presupposes that bonding and education can take place in brief time bursts, on the run. Quality time occurs within quantity. As you spend time with children—fishing, gardening, camping or "just" eating a meal - there are unpredictable moments when an opening occurs, and education takes hold. . . . We have made a mistake in entrusting strangers with the personality formation of infants and toddlers.[63]

We have lost our respect for nuance. If the subtleties of a child's existence, those details so nebulous that we would not think of putting them in an instruction list, are left to others, then raising a child is an abstraction. It means that a good part of our children's lives are left to chance—the chance that this babysitter who seems so good *is* so good—and the chance that, when confronted with a situation, she will respond similarly to the way we would. The question is whether we are willing to bet on the kind of care our infants and babies are receiving or whether we must know.

Each parent has his or her own sense of what response to a given situation is appropriate. More often than not, the responses of childcare workers to their child will be strikingly different from their own. A parent who believes that manners should be taught gradually and flexibly, with an understanding of what is appropriate for each age, might find their child with a person who, upon encountering a transgression at the lunch table, responds with disgust and a firm reprimand. A parent might express the opinion that children often misbehave because they need love and yet discover that their child is with a person who takes a child's every action literally. A parent might believe children require clear, age-appropriate limits while leaving their child with a person who does not care enough about the child to endure the persistence and attentiveness, which limit setting requires. Indeed, in her book *Other People's Children*, Julia Wrigley shows that parents and care givers usually find themselves embroiled in "clashes of values" and "become tangled in issues of power and control."[64]

How an adult responds to a child's cry of exasperation, to a smile or a question, to an injury received or an insincerity presented depends upon the character and upbringing of the adult. But *it also depends upon whether the adult loves the child. For, love and lack thereof show through one's actions no matter how virtuous the actions themselves.* Moreover, as much as we have been convinced otherwise, a child relies upon and is comforted by the response of those she loves much more than she relies upon and trusts the response of those she does not love. She receives a different degree of comfort from care givers and parents even if their actions and words are identical. A mother experiences as inevitable the difference between her response to her own child's needs, injuries, smiles, questions, etc. and her response to the needs, injuries, smiles, questions, etc. of another child. As much as she might try to demonstrate impartiality, she and her children know that her deepest emotional resources are reserved for her own children. The unique quality, intensity, and commitment of a mother's love has been assumed in all generations and in all places until our own. Now, we doubt that the constant of a mother's love is necessary and believe it can be easily substituted for. Dr. Hojat argues to the contrary:

Assuming that a family is functional, and parents are mentally healthy, attentive, and lovingly responsive to their child's needs, the home and family environment is certainly the most ideal setting for full and harmonious personality development. I believe that no social, behavioral or medical scientist in his or her right mind would dispute the fact that such a family setting is the most desirable environment for healthy growth. . . . Parents can give unconditional and constant love, appropriate response to their child's needs, and undivided attention in a warm familiar home setting. Such love, cannot, of course, be purchased at any price in an alternative care setting.[65]

As we shall explore further, studies touting the "advantages" of out of home care tend to be based upon disadvantaged children whose parents are less than attentive—who are not "good enough." Indeed, many of the children in these studies come from abusive families where child neglect, swearing, drug use, and promiscuous behavior are the norm. The magazines pushing these studies, however, all too often leave out the fact that the children are disadvantaged. Many day care advocacy articles "showing" day care to be OK are based upon model day cares having as their clientele such deprived children. For example, advocates of federal day care typically cite the Ypsilanti, Michigan High/Scope study. This study, however, was based upon low-income, high-risk children in highly superior day care centers. The "positive results" were that the children avoided juvenile delinquency in higher than expected numbers. As Dr. Hojat warns, "Possible psychological improvements among children from dysfunctional families who have received purchased care should not be an argument against the superiority of maternal care in perfectly functional families."[66] Another often referred to study, for example, is based upon a model infant day care center run by a school of education for babies between the ages of two and twenty-two months for only twenty hours a week (Edwards, et. al., 1987). When we are not informed that these children spent twenty or less rather than forty to fifty hours a week away from loved ones, we are blatantly misled. "Findings" on day care are often based on financially subsidized university settings where day care centers tend to be much better than average and where the parents using the centers tend to have shorter, more flexible work hours. We must insist that the press turn their skeptical eye toward such "findings."

The ideological motivation and the distortion of data in those studies that tend to make it to the public view have blurred our vision. Visionary Horkheimer foresaw this trend as well: "The so-called facts ascertained by quantitative methods, which the positivists are inclined to regard as the only scientific ones, are often surface phenomena that obscure rather than disclose reality. —Thought today is only too often compelled to justify itself by its usefulness to some established group rather than by its truth."[67]

Advocacy articles often simply assume the availability of high-quality care. A national report referred to by Richard Gill resulted in one such article. Children can benefit from "multiple mothering," it insisted, if "it provides affection, warmth, responsiveness, and stimulation in the context of enduring relationships with a reasonably small number of care givers . . . who have come to know the child's individual needs and style." In an article entitled, "Day Care or Parental Care?," Gill asks, "What can be made of such statements?" He points out that even with the best state-enforced and funded day care, parental care is still the most likely to provide, "enduring, stable and responsive" care, sensitive "to the child's individual needs and style" while day care is "intrinsically characterized by transitory relationships even when care is of high quality."[68]

What is really frightening about all this is that those whose role it is to advocate day care actually benefit from social decay. The more insufficiently loved and badly brought up children there are, the more children who can be used to tout the "harmlessness" or even the benefits of non-maternal care. The irony and tragedy of such babies as these being the subject of articles that imply that babies can do with less parental love and interaction than previously thought has yet to hit us. Any benefit these babies receive comes not from the "advantage" of a group environment but from the advantage of receiving any attention and affection at all! Why are we not able to confess to ourselves what all other generations have known—that love and attention are always to a baby's advantage? (See Chapter 2 for abundant research supporting this.)

Many "reports" on modern childrearing practices go beyond the misrepresentation of facts and toward the abandonment of common sense. An article I encountered several years ago insisted that day care was a good thing and used the "dramatic" results of a new survey to support that claim. Researchers had interviewed first graders and found that the majority whose mothers worked, when questioned, said they were "glad" their mothers did. All kinds of conclusions were drawn from this, the most important being that a working mother's guilt is unfounded. I found it amusing that the researchers neglected the fact that six and seven year olds need to revere their parents and tend to compete with peers regarding whose parents are the smartest, nicest, etc. What first grader would come right out and say that they wished their own parents were more like the parents of some of their friends? Moreover, with society proclaiming with such loud unanimity that liberated motherhood is a good thing, it would take a brave little soul to declare it a difficult thing. What was surprising to me was that almost half in this survey admitted to wishing their mother did not work. Interestingly, the researchers did not ask (or did not publish) the results of how many children whose mothers did not work were glad they did not. That such dubious "research" goes unchallenged is intriguing in a culture that glorifies the scientific study and depends greatly upon the reporting of statistics. Horkheimer foresaw that, combined, our emphasis upon the scientific study and our view of truth as "relative" (as having more to do with preference than with reality) would lead to studies being "used" in support of preferences: "In face of the idea that truth might afford the opposite of satisfaction and turn out to be completely shocking to humanity at a given historical moment and thus be repudiated by anybody, the fathers of pragmatism made the satisfaction of the subject the criterion of truth. For such a doctrine, there is no possibility of rejecting or even criticizing any species of belief that is enjoyed by its adherents."[69]

On the big story level, the press's reaction to Marilyn Quayle's speech at the Republican Convention of 1992 was especially revealing. With the caveat that she herself was a working mom and that it could be done successfully, Quayle dared to suggest that women who decided to stay at home deserved respect and that time spent with children did make a difference in their lives. For this, Quayle was pounced upon by the media with such a vengeance and with such a degree of hostility as one would have expected had she suggested that the holocaust had not occurred. She was branded an extremist and depicted as a dim-witted reactionary with no understanding of modern women and modern times.

It was, perhaps, not modern times Quayle was unprepared for but the modern press. For, at about the same time she was being depicted as extreme, Susan Faludi's book *Backlash* was being received as the voice of reason. Unlike Quayle, who actually paid her respects to the working mother, Faludi described the kind of woman who stays home with her children as "childlike, silenced and homebound." Women who questioned this assumption were stereotyped, belittled, and accused of undermining the feminist cause. According to Faludi, the only alternative to being a feminist was being a "masochist."[70] Notable in her book was the absence of respect for the woman who chooses to postpone her career during her children's early years. Also absent was any careful consideration of what is good for the child. Faludi's book received lots of publicity wherein "reporters" "described" the book to the information-hungry public. Displays were to be found in all the big bookstores; mentions which sounded more like endorsements were heard on the evening news.

What Quayle's vilification and Faludi's acceptance indicate is, again, an inversion of extremes. Change had come with such full force that to suggest that time spent with parents made a difference in children's lives was to be branded an extremist. Were we so certain about our course that it was inappropriate to think about it? Penelope Leach observes the following about modern culture:

> Lies, half-truths and truths left untold are combining to convince people that women's sense of symbiosis with young babies arises from their needs, not their infants; that parents' dreams of close companionship with growing children are unrealistic; that their desire to be the prime influence on their offspring's development is atavistic arrogance. Parents are being told that the care compromises which circumstances force upon them are actually better for their children, that "quality time" is enough of their time and the rest should go to the linked achievement of "self-fulfillment" and the salary check. The subtext must be that parents are not very important to children or that children are not very important to society.[71]

Just as the entertainment industry has painted a distorted image of the working and care-provider-finding experience and just as both popular magazines and academic journals have apotheosized non-maternal care, so too the news industry has painted an embellished image of the working woman by using statistics in such a way as to make full-time employment outside the home seem a highly preferred trend with only rare exceptions. Statistics on how many women work full time have been exaggerated as innumerable articles have downplayed and ignored the mother employed part time, the job-sharing mother, and the mother who works only during school hours, only during her husband's off hours, or only during the school year. The woman who has tried to lessen her working hours for the sake of her children, to postpone her career until her baby is a toddler, or to find a new career with flexible hours has been under-represented to the point that she is usually denied any acknowledgment or visibility whatsoever.

For example, throughout the 1980s, when stating the fact that more than 50 percent of mothers worked outside the home, reporters rarely, if ever, mentioned that the percentage was less for mothers of young children. Nor was the diversity within the ranks of those working mothers mentioned. The large numbers within that group that worked part time or during off hours were as invisible as the stay-at-home mom. In an article entitled "A Close Look at Labor Statistics Bursts the Supermom Myth," journalist Deborah Churchman discovered that official government statistics often quoted in the news failed to represent the part-time worker. In 1985, 62 percent of American mothers with children under eighteen were reported to be "in the work force." And yet, underlying the loud reporting of this statistic lay the fact that only 41 percent of mothers worked full time. Churchman discovered the perpetuation of a "myth" that 62 percent of women worked out of the home forty hours a week; only 23 percent of married mothers had worked full time year round in 1985. Churchman also discovered the perpetuation of a myth regarding the kinds of work women do. According to Churchman, the idea that this country is full of "super moms, who wear power-suits, drop the baby at a day-care center, work downtown forty hours a week" distorts the reality of mothers in the United States today. "The profile of the real working mother is someone who may often be tired, guilty, underpaid, or stressed even when she likes her job but especially if she doesn't. She works in an office, hospital, school or factory. She is not very glamorous, and that's the main reason she doesn't wind up in too many perfume adds."[72] By keeping such kinds of work in the background, the media is able to glamorize the workplace and to heighten the pressure upon new mothers to seek satisfaction therein.

It should be noted that, since Churchman made these observations, times have changed. By 2005, 73 percent of working women had white-collar occupations, while women in professional and related categories accounted for about 25 percent of all working women.[73] As of the year 2000, according to U.S. Labor Department statistics, more than seventy percent of women in their "prime years" were employed. At the same time, the number of married working women on part-time schedules has grown enormously, according to an article in the *American Journal of Economics and Sociology*, which cites multiple studies.[74] A study by Hewlet and Luce found large numbers of women "opting out" of the workforce altogether if they had children.[75] A recent, fascinating study of Ivy League women found that the majority planned to stay home with their young children.[76] On the other hand, a recent study by the Simmons School of Management, found that the majority of the women it surveyed, rather than "opting out" or working part time, were seeking "flexible work arrangements" such as telecommuting and flexible hours.

What is clear is that, while the number of mothers of young children who are working is larger than ever, proportionate attention must be given to women who have managed to redefine work and to mothers who are reassessing the costs and benefits of working full time.

Even in the 1980s, Dr. Jack Westman cited evidence that many families decide that the financial costs in settling for a part-time income are easier to bear than the "emotional costs" of trying to earn two incomes.

This was suggested to him by the fact that (as of 1988) 34 percent of mothers of children under the age of three were employed only part time. Thus, nearly two-thirds of the mothers of infants and toddlers did not work away from home or had part-time jobs. In the 1990s, Arlene Rosen Cordozo argued that the often-quoted statistic that two-thirds of mothers worked disguised the fact that about only one third of *married* "working mothers" worked full time.[77]

Women who use relatives and friends rather than institutions and "child care professionals" to look after their children are hurt by another misconception: that "affordable, quality" day care would solve the needs of working parents. A little publicized Rand Corporation study found that "child care by relatives was more likely to satisfy parents' criterion for what is important than was institutional care: the small group sizes, loving environment and transmission of family and cultural religious values." By contrast, the structural elements of child care that are currently the focus of licensing were found to be "largely irrelevant in terms of what parents demand."[78] The great majority of parents view day care as an undesirable option.

In yet another distortion, those seeking massive funding for day care often conjure up the image of huge numbers of women working out of economic necessity. When it is useful, the glamorous image is replaced by the image of desperation. Observing the employment of the later imagery, Penn State University researchers concluded that it was misleading. They found that "the rising proportion of *married* mothers entering the labor force since 1960 is largely due to family decisions to earn a second income so that the family may enjoy a higher standard of living." They noted that while, in the 1950s, "providing basic necessities for the family appeared to be the predominant economic motive, by 1980, standard-of-living preferences dominated the economic motive." Since economic necessity is generally not the reason for a second income for married women, the PSU researchers ask, "Is it possible that families will scale back their income needs to devote more time to family and leisure?" They conclude, "if the recent past is any indication of the near future, this does not seem likely." And yet, they imagine "a scenario in which families begin to choose a simpler lifestyle."[79]

Although economic necessity does *contribute* to the numbers of working mothers, the numbers working out of necessity are, in turn, greatly influenced by higher divorce rates and by the phenomenal increase in single parenting. Indeed, multiple studies have shown that the growth of the poverty-ridden family is directly related to the growth of the family headed by the single mother. Moreover, it can be demonstrated that our definition of what is "necessary" has changed, often including consideration of what is "desirable" (see Chapter 3). Most *married* women work for self-fulfillment and a higher income. The blurring of the distinction between those who work out of necessity and those who work for fulfillment makes it easier for "women's groups" to claim to speak for all women.

The misleading reporting of "facts" regarding working women and day care preferences, especially on television, has tremendous influence upon our collective consciousness. News is supposed to be "objective." Living in a free country as we do, we assume the absence of propaganda (even if we observe "biases") in our nightly news programs. The "visuals" that back up the reports embed the "facts" further within our minds. In an address entitled "Electronic Democracy: How TV Governs," Anne Rawley Saldich of the University of California, Berkeley, explained:

> Television's immense political power flows from a combination of several qualities that are not found elsewhere. Its powerful imagery gives viewers a you-are-there feeling, which tends to shut down one's critical, analytical faculties. This, in turn, gives the medium high credibility. People are inclined to believe what they see even if it contradicts their knowledge or experience. Because television news has the highest credibility of all media it also enjoys the kind of authority that every institution in America envies. Credibility is the keystone of all power relationships because belief is the engine of action.[80]

The imagery is all the more powerful because it is impossible to escape. Living in America today, we are consumed by images, and consume them. Given that one now finds television and computer kiosks in airports, stores, restaurants, dorm rooms, exercise facilities, coffee houses, hotel lobbies, and libraries, surely even the extraordinarily high estimates of the amount of time Americans spend under the spell of media information is underestimated.

Regarding the subject of day care, the media has taken relentless advantage of its "information-providing" power. Those lobbying to make day care a federal industry for which we all pay have benefited the most from media distortions. Day care advocacy groups and their willing partners in the press leave out essential information about child development, ignore the diversity within the ranks of working mothers, and distort true working patterns because they fear funding for day care would be cut if the truth were out. Distorted statistics regarding how many families "needed" day care and the distorted impression given regarding how many families saw day care as a desirable child care "option" were tailor made for the passage of a national day care bill.

Witness the positive press given to the "Children's Defense Fund," which has just such a priority. Witness Marian Wright Edelman's priorities during consideration of the ABC bill in Congress. ABC was to provide federal subsidies to increase day care's affordability and licensing provisions, which supposedly would increase both the quantity and the quality of day care centers. Jessica Gress-Wright astutely portrays the bill's supporters:

> ABC was supported by a broad coalition of unions, feminists, advocacy organizations and policy elites, each of whom had a financial and ideological stake in the bill's passage. Thus, the teachers associated with NAEYC, desperate for higher pay, were relying on ABC to restrict competition from low-wage family day-care providers and church-based day-care centers, as well as to provide the subsidies which would make higher salaries possible. Unions hoped to recruit badly needed new members from the ranks of the subsidized teachers. Feminists wanted to enable women to stay in the work force. The Children's Defense Fund wanted to recover the influence and patronage it had lost under Reagan. And the "liberal developmental intelligentsia" (in Jay Belsky's wry self-characterization) wanted a chance to apply its expertise in child-rearing on a national scale.[81]

ABC was a bill crafted by and for interest groups. It was not lobbied for by large numbers of parents but *by those who claimed to know what was best for parents.* In effect, it bolstered government support for institutional day care while threatening to put the home and church-run childcare, which parents tended to prefer, out of business. Interestingly, the question of whether day care is good for children, of whether it is something the national government should actively encourage and of whether a national bureaucracy was up to the task of "child development" was kept far in the background by the bill's advocates. They and their supporters in the press used language in such a way as to make government-sponsored day care and "caring for children" synonymous.

As Cannaught Marshner explained in an article entitled "Socialized Motherhood: As Easy as ABC," the bill's sponsors learned from the 1971 defeat of Walter Mondale's attempt to lead the Federal government into the realm of child development:

> No longer praising the destruction of the nuclear family, they go to great lengths to usurp the pro-family rhetoric of the Right. Rather than argue over whether day care is good for children, they take the line that since women must work, the Federal Government must help them raise their children. A spokesman for the House Subcommittee on Human Resources told me that hearings on the bill will "focus on individual provisions of the bill rather than the issue as a whole." In other words, the members of congress will not allow witnesses to question whether encouraging day care is good for children or families.[82]

In spite of a well-orchestrated publicity campaign, the bill did not pass easily. New president Bush threatened a veto, while House members George Miller and Tom Downey proposed an alternate bill which would have combined an earned income-tax credit which put funds directly in the hands of working parents and a childcare entitlement to the states. Throughout 1990, the CDF and the childcare lobbyists pushed hard. Finally, in the spring of 1990, Congress passed a compromise bill entitled "The Early Childhood and Development Act." It provided tax relief for working families and provided federal support to the day care industry, something the lobbyists sought above all else. It provided 2.5 billion for five years instead of the hoped-for 2.5 billion for the first year, but it set no limits on future authorizations. The 1990 bill put government clearly in the business of providing financial aid to working families and set the precedent for massive federal involvement in day care. As Marshner observed, while it did not satisfy the scope of the day care lobbyists, it provided them with a toehold from which to fight.

In "Day Care or Parental Care?" Gill asks, "Should the government actively promote out-of home care as an alternative to parental care in the rearing of infants, toddlers and preschoolers?" He claims that "the present younger generation has been subject to a curious and possibly shameful national neglect from infancy through adolescence." He points to "an abundance of disturbing statistics on broken homes, child poverty, emotional problems, teenage suicide, and inadequate, unstable, sometimes unsanitary infant and child-care arrangements." And yet, observes Gill, "with surprisingly little fanfare, Congress enacted a bill that provides for closer regulation and inspection of day-care facilities, a program of federal grants to the states aimed at making child-care more affordable for working families and funds for improving the quality of day care services."[83]

During consideration of these bills, the press was firmly behind the ideological stance of the bills' supporters. Supporters fed a steady diet of misinformation to the press regarding the so-called "day-care crisis." A document developed by the Democratic National Committee as part of their 1988 campaign strategy outlined a strategy for addressing family concerns in such a way as to split Republicans in two over its failure to reconcile itself to the "modern family." Meanwhile, advocates of a Federal day care program were planning for a six to eight month media campaign on the "day-care crisis." The strategy worked in that the "crisis" achieved saturation coverage during the spring and early summer of the presidential election year. On the evening news and in articles in *Parade Magazine, The New York Times,* and other magazines and newspapers, American citizens were "informed" about the crisis.

Did the "crisis" really exist or was an ideology, the credibility and popularity of which relied upon positive findings about day care, the underlying motivation for these stories? Evidence shows that there was no chronic shortage of day care. In an April 21, 1989 conference entitled "The Economics of Day Care," Robert Recter recalled that, "perceptions on day care have been so distorted that in 1988 he found it almost like spitting into a hurricane to testify before congress that there was no day-care crisis nor a shortage of day care." He pointed out, "even the Urban Institute has issued a report finding no shortage of day care and that economic data on day care show the market is working quite well: for-profit centers such as Kindercare and Gerbers operate with average vacancy rates of 25 percent." Still, he noted, advocates "persist in their illusory reports of a chronic shortage of day care."[84] Why, wondered Stephen Chapman, columnist for *The Chicago Tribune* also at the conference, does the press respond the way it does to the interest groups promoting day care?"[85] Recter explained, "because of the ideological bias documented by Robert Lichter and Stanley Rothman, the Children's Defense Fund will find it much easier to plant stories than, say the Cato Institute." In fact, he added, *Newsweek, The Washington Post,* and *The New York Times* contribute generously to the Children's Defense Fund.[86]

Thus, the interest groups which, for various reasons, wanted federally funded and guided day care, knew they needed the public perception of a crisis in order to achieve it and the press willingly fulfilled that need. Allan Carlson, who was also at the day care economics conference, traced the use of "crises" to justify state intervention in the family as far back as the 1930's. He recalled attending a public-policy conference in Michigan where he was the only one voicing concerns about full-time day care's effect on children. For other participants, the conference was "almost a religious revival in favor of ABC." The mood reminded Carlson of a scene in Cabaret in which a young Nazi boy sings, "Tomorrow belongs to me." Carlson observed that "there was a sense that it was going to be their world; the future, history was moving in their direction."[87]

Opponents of national day care legislation were portrayed by the press as enemies of both children and progress. Reporters precluded the question of whether day care is harmful to children by keeping the question of when government would "solve the crisis" in the forefront, and by transfiguring those who questioned their proposed "solution" into mean-spirited reactionaries. Never mind that, at the time the bill was under consideration, 76 percent of preschool age children were in the care of parents or relatives and that, of the remaining 24 percent, half were in unlicensed, informal day care not covered under ABC. Never mind that, even for licensed day care, the ABC bill would offer coverage to church-based day care only if they were engaged in no religious activity. Never mind that the bill would force more children into institutional settings. The bill's proponents had both a vested interest and an ideological interest in its passage, viewing it as the wave of the future. Jessica Gress-Wright understood the real effect of ABC, an effect that resonates today, dominating every political discussion of "children's issues:"

> ABC would not, in fact, improve the availability, affordability, and quality of child care for ordinary parents. "Availability" and "affordability" were carrots, vote-getters; in fact, the amount proposed—2.5 billion for one year, only 70% of which could be used for subsidies—was derisory compared to the 75-100 billion it would cost to implement ABCs promises nationwide. Under the provisions of the bill, moreover, the state would have to go after all providers who broke licensing rules, which meant that upward of 90% of all current day care in America would be ineligible for subsidy. This was the stick of "quality' and its enforcement would deprive parents of most forms of family day care—in which, typically, a young mother or an empty nester takes in a few children from the neighborhood. Perhaps most significantly, by using government funds to establish nationally standardized day care and by subsidizing that care, ABC provided a financial boost to working parents and a financial disincentive to parents who chose to stay at home. The bill created a new bureaucracy in the Health and Human Services Department and authorized 2.5 billion in federal aid to day care centers.[88]

The blurring of our vision, achieved through incomplete and fragmented statistics and lopsided media images and news reports, holds powerful sway in a country where majority opinion is revered and where majority opinion has such a cogent effect on so many politicians. What we have seen is that the part-time employed mother, the job-sharing mother, the mother who works only during school hours, the woman who tries to put her career on hold until her children enter kindergarten, and the woman who works but would never leave her child in the hands of a stranger are downplayed and, even worse, removed from our sight. When we are made to believe that certain trends are nearly universal, it is emotionally difficult to buck the trend. We feel that society will not and cannot support us in our decision to raise our own children.

Politicians on both sides of the political spectrum believe the public will not support them if they question the seemingly inevitable march toward more publicly sponsored day care and more disincentives for those who prefer other kinds of child care. Lest we think the fear of questioning recent (misleading) portrayals of "what parents want" is not so great, look at virtually any high profile political campaign. "Children's issues"—education, crime, and drugs—are addressed while the issue of how children's upbringing or lack thereof affects American society is absent. Even "conservatives" fear that to raise the documented connection between parental absence and crime, drugs, poor performance in school, teenage depression, and weakened relationships would be to bring on their own demise.

In politics and in journalism, the incentive is toward creating change, for one receives much more credit for transforming society, than for simply letting it be. How many times have we heard campaigning politicians declare: "The country is ready for change," or "The people are hungry for change," or "It's time for a change?" How many journalists win awards for pointing out that what is "already there" is good or that it works? Our societal emphasis on image reinforces the drive for catchy new "solutions" that capture the limelight.

The political precedent of treating day care as the method of child care preferred by parents and as the best solution to the child-rearing problems of society as a whole continued on after ABC. With this rationale, the Clinton administration proposed a twenty one billion program of new spending and tax breaks to subsidize day care. In an unusual journalistic move, a January, 1998 edition of the *Wall Street Journal* criticized the administration's use of misconception to advocate and fund the program:

> Now it is important to understand that the Clintons and their allies in the multibillion-dollar child-care industry have a specific idea in mind when they talk about "quality care." They don't mean finding better baby-sitting in the home, or even, heaven forbid, staying home one's self with a lonely child from time to time. No, they envision building great numbers of brightly lit centers where child experts stimulate infant brains by waving flash cards before their cribs. Indeed $3 billion of the money will create an early learning fund. . . . The pumping has begun. With billions to offer, it's likely that parents, politicians, academics, trainers and corporations will take the money and run.

Overall, the press was tremendously supportive of the Clintons' day care policy. The American public received the message that a study by the National Institute of Health released at the time resulted in nothing but positive findings about "quality care." *USA Today* declared day care "not harmful to growth or bonding." *Time* announced that the "kids are all right." The Associated Press notified us that day care's effect was good as long as it was of high quality. What we did not hear about was the study's finding of a negative correlation between hours spent in day care and good mother-child interaction, nor that the study was preliminary, nor that the preliminary results pointed to some likely negative behavioral outcomes. More essential, we did not hear about the *many reputable studies and mountains of evidence* which show a negative correlation between day care, even "high quality" day care, and just about every essential aspect of a child's development. These include the development of a kind disposition, the capacity for close relationships, intellectual curiosity and intelligent thought processes, skills of concentration, ability to control anger and to resist drugs, alcohol, and depression (see Chapter 2).

Focus upon the slogan "quality care" combined with inadequate attention to what actually goes on in day care centers and to the actual results of day care studies distorts our vision. Most of us have never been inside a day care center. We therefore have little recourse from the imagistic slogans with which we are presented. *If we value knowledge, we must expose the modern imposters of knowledge—strategically placed "information" and media-induced "impressions."*

For obvious reasons, those who advocate day care, who go beyond just accepting it, tend to be found most often on the progressive side of the political spectrum. The fact that the American media tends to be progressive, in turn, means that day care advocates and day care itself will be positively "positioned" in movies, shows, and news stories. A belief that they should promote social reform in order to move Americans toward a vision (their vision) of the good society often lies at the heart of media distortions and rationalizations. *And That's the Way It Isn't* by Brent Bozell III and Brent H. Baker reveals some of the ways in which journalists and reporters make the facts fit the viewpoint when it comes to issues affecting children and the society in which they are raised. One of the most common methods is labeling. By giving an institution or person the label right wing, for example, journalists give the impression that the person is extremist or at least ideologically biased. Bozzell and Baker found that conservative groups were labeled an average of 58 percent of the time while liberals were identified a mere 2 percent of the time; the conservative Concerned Women for America was tagged almost twenty times more frequently than the liberal National Organization for Women. The use of labels is highly effective. One congressional staffer confided that congress people are "scared to death" to oppose day care legislation. "They're afraid of being labeled anti-woman in their campaigns." Other interesting findings included these: 55 percent of newsroom reporters considered themselves liberal, compared to just 17 percent who identified themselves as conservative; newspaper journalists are far more liberal than others surveyed; less than one-fourth of the public and only 38 percent of college-educated professionals described themselves as liberal; of nearly four million dollars contributed to political organizations, the foundations for ten of the biggest media empires allocated 90 percent to liberal organizations (i.e., the Children's Defense Fund); one time progressive activists are far more readily accepted into media jobs than those who used to work for moderates or conservatives.[89]

Other research confirms the findings of Bozell and Baker. Lichter, Lichter, and Rothman conducted a quantitative study of the ideological beliefs among motion picture and television producers, writers, directors, and executives. They found the "Hollywood elite" to be consistently liberal in "all three dimensions of political ideology:" economic, social, and foreign policy.[90] David T. Prendle of the University of Texas at Austin and James Endersby of the University of Missouri at Columbia expanded upon this research by comparing the ideological attitudes of the Hollywood elite to that of the general public. They discovered a huge discrepancy, but were struck by the suffusion of Hollywood ideology into everyday lives:

> The motion picture and television industries together constitute a gigantic potential propaganda machine. The average adult watches TV about three hours a day; the average child about four hours. Young people are so attentive that by the time the typical American has graduated from high school, he or she has been exposed to video for 17,000 hours, more than any other life activity than sleeping. Further, Americans purchase roughly a billion movie tickets annually, and this behavior is also skewed toward the youthful age groups. . . . The general consensus of scholars is that these media function as a powerful vehicle for mass learning. If this is so, then a consistent political bias in Hollywood's product might have profound, long-term consequences for public opinion.[91]

It is simply clear that, as parents search for accurate information, the ideological motive of those reporting on day care must be considered.

It should be noted that such an ideological motive exists not only in the mediums of popular print, television, and the motion picture industry but also in many academic journals. Many academic researchers, also much more progressive than the general public, have been unwilling to inspire a thoughtful and thorough discussion of children's issues. (Recall the pressure put upon researchers who found innate differences between the sexes.) Although this is perhaps less true now that brain imaging and cross-cultural studies make it hard to deny the unique quality and attributes of the mother-child relationship, those who discovered truths that did not fit progressive ideology often suffered the consequences. As an example, Otto Weininger, one of Canada's premier psychologists, was for many years unable to publish in any professional journal a watershed work on the effects of day care. It finally appeared in *The Journal of Family and Culture*. Some academicians have actually suggested that any information leading to negative conclusions about non-maternal care be suppressed. Cummings and Beagle-Ross argued that the issue of whether day care is good or bad for infants is "useless from a social policy perspective" and that "the need for out-of-home care for infants will continue to be an inevitable byproduct of changes in economic conditions and parents' roles."[92]

In an article entitled "Abandoning Research on Consequences of Non-maternal Care: A Disservice to the Science," Dr. Hojat criticizes a similar article by Louis Silverstein suggesting that "psychologists must refuse to undertake any more research that looks for the negative consequences of other-than-mother care" and must "interrupt" all research in which the hypothesis of risk factors associated with non-maternal care is being tested. This approach, warns Hojat "provides ammunition and further division of the already frail discipline of psychology into a battlefield in which the accumulated knowledge will be disgraced for the reason of not being feminist."[93] Hojat laments the compromising of scientific procedure for the sake of ideology.

Sharon Landesman Ramey, the prominent Georgetown University researcher who has taken part in numerous large studies on the effects of "parenting" and day care, finds a problem not with the scientific research itself but with the way the research is interpreted. Emphasizing that the research clearly shows "what parents can do, actually do, and fail to do for their children encompasses a very broad spectrum and potentially influences many far-reaching aspects of a child's total development," she laments the lack of attention given to "the impressive and growing body of scientific literature that unequivocally supports the conclusions that children's cumulative life experiences matter."[94] She argues that recent radical suggestions, based upon selective research and claims of genetic determinism, that parents have no influence upon their children have not emerged directly from the scientific community. "Rather, the corporations that publish these books and manufacture new products for parents are the ones that launch vigorous and expensive promotional campaigns to capture prime-time media coverage." She adds, "The sound knowledge base, accruing from decades of research on typically developing children and children with identified disabilities, alas, does not readily lend itself to a few dramatic headlines, much less conclusions that totally overturn what many parents already think and do."[95]

What *has* emerged from diverse areas of the scientific community are dramatic new findings on the vital importance and lasting significance of the mother-child bond. Partly because of this, significantly more research detailing the positive effects of active parenting, maternal attention, and attachment is appearing in academic journals now than at the time Weineger tried to publish his article. As James E. Swain of Yale, Jeffrey P. Lorberbaum of Penn State, Samet Kose of the Medical University of South Carolina, and Lane Strathearn of Baylor College put it in a joint article, "Over the past decade, a diverse spectrum of research has begun to explore the neural basis of attachment—at molecular, cellular and behavioral levels" (Insel & Young, 2001; Strathearn, 2007). This research has uncovered many parallels between Bowlby's original thesis and the biological systems which may underlie attachment and stress reactivity."[96] They point out that "empathy, defined as appropriate perception, experience and response to another's emotions" has become one of the central interests of psychodynamic clinicians studying the mother/child relationship.[97]

Hopeful signs of unbiased research are still outweighed by slanted reporting and repression or distortion of findings. There is a reason that Landesman Ramey, in a publicly reported statement regarding the large-scale NIH study showing a link between day care and poor behavior of which she was a co-author, commented: "I have accused the study authors of doing everything they could to make this negative finding go away, but they couldn't do it. They knew this would be disturbing news for parents, but at some point, if that's what you're finding, then you have to report it."

Reporters and academicians alike learn to ask certain questions rather than others and to phrase their questions in ways most likely to produce a desirable outcome. As Jon A. Krosnick remarks in an article entitled "The Uses and Abuses of Public Opinion Polls," "Because public opinion is often so sensitive to detail, a slight change in the way a survey question is asked can sometimes greatly alter people's answers."[98] Rather than ask the big, important questions such as, Are our children thriving or are they floundering under the new approach to child-rearing?, researchers assume the children are OK, assume that more quality day care is the benchmark of social progress, and proceed to the question of how society can best approach that benchmark.

The discussion of childcare has so far reminded me of a train so intent upon reaching its destination that it does not stop to let the people on. The parents who know in their heart that no one can do for their children what they do, the researcher who connects early development of the brain to one-on-one contact with and stimulation from a loving other, the philosopher who wonders if we are raising a generation better geared for survival than for thinking and contributing, and the teacher who sees countless behavioral and emotional problems which she did not see in the past are not given a seat on the train of progress. In an inversion of extremes, these people who want nothing more than moderation, a kind heart and a careful, reasonable approach to childrearing are relegated to the lunatic fringe. Meanwhile, those who would impose upon us and our children a "brave new world" march confidently "forward" in the knowledge that, because they have the correct "social vision," Hollywood, the press, and much of academia will treat their assertions as authoritative, their "findings" as conclusive.

And yet, it is most certainly weak to believe something simply because it bolsters our social agenda. Much more strength is to be found in the ability to make well-informed choices and in the ability to think clearly about potential consequences. Indeed, the combination of cloudy thinking and irresponsible actions is the stuff tragedies are made of.

To say that statistics and images have been distorted is not to deny that a social revolution has occurred. There is no denying that, whether because of their mother's full-time employment or because of her part-time employment, children are receiving huge quantities of non-parental care. Moreover, there is no denying that the numbers of children receiving such care has grown steadily over the last thirty years, and is only now beginning to fall off. It is simply to point out that, by exaggerating the uniformity of modern mothers and by failing to give a voice to those who have qualms about the effect of modern choices upon modern children, the media has contributed to a one-sided definition of progress. Over those same years, many women feared that they placed themselves within the confines of a reactionary fringe if they chose to concentrate on their young children. We must remember that the media exist in their own agenda-laden confines, *confines that prevent them from seeing the truth about us.*

In sum, the effect of the illusory upon the modern American consciousness is phenomenal. Both the images and the information we receive are misleading. What we have seen over the last twenty five years is the following: (1) the glamorization and visibility of the working mother and the degradation and invisibility of the mother who stays at home while her children are young; (2) blurring of the differences between those who work out of necessity and those who work for fulfillment and an unwillingness to scrutinize the new definitions of necessity and fulfillment; (3) exaggeration of the number of women who work full time (4) the lack of attention given to families who prefer alternatives to day care; (5) the omission of findings regarding the damage which accrues to children who lead predominantly separate lives from their parents; (6) the high visibility of the *ideal* and *goal* of high-quality day care combined with the low visibility of actual day care centers; (7) trivialization of the working mother experience and the babysitter-hiring experience and inattention to real-life difficulties in those areas, and (8) the reformulation of human-nature to the end that any special maternal function is denied.

Our willingness to buy into the superficial and partial picture painted for us has stemmed in part from our belief in the larger social cause. The cause of women's liberation has been thought so worthy that we have been willing to accept less than clear thinking and less than accurate reporting in support of it. Many never lost the spirit of fighting against social injustices, which inspired them when they came of age in the late 60s and early 70s. What has struck me about this activism has been its often-abstract nature. As attention to big social issues has increased, attention to kind behavior between one person and another has decreased—for what is most important is every individual's subordination to higher social ends. Thus, the righteousness of an idea is allowed to overshadow the details or lack thereof in the thinking that supports it. Thus, the man who supports feminism might feel free to sleep with a woman at night and disown her the next day since they are both "liberated." Thus, the social worker might leave her children in an uncertain childcare situation because her work with other children is so important. Thus, a journalist will rail against the "mindlessness" of domesticity while not permitting *intelligent* debate of "women's issues" in his journal. In all of these instances, the impersonal cause assumes priority over personal relationships.

In 1976, Jean-Francois Revel wrote *The Totalitarian Temptation.*[99] Revel analyzed the rhetoric and methods of the advocates and apologists of communism. The methods he describes are strikingly similar to the methods used in this country to support the idea that full-time childcare is the preferred alternative to parental care and that children are "just fine" with minimal input from their parents. A brief deviation into this book is worthwhile for it warns us against succumbing to the slogans and distortions described above and reminds us to keep our hearts and our minds alive. To those who have given in to the "temptation" to distort the truth and block the voice of dissent, this book provides reason for sober restraint.

Of Communism, Revel makes the following points: (1) It is based on an abstract theory which is not rooted in a rational understanding of human nature. (Child care advocates deny the existence of maternal feelings and ignore the natural and documented need of babies for their mothers.) (2) Its self-esteem is not based on success. On the contrary, it thrives on despair. (Advocates of child care thrive upon the idea of the unhappy "housewife," the family in desperate economic straights and the day care "crisis.") (3) The goal is power for a certain group, not the greatest good for the whole. (Policy has catered to interest groups, not to overall parental preferences. The focus has been upon making life convenient for parents who prefer institutional day care.) (4) The faults of society are magnified and distorted so that any underlying oppression can be justified as necessary in order to achieve "liberation" from society's wrongs. (By portraying women and girls as victims of male chauvinism and portraying the family as an instrument of oppression, and by reinterpreting history in this light, whatever parents do becomes justified so long as it is "liberating.")

Of the Western press's reaction to communist states, Revel noted that "the refusal to judge them doubtless reflects a decision to approve them no matter what" and that "the fact that the water is bad never suggests that the well from which it is drawn is poisoned."[100] The refusal to judge the effect of modern choices upon modern children, no matter the outcome, is manifest. For example, we are quick to attribute the phenomenon of troubled children to the living conditions of poor parents but never attribute the phenomenon to the nurturing conditions of wealthy parents. We are thus incapable of even beginning to understand the psychological and behavioral difficulties evident across all income groups.

Revel added: "From the moment that people are in a position to evaluate totalitarian rule from their own experience, they no longer have the ability to abolish it, or criticize it, or alter it, or even to escape it. Then, after a generation, a people subjected to a totalitarian regime has scarcely any means of comparing their society to others . . . News having been entirely supplanted by propaganda, it becomes impossible for residents of a totalitarian state to conceive of, or to remember, a society different from their own."[101] *We live in a democracy, but we also live in a society consumed by the disease of forgetting—forgetting what other cultures and other times have known about young children's needs and forgetting all historic, biological, and literary references to the maternal.* We find the maternal ideal unliberated, therefore we remember the special bond between mother and child only in order to dismiss it. We leave ourselves without an alternative to the status quo. Of the Communists, Revel further says:

> You are not seeking the right to explore, to experiment. Rather, you claim the right of total social surgery, like the quack physician who claims to know, as if it were a routine operation he has successfully performed a thousand times, how to replace all the patient's organs at a single stroke. You also make excuses, to the point of turning our stomachs, for all your friends' surgeons whose patients expired on the operating table. For years and years you go on maintaining that the operation was a complete success and that the patient will exhibit the flourishing state of his health as soon as certain unfavorable conditions and maleficent adversaries have been eliminated. Should the deceased insist by chance on remaining dead, the latter will bear responsibility for the crime—you political geniuses! You have invented a new art of government which, according to you yourselves, can only succeed when it meets no obstacles and faces no enemies.[102]

It is a very modern idea that in order to improve upon the past you must destroy it. Baby boomers did not just modify childhood—they radically transformed it. The idea of childhood has been so thoroughly upended that it is the "new normal" to put babies into day care centers and toddlers into endless structured activities and academic lessons. In spite of some recent efforts to resurrect the idea, we have almost abolished the ideal of the two-parent family. Monogamy, fidelity, the sacrificing of self for children, and the idea of motherhood have been attacked with such full force as to construct a great divide between current generations and all generations prior. Tradition threatens to undermine the myth upon which social engineering depends. And so it is discarded.

Revel describes the Communist's ability to explain away the short-comings of their government (from economic, to academic, to political) by the belief that "a leftist government is not required in the short run to do better than a rightist one. It is in any event superior because it is a good government, while the rightist regime is a bad one."[103] We too are tacitly warned not to draw attention to our own shortcomings. The message we have received is that the "liberated" mother does not have to *do* better or as well as the "un-liberated" mother for her children; she simply *is* better by virtue of being true to her cause. The future belongs to her, an idea that holds powerful sway in a forward-looking country whose identity depends so greatly upon the future.

Revel goes on, "The description of free and democratic societies as totalitarian rests on several lines of reasoning that have in common under their apparent diversity making the exception appear to be the rule, the marginal appear to be the basic phenomenon."[104] It is still reprehensible or at least shocking, in most quarters, to question the assumption that childrearing decisions, in the end, do not really matter. This is thought to be too "judgmental." Revel asks why it should be so shocking that people have "honest reservations" about and "serious reasons" for questioning socialism. It cannot be denied that honest reservations about and serious reasons for questioning modern childrearing trends have been treated similarly to the way honest reservations about Communism were treated. Although there have been recent signs of resistance, we have come perilously close to the elimination from our public forum of doubting voices.

Instead of an evaluation and a study of the changes, which have come with full force to families and children, we have seen a constant rationalization of that change, a *comforting self-congratulatory stance that holds difficult questions at bay*; that stops "admittedly regrettable events," that are the result of new policies, from being discussed. "Should we therefore understand that scientific analysis must not be permitted to derive the cause from its effects?"[105]

One of the most effective methods of the Communists in their self-reinforcing process, Revel observed, was to make the most noise and to apply labels to their opponents volubly and frequently. So too, those who have observed negative behavioral and emotional outcomes in children who have received too little parental guidance and love minimize and pass over this knowledge in order to avoid the label of reactionary close-mindedness. The use of invective has succeeded in causing the American people to walk on eggs as far as "children's issues" are concerned. We all know not to say certain things, not to articulate certain ideas. Revel's treatise on Communism bears a warning for all modern societies. For, ideology and propaganda are fearsome companions in the modern race toward "progress."

Stop and think about the message we are receiving. If people are so careful of our "feelings" that they do not dare breathe a word questioning the feminist framework and if that framework dictates what women may and may not say, then we must be delicate creatures indeed. Moreover, we must be a dull lot, resigned to touting the group line or no line at all. If one viewpoint is apparently widespread and acceptable while the other is rare and unacceptable, how are we to think about our choices in any meaningful way? If we have the ability to make choices but fear our ability to question them, then choice is no more than random preference; it takes on the character of flightiness, precisely the characterization strong women seek to avoid.

It would be a sad irony if feminism were to encourage the trivialization of life by insisting upon women's acceptance of simplistic platitudes. Must the press coddle us with "feel good" articles congratulating us for our advances while misinforming us about something as vital as our children? If the only articles available convince us that our young children do not need us as much as they truly do, then we have indeed been victims—of a cover-up underlain by the belief that women would rather be ingratiated than informed.

If we do not need protecting, as feminism insists, then we must insist that the media and the press stop protecting us—protecting the image of us, which it deems appropriate. By keeping the discussion of children's issues on a superficial level lest a fact that does not fit the agenda pop up, the media and the press insult the intelligence of all parents. For beneath that protection of the illusory image of us there is an oppression. Beneath the relativistic insistence that preference is what matters is the incessant packaging, selling, and promotion of one preference.

Can anyone really believe that the decision whether to be the predominant influence in our young children's lives is simply a matter of preference? Rather, it is a decision with far-reaching consequences requiring careful thought and accurate information. Women I know who have made the decision to be that predominant influence are quick to point out that the important thing is having the choice and that they would never pass judgment on the full-time working mother. And yet, society has clearly passed judgment on them, relegating to the status of "housewife" these intelligent, interesting, busy women, many of whom are rarely "at home." While their image is that of subservience, these women are certainly not subservient. They have part-time babysitters and, if they can stretch it financially, help cleaning the house. They are not domestic drudges. They do not feel obligated to put a hot meal on the table every night nor to have perfectly pressed clothes for their children and a sparkling kitchen. Over the years, I have seen one such friend thrive as a sculptor, another as a painter, another as a participant in city planning, another as part-time editor. I have seen others thrive upon committee or volunteer work at their children's schools and others upon having welcoming houses, a close network of friends, and the interesting conversations and good times that ensue. I have seen women return successfully to full-time work after taking a few years off, even though this is a hard thing to do, especially given corporate inflexibility in these matters.

These women have pursued interests and friendships within the framework of motherhood and have learned not to expect the path to fulfillment to be one smooth road. An artist friend of mine, for example, agonized during her child's early years over the missed time painting. She wanted to be with her baby but worried that she would never return to the empty canvasses in her studio. When her second baby started nursery school three mornings a week, she found those mornings ideally suited for painting and actually found herself more inspired and more disciplined in the task than when, as before motherhood, all her days had been free. She never regrets the time spent away from the oil and brush. She now spends hours a day at it. She finds she brings new depth to her painting, having savored her children and surrendered to the depths of feeling to which they brought her.

A dependency upon the group image will permit us to rationalize too much and reason too little. Rationalizations allowed the Communists to think they were strong until the wall came tumbling down. Communist "strength" depended upon people buying into the group vision of utopia or, at least, being afraid to speak out against it. Underneath the surface of invincibility was the weakness inherent in any system dependent upon propaganda. The most important thing adults can do for children is to insist that the complex truth come out. The modern American child's behavioral, emotional, and learning difficulties, most especially his and her inability to thrive, warns us of the fragility of our illusions. Those illusions have created a false harmony for us; they have smoothed over the rough edges of modern life. Many intelligent people believe that the wall is tumbling down. It is time that their voices be heard.

Notes

1.   Francine du Plessix Gray, *Soviet Women, Walking the Tightrope*. New York: Doubleday, 1989: 131.
2.   Steven Pinker, *The Blank Slate: The Modern Denial of Human Nature*. New York: Penguin Books, 2002.
3.   Mark Bornstein, *Handbook of Parenting*. Mahwah, NJ: Lawrence Erlbaum Associates, 1995: 3-39.
4.   Daniel L. Olds, Lois Sadler, and Harriet Kitzman, "Programs for Parents of Infants and Toddlers: Recent Evidence from Randomized Trials," *The Journal of Child Psychology and Psychiatry*, 48. (March/ April 2007): 356.
5.   Jack Westman, "The Risks of Day Care for Children, Parents, and Society," in *Day Care: Child Psychology and Adult Economics* edited by B. Christensen. Rockford: The Rockford Institute, 1989: 1-67.
6.   Robert Rector, "The Risks of Day Care for Children, Parents, and Society," in *Day Care: Child Psychology and Adult Economics* edited by B. Christensen. Rockford: The Rockford Institute, 1989: 121.
7.   Penelope Leach, *Children First*. New York: Alfred A. Knopf, 1994: 66-67.
8.   *Ibid.*, 78.
9.   Tony Schwartz, *The Responsive Chord*. New York: Doubleday, 1974.
10.   Canadian Broadcast Standards Council Columbia Regional Council Web Site

(report on 10/14/1999 decision) September 11, 2006: <http://www.cbsc.ca/english/decisions/decisions/1999/991014.htm.>.

11. *Amercian Family Association Journal.* (July, 1998).
12. *Ibid.*, 1999.
13. *The Effects of Electronic Media on Children Ages Zero to Six: A History of Research.* (Menlo Park: The Kaiser Family Foundation, 2005).
14. "Study Sheds Light on Marketing of Violence." Duke University News and Communications Web Site. (September 15, 2000; January 20, 2007): <http://www.dukenews.duke.edu/2000/09/violence915.html>.
15. John Thorton Caldwell, *Televisuality: Style, Crisis, and Authority in American Television.* New Brunswick, NJ: Rutgers University Press, 1995: 4.
16. *Ibid.*, 93.
17. Christine Davidson, *Staying Home Instead: Alternatives to the Two-Paycheck Family.* New York: Lexington Books, 1993: 9.
18. *Ibid.*, 9.
19. Mohammadreza Hojat, "Can Affectional Ties be Purchased? Comments on Working Mothers and their Families," *Journal of Social Behavior and Personality* 5. 1990: 493-502.
20. Davidson, *Staying Home Instead.* 24.
21. Barbara Defoe Whitehead, "The New Family Values," *Utne Reader* 57. (May/June 1993): 61-66.
22. Westman, "The Risks of Day Care for Children, Parents, and Society." 24.
23. *Ibid.*, 11.
24. John Bowlby, "The Making and Breaking of Affectional Bonds" in *British Journal of Psychiatry,* 1977: 204.
25. D. W. Winnicott.
26. Selma Fraiberg, *Selected Writings of Selma Fraiberg.* Columbus: Ohio State University Press, 1987.
27. Michael Rutter, "Social-Emotional Consequences of Day Care for Preschool Children" in *American Journal of Orthopsychiatry.* (January, 1981).
28. Thomas Fleming, *The Politics of Human Nature.* New Brunswick, NJ: Transaction Publishers, 1993: 83-84.
29. Karen Sacks, *Sisters and Wives: The Past and Future of Sexual Equality.* Westport, CT: Greenwood Press, 1979: 83-84.
30. Fleming, *The Politics of Human Nature.* 84.
31. Steven Goldberg, "Utopian Yearning Versus Scientific Curiosity," *Society,* 23, no.6. (September/October, 1986).
32. Gerda Lerner, *The Creation of Patriarchy.* New York: Oxford University Press, 1986. * Please see Fleming's discussion of this and other works.
33. Phillipe Aries, *Centuries of Childhood-A Social History of Family Life.* New York: Knopf, 1962.
34. Peter Fuller, "Uncovering Childhood," in *Changing Childhood,* edited by Martin Hoyles. London: Writers and Readers Publishing Cooperative, 1979.
35. Valerie Polakow, *The Erosion of Childhood.* Chicago: University of Chicago Press, 1983: 10-11.
36. *Ibid.*, 15.
37. Shulamit Firestone, *The Dialectic of Sex: The Case for Feminist Revolution.* New York: Morrow, 1970.
38. Catherine MacKinnon, *Toward a Feminist Theory of the State.* Cambridge: Harvard University Press, 1991.
39. Reinhard Kuhn, *Corruption in Paradise: the Child in Western Literature.* Hanover, NH: Brown University Press, 1982.

40. John Demos, *Past, Present and Personal: The Family and the Life Course in American History.* New York: Oxford University Press, 1988.

41. Barry Levy, "Tender Plants: Quaker Farmers and Children in the Delaware Valley, 1681-1735," *Journal of Family History 3.* (Summer 1978): 116-129.

42. Allan Carlson, "The Natural Family Under Siege," *The Family in America.* The Howard Center for Family, Religion, and Society 13:4 (April, 1999): 2.

43. Fleming, *The Politics of Human Nature.*

44. Lloyd E. Sandelands, *Male and Female in Social Life.* New Brunswick: Transaction Publishers, 2001: 125.

45. G. M. Alexander and M. Hines, Sex differences in response to children's toys in nonhuman primates (Cercopithecus aethiops sabacus). *Evolution and Human Behavior,* 23. 2002: 467-469.

46. ABC News, *Journal Graphics, Inc.* Denver, CO.

47. Deborah Blum, *Sex on the Brain: The Biological Differences Between Men and Women.* New York: Penguin Books, 1997: 66.

48. *Ibid.,* 69.

49. M. Hojat, "A Mother's Love: What Children Will Not Receive in Day-Care Centers," *The Family in America* 8:12. (December, 1993): 2.

50. Jennifer Harper, "MRIs Show Dramatic Evidence of Male-Female Brain Differences" *The Wahington Times.* (December 2, 2005): worldandI.com: A Chronicle of Our Changing Era. (December 5, 2005): <http://www.worldandi.com/subscribers/headlines-detail.asp?num=10440>

51. Richard Haier, "All Too Human? Monkeys Mimic Children in Toy Picks," *The Seattle Times.*

52. Mona Lisa Schulz, M.D., Ph.D., *Awakening Intuition.* New York: Harmony Books, 1998: 57.

53. Joan Borysenko, Ph.D., *A Woman's Book of Life.* New York: Riverhead Books, 1997.

54. Joseph Adelson, "What We Don't Know About Sex Differences," *New Perspectives IV.* (Spring, 1985): 10.

55. M. Rutter, "Nature-Nurture Integration: The Example of Antisocial Behavior," *American Psychologist* 52:4. (1997): 396.

56. Linda Carroll Martin, "Mom's Journey: From Loose Ends to the Leading Edge," *Eastside Weekend Magazine.* (September 17, 1997): 16-17.

57. Leach, *Children First.* 40.

58. Max Horkheimer, *Eclipse of Reason.* (New York: Oxford University Press, 1947), 52.

59. *Ibid.,* 77.

60. Westman, "The Risks of Day Care for Children, Parents, and Society."

61. Patrick McNamara, Jay Belsksy, and Pasco Fearon, "Infant Sleep Disorders and Attachment," *Sleep and Hypnosis 2003,* 5 (1): 7-16.

62. Sandra Scarr, *Mother care/Other care.* New York: Penguin Books, 1987.

63. Amitai Etzioni, "'Children of the Universe," *Utne Reader* 57. (May/June 1993): 54.

64. Julia Wrigley, "Clashes in Values," *Childhood Socialization* edited by Gerald Handel. New Brunswick: Aldine Transaction, 2006: 345.

65. Hojat, "A Mother's Love: What Children Will Not Receive in Day-Care Centers," *The Family in America* 8:12. (December, 1993): 1.

66. *Ibid.,* 2.

67. Horkheimer, *Eclipse of Reason.* 82-86.

68. Richard T. Gill, "Day Care or Parental Care?" *Public Interest* 105. (Fall, 1991): 3-16.

69.   Horkheimer, *Eclipse of Reason.* 52.

70.   Susan Faludi, *Backlash: The Undeclared War Against American Women.* Anchor, 1992.

71.   Leach, *Children First.* 26.

72.   Deborah Churchman, "A Close Look at Labor Statistics Bursts the 'Supermom' Myth," *The Christian Science Monitor.* (July 9, 1987): 18.

73.   "Professional Women: Vital Statistics," Department for Professional Employees AFL-CIO, Fact Sheet, 2006.

74.   Bijou Yang Lester, "Part-time Employment of Married Women in the U.S.A.: a Cross-Sectional Analysis," *American Journal of Economics and Sociology.* (January, 1996; June 1, 2007): <http://findarticles.com/p/articles/mi-m0254/is-n1-v55/ai-18074643/print>.

75.   "Optioning In versus 'Opting Out': Women Using Flexible Work Arrangements for Career Success," CGO Insights, briefing note 25, January, 2007: 2.

76.   Louise Story, "Many Women at Elite Colleges Set Career Path to Motherhood," *New York Times.* (May 9, 2007).

77.   Arlene Rossen Cardoza, Ph.D., *Sequencing.* Minneapolis: Brownstone Books, 2000.

78.   Linda J. Waite, Arleen Leibowitz, and Christina Witsberger, "What Parents Pay For: Child Care Characteristics, Quality, and Costs," *Journal of Social Issues* 47:2. (1991): 33-48.

79.   "Working for Frills," *The Family in America.* (February, 1991): 1.

80.   Anne Rawley Saldich, "Electronic Democracy: How TV Governs" *Television and American Culture* 25, edited by Carl Lowe. (New York: H.W. Wilson Co., 1981). Reprinted with permission of Vital Speeches of the Day 46: 487-495.

81.   Jessica Gress-Wright, "Liberals, Conservatives & the Family," *Commentary.* (April, 1992): 43.

82.   Connaught Marshner, "Socialized Motherhood: As Easy as ABC," *National Review.* (May 13, 1988): 28.

83.   Gill, "Day Care or Parental Care?" 4.

84.   "The Economics of Day Care: Summary of a Discussion," in *Day Care: Child Psychology and Adult Economics* edited by B. Christensen. Rockford: The Rockford Institute. (1989): 113-146.

85.   *Ibid.*

86.   *Ibid.*

87.   *Ibid.*

88.   Gress-Wright, *Commentary.* 44.

89.   L.Brent Bozell III and Brent H. Baker, *And That's the Way it Isn't.* Alexandria: Media Research Center, 1991.

90.   S. Robert Lichter, Linda S. Lichter, and Stanley Rothman, *Watching America.* New York: Prentice Hall, 1991.

91.   David F. Prindel and James W. Endersby, "Hollywood Liberalism," *Social Science Quarterly,* 74:1. (March, 1993): 136.

92.   E. Mark Cummings and Jessica Beagle-Ross, "Towards a Model of Infant Day Care: Studies of Factors Influencing Responding to Separation in Day Care" in *The Child and the Day Care Setting: Qualitative Variations and Development* edited by Ricardo Ainslie. New York: Praeger, 1984.

93.   Hojat, "Abandoning Research on Consequences of Nonmaternal Care: A Disservice to the Science," *Journal of Social Behavior and Personality,* 8:1. (1999): 5-8.

94.   John G. Borkowski, Sharon Landesman Ramey, Marie Bristol-Power, *Parenting and the Child's World.* (Mahwah, New Jersey: Lawrence Erlbaum Associates, Inc., 2002): 58.

95.   *Ibid.*, 49.
96.   James E. Swain, Jeffrey P. Lorberbaum, Samet Kose, and Lane Strathearn, "Brain basis of early parent-infant interactions: psychology, physiology, and *in vivo* functional neuroimaging studies," *The Journal of Child Psychology and Psychiatry*, 48:3/4. (March/April, 2007): 264.
97.   *Ibid.*, 279.
98.   Jon A. Krosnick, "The Uses and Abuses of Public Opinion Polls," *Chronicles*. (February, 1990): 47.
99.   Jean-Francois Revel, *The Totalitarian Temptation*. New York: Penquin Books, 1978.
100. *Ibid.*, 26, 72.
101. *Ibid.*, 27-28.
102. *Ibid.*, 160.
103. *Ibid.*, 225.
104. *Ibid.*, 214-215.
105. *Ibid.*, 72.

2

Love and Stability:
The Fundamentals of Early Childhood,
which Day Care Cannot Provide

The world is too much with us; late and soon,
Getting and spending, we lay waste our powers:
Little we see in Nature that is ours;
We have given our hearts away, a sordid boon!
The sea that bares her bosom to the moon;
The winds that will be howling at all hours,
And are up-gathered now like sleeping flowers;
For this, for everything, we are out of tune;
It moves us not. —Great God! I'd rather be
A pagan suckled in a creed outworn.
So might I, standing on this pleasant lea,
Have glimpses that would make me less forlorn;
Have sight of Proteus rising from the sea;
Or hear old Triton blow his wreathed horn.
                              —William Wordsworth

The growing ranks of children who are unable to listen, concentrate, or articulate ideas; the sad litany of statistics regarding teenage apathy and depression; and the psychological and behavioral problems therapists and teachers are seeing at a younger and younger age require our attention. When about 20 percent of teenagers are said to be involved in "cutting," when suicide rates rise dramatically (not just for teenagers but also for children), when hitherto unheard of kinds of cruelty become a societal routine, and when both heartless behavior and self-destructive behavior become societal norms, something is wrong. At a minimum we must ask, Are American children being well-enough brought up and well-enough loved? Once we have paid serious attention to this question, we must ask, What makes a child thrive as opposed to just getting along? One of the dreariest circumstances of modern life is the "inability to thrive," now accepted as a commonplace disorder of babies and young children. Why aren't these children thriving? What makes the difference between a child who is thriving and one who is barely OK?

Reason, common sense, instinct, and the "evidence" all point to the fact that children thrive upon love. And, since their parents are the ones who love them most, it makes sense that time spent with parents makes a huge difference in children's lives. From the generation which proclaimed "love as the answer" there has been an ironic inattention to love with regards to our own children. We discuss how well our children are "taken care of" during the day and how well they are "doing" in their daytime activities, but we do not discuss how well they are loved. We have convinced ourselves that love is something young children, even babies, need only on weekends and at the end of the day. Many of us, however, have qualms about this theory. We suspect that children need not the Orwellian "attending to" of the professional but the love of their parents.

Parents and children suffer when their true feelings and experiences simply refuse to fit the project-which-must-succeed. A pioneering spirit has contributed to our strength and national character. But when applied to our children it can have sad consequences. We try out new methods of childrearing and tell ourselves that, being the can-do Americans that we are, the experiment will, of course, work out. The American experiment with day care has been like the trying on of a new hat, way too large, and insisting that it fits because it only comes in one size. We have insisted that babies and infants are ready for group environments because it is the only conclusion our modern agenda permits. Let us, instead, look honestly into the world of day care; let us investigate whether day care can provide young children with what they really need.

Everything children do from the moment they are born indicates their need for love. From the beginning, they cry to be held; they prefer their mothers; they respond to her voice; they are soothed by her incantations and her gentle caress; they reveal the need to bond with one loving person. If that bonding with a loving adult is permitted to occur, they cry or are frustrated when she leaves; they are comforted and relieved when she returns. They are relatively nervous around strangers; they are relatively calm in their mother's arms. Observes Penelope Leach, "Whether they are six or sixteen months old, most babies try to keep a beloved adult with them all the time and, while they are awake, many are successful."[1]

Babies give us infinite signs that they need reassurance about just how committed we are to them, how much we think of them, and whether we are there for them. Babies do not reveal themselves to us as sturdy souls but as insecure and vulnerable. Their very neediness is a request: for loving care and reassurance from those who love them. Indeed, reassurance is the wrong word for it implies the strengthening of something already there. Babies have no already-there confidence, although their actions indicate a desire for it. It is up to parents to instill in them the trust in another, which gradually allows them to trust in themselves, the trust they are born desirous of, but which they do not yet possess.

The most important conduit of confidence in self and trust in another is the mother's consistent and reliable responsiveness to her baby's signals. As opposed to the image of the infant as passive, recent research recognizes the infant as an alert and curious creature who becomes intensely attached to the mother and actively solicits interaction with her. Indeed, we now know that the baby actually regulates the behavior of the adults in her life, giving them clear signals as to what she needs and when. Reports Dr. Edward Tronick in an article entitled "Emotions and Emotional Communication in Infants:"

> Regardless of what the infant's affective repertoire is eventually discovered to be, it is well established that parents are acutely sensitive to their infant's emotional expressions and behavior. . . . Parents (also) "frame" their infant's gaze by looking at their infant until the infant looks away from them (Kaye & Fogel, 1980). . . . After a decade of controversy, it is now well established that the face-to face interactions of infants and adults starting as young as three months are bidirectional (i.e. mutually regulated) rather than just being the product of adult social skills. That is, infants modify their affective displays and behaviors on the basis of their appreciation of the mothers' affective displays and behavior. (Cohn & Tronick, 1987; Lester, Hoffman & Brazelton, 1985)[2]

Confirms Daniel N. Stern, "In this light, it becomes obvious that infants exert major control over the initiation, maintenance, termination, and avoidance of social contact with mother; in other words, they help to regulate engagement. Furthermore, by controlling their own direction of gaze, they self-regulate the level and amount of social stimulation to which they are subject."[3] (There will be times when the infant prefers not to interact—when he prefers quiet and repose.)

According to Stern, infants begin to experience a sense of an emergent self from birth:

> They are predesigned to be aware of self-organizing processes. They never experience a period of total self/other undifferentiation. There is no confusion between self and other in the beginning or at any point during infancy. They are also predesigned to

be selectively responsive to external social events and never experience an autistic-like phase.[6]

Rather than seeing infants as suddenly developing a sense of self and a recognition of mother, we now know that the infant "is endowed with observable capacities that mature." "When these become available, they are organized and transformed, in quantum mental leaps, into organizing subjective perspectives about the sense of self and other."[4] From the beginning, infants give signals to their mothers, receive messages form their mother, and develop an awareness of that interaction.

University of Chicago psychologist Amanda Woodward has established that children begin to develop reasoning skills as young as seven months of age and are able to comprehend words as well at thirteen months as they do at eighteen months when they begin to speak with an expanded vocabulary. "The fact that even young infants interact with their caretakers in well orchestrated sequences suggests that infants have the ability to reason and make predictions about the behavior of others."[5]

Thus, an infant's healthy development depends in part upon their own initiation of social contact receiving appropriate and consistent responses. The infant develops a sense of individual *capacity, as opposed to futility,* by having its signals taken seriously. The more responsive the parent is to the baby's signals, whether those signals indicate a desire for verbal interchange, a desire for calm and comfort, or a desire for loving praise, the more responsive the baby is to the parent. This reciprocity creates within the baby a confidence in her own ability to communicate and the trust that she is loved. This confidence and trust becomes the cornerstone from which she dares to explore the world and because of which she will be capable of relating positively to others.

In the *Journal of Child Psychology and Psychiatry*, Ruth Feldman describes her research into the biologically natural rhythms of interaction between mother and infant that create an opportunity for the mother and infant to co-create relational moments. "Between the age of 2 and 3 months, parent-infant interactions begin to show a clear temporal structure, in terms of behavior matching, sequential relations, and time-series parameters. Interactions at this age involve repetitive-rhythmic cycles of behaviors in different modalities, including gaze, touch, affective expression, body orientation, manual actions and arousal indicators."[7] These processes of rhythmic interpersonal interaction, or "synchrony," in turn "are likely to shape neural pathways" and "form the basis for healthy future I-thou relationships." Feldman's work is worth exploring in detail, but she sums it up for us as follows:

Infants enter into the social world through the sensitive moment-by-moment adaptation of an attuned and caring adult during social interactions. Such interactions are adjusted in micro-shifts in infant affect and arousal, coalesce into patterned configurations of vocal, visual, and affective sequences, and organize the infant's biological rhythms and attentive states into a lived experience that highlights the present moment. As seen, this early experience is critical for the development of symbol use, empathy, emotional resonance and self-regulation and lays the foundation for the child's later capacity for intimacy throughout life.[8]

The infant's sense of frustration and even despair when mother does not respond to his or her signals has also been firmly established. Even short periods of indifference to baby by the mother can result in the baby becoming frightened and confused. The combined research of TB Brazelton, E. Tronick, L. Adamson, H. Als, and S. Wise resulted in this summation of the effects of a mother's indifference as documented on videotape:

> When she violates his expectancy for rhythmic interaction by presenting a still, un-responsive face to him, he becomes visibly concerned, his movements become jerky, he averts his face, then attempts to draw her into interaction. When repeated attempts fail, he finally withdraws into an attitude of helplessness, face averted, body curled up and motionless. If she returns to her usual interactive responses, he comes alive after an initial puzzled period, and returns to his rhythmic cyclical behavior which has previously characterized their ongoing face-to-face interaction. This attentional cycling may be diagnostic of optimal mother-infant interactions and seems not to be present in more disturbed interactions.[9]

Secure attachment to mother, known and acknowledged to be essential to a baby's emotional well-being, depends not only upon the mother's responsive interaction with her baby. It also depends upon the amount of time they spend interacting. Researcher Victoria Hamilton writes, "Research on attachment shows that the two most important variables in the creation and maintenance of a secure attachment are the sensitivity of a mother's responsiveness to her baby's signals and the amount and nature of interaction between the two." She adds, "Human beings come into the world genetically biased to develop certain behaviors that, in an appropriate environment, result in their keeping close to whoever cares for them. This desire for proximity to loved ones persists throughout life. Only when children feel secure in their primary attachments can they go out with confidence to explore and make the most of their world."[10]

"Attachment" is a fluid process. The relationship between mother and baby is not stagnant but expansive. Each successful interaction opens the door to the next successful interaction. Every mother who spends con-tinual time with a baby is aware of this continual building of closeness. In an article entitled "The Making and Breaking of Affectional Bonds,"

John Bowlby observed, "The more experience of social interaction an infant has with a person the more likely is he to become attached to that person. For this reason, whoever is principally mothering a child becomes his principal attachment figure. Attachment behavior remains readily activated until near the end of the third year; in healthy development it becomes gradually less readily activated thereafter."[11]

The opportunities for the baby to attach to one special person are obviously less if he or she is subject to a series of caregivers and even less if he or she is subject to the crowded and turbulent world of day care where many other children compete for adults' attention and where the job of care giving, by its nature, prohibits the care giver from treating one child as "special." Professor Alice Sterling Honig argues that day care workers do not usually make good surrogates for parents because of this fact. Care givers, she warns, "cannot by their cheerful daily ministrations substitute for that intense intimate relationship between a parent and child." Young children need the specialized care of one adult who "is crazy about the kid." She warns that when a mother must leave a baby before their love relationship has grown comfortable and reasoned, "a certain amount of deep internal mourning is generated." Defenses to ward off this mourning include the formation of a less passionate commitment to the parent-child relationship. In place of the attuned and responsive parent, Honig fears more of the "efficient" kind of parenting which may be the "curse" of this generation of children.[12]

The inborn need of infants to attach to one adult, preferably mother, is ignored by the modern media, by popular culture, and by most forward-looking Americans. Ignoring that need puts children and families at risk. In an article entitled, "The Risks of Day Care for Children, Parents, and Society" Dr. Jack C. Westman describes the yearning for and the seeking of "attachment" on the part of babies as something families ignore at their own peril:

> The attachment bonds of infants are their emotional lifelines and the foundation on which self-esteem builds. Since we cannot see these bonds, we infer their existence by observing certain behaviors considered to be "hallmarks of attachment." These are proximity-seeking and proximity maintaining behaviors and protest responses under separation. Examples are the close following of a mother by a toddling child and the despairing cries of outrage when the mother goes away, and the child is prevented from accompanying her. Prior to toddlerhood, the baby enhances the mutual bonding process by smiling and by clinging to the person who embodies the essence of protection, security, and survival. . . . Separation of a developing attachment relationship, such as by hospitalization, results in protest behavior as part of an anxiety reaction and may affect personality development. Even brief separations can affect young children who lack an appreciation of time and perceive any separation as permanent.[13]

Westman describes the bond between mother and child as the product of "a complex sequential development during the first 18 months of life." A dialogue occurs between infant and mother in which "messages from the mother are taken as signals by the baby." Westman recalls Fraiberg's studies which revealed the attachment process as "falling in love:" "Two people arouse in each other sensual joy, feelings of longing, and the conviction that they are indispensable to each other."[14]

Objective researchers in child development are in increasing agreement over what babies need and what conditions allow them to thrive. By paying closer attention to the signals and responses that babies and children themselves provide, even those researchers who have tried to make the facts fit the agenda are beginning to admit that babies need more of the steady and responsive kind of love, which mothers have been known to provide. As David Elkind states, it is becoming increasingly difficult to disagree with Erik Erikson's assertion that the infant's task is to acquire a sense of trust that is stronger than his or her sense of mistrust. Elkind explains, "The sense of trust involves a feeling that the world is a safe place and that one's needs will be met. The sense of mistrust, on the other hand, involves the sense that the world is unsafe and unreliable, not trustworthy. The sense of trust is to a large extent a derivative of the child's attachment or "bonding" to the parents." Elkind describes the positive effect of attachment upon children's emotional make-up: "Research suggests that children who are securely attached to their parents at twelve to eighteen months were later rated (by their preschool teachers) as more emotionally positive, more empathetic, and more compliant than children who were less securely attached."[15] In effect, he observes, they were more "trusting" than were children with less solid attachments.

Elkind is quick to suggest that it is not the "absolute time" a child spends with the mother which determines whether the child is attached. "A baby, for example, can be with adults other than the mother and still be primarily attached to the mother."[16] It appears, however, that he makes this stipulation due to societal pressure, for his own logic proceeds to undermine it. The very reasons he gives for the attachment between mother and child, even when the care giver is the dominant influence, speaks to the problematic nature of the relationship between the care giver and the baby:

> Perhaps because we are genuinely committed to the infant, and to the long-term relationship, we interact differently with our baby than does a care-giver. We are more sensitive to the variety of different messages babies send through their body

language and the gurgles and their cries. . . . In contrast, a care-giver does not feel and cannot convey commitment to a long-term relationship with the infant. Care givers are wary of becoming attached to the infant because they know that at one point or another the attachment will be broken and they do not want to subject themselves to the pain of that loss.[17]

If a care giver is leery of feeling too much attachment and is less responsive to a baby's signals, when a baby needs and thrives upon the responsive interaction of a loving adult more than anything else, then it is simply illogical to suppose that an infant spending most of their days with a paid care giver will experience optimal conditions for that wonderful condition called "thriving." Indeed, Elkind qualifies his assertion that the quality of interaction between parent and child is enough to ensure attachment by declaring that "a certain quantity of time is necessary to convey commitment and to encourage trust." "Quality time," he finally adds, "is really not enough; quantity is essential too." In a footnote, he further qualifies his assertion by indicating that infants are capable of attachment "only when the non-parental care is of high quality."[18]

If we are to face reality, we must admit to ourselves that even this qualification falls short. As we shall see, many thorough studies conclude that even children who receive quality infant day care are less socially responsive, less exploratory, and less content than those cared for by their parents. As many questions as answers emerge from Elkind's analysis. If the whole attachment process falls apart if care is not of "high quality," we must think long and hard about what the odds are that we will find "high quality" care for our babies. Moreover, one cannot in one breath say that infants need love and responsive interaction more than anything else, and in the next say that they are just as well off spending most of their time with a care giver who loves them and responds to them less—than with parents who love and respond to them more.

If the very advantage to being attached is that infants develop a sense of trust, a sense of empathy for others, and a secure base from which to explore, then *it is not simply the attachment we must be careful of but also the trust, security, and loving feelings which go with it.* We must ask ourselves what it does to an infant's trust when we suddenly go back to work full-time, when one care giver is suddenly replaced with another, or when the babbling which provoked sonoric responses from the mother or the previous care giver provokes no such response from the new person in charge. What happens when the tears which used to provoke meltingly warm words and a tender hug now provoke only a silent check to see if the diaper is dirty or an efficient preparation of the bottle? What happens when the baby, beginning to "talk," realizes that the new adult in her life does not hear those words as words? What sounds like incoherent babble to the new person was intelligible conversation to the person familiar with that baby's particular "accent." Warns Penelope Leach, "A baby who expects particular people to respond to her particular signals in their particular ways is confused and distressed when they do not. . . . What upsets that baby is her unexpected failure to manage and control the interaction and evoke a response. . . . But it is only by being allowed, even helped, to find reliable ways of controlling some aspects of adult behavior that a baby can build vital competence and confidence in her own powers of communication."[19] Babies are thus dependent upon a mother's unique *kind* of responsiveness and upon the reliability of that responsiveness. Leach further intones:

> An outside care giver has less reason than a mother to celebrate an infant and there-fore needs less cause to be indifferent to him. A nursery worker has less reason still to celebrate this infant because she has others to care for who may overload her or whom she may prefer. How well an infant thrives despite any of those situations probably depends on how much time he also spends with someone who cares not just for but about him. . . . By around three months or so, infants realize that they are separate from the mothers and others on whom they are totally dependent and then only consistent and dependent responses can protect them from the lonely fear of being abandoned and from anxiety about their needs being met.[20]

Ineluctably, it is both the quality of care a baby receives and the continuous nature of that care which matters. As Leach points out, the *consistency* of care makes a huge difference in babies' lives:

> Responsive and overtly affectionate adults are crucial to all aspects of infants' de-velopment. Every time a baby's very existence is celebrated in another spontaneous hug; every time her sounds, expressions and body language are noticed and answered; every time somebody does something just because she seems to want or enjoy it, a tiny piece is added to the foundations of that baby's future self-image, self-confidence and social competence. The more of that sensitive, tuned-in experience a baby gets (and the less of its opposite), the better. . . . Only adults who know, have known and will go on knowing an individual baby can provide that vital sense of trust and empowerment. Even the best-intentioned and qualified stranger cannot do it because however much she knows about babies in general, she knows nothing about this one.[21]

When babies cry when their mother leaves, but she leaves anyway for long periods of time over and over again, the babies learn to harden themselves against disappointment. When they indicate curiosity about things but receive only an occasional response because the child care provider is too busy or too uninterested to respond, they become less curious. When they are met with disapproval when they express their needs loudly and insistently, they learn to need less. From the beginning of life, they learn to lower their expectations in order to avoid pain. A hardened child makes for a hardened adult, as insensitive to others' needs as the adults in his life were to his.

In 2004, The Child Study Center at Yale brought together psycho-analysts, molecular biologists, developmental psychologists, early interventionists, and social policy experts to explore the question of "risk, resiliency, and recovery" in young children. Findings confirmed that poor parental bonding *not* considered abuse or neglect was associated with increased risk for several psychological and cognitive risk factors. The March/April 2007 Annual Research Review edition of the *Journal of Child Psychology and Psychiatry* compiles articles documenting these findings. In one article, entitled *Brain basis of early parent-infant interactions: psychology, physiology, and invivo functional neuroimaging studies*, co-authors James E. Swain, Jeffrey P. Lorberbaum, Samet Kose, and Lane Strathearn present an eloquent endorsement of John Bowlby's theory of attachment vis-à-vis modern developments in research and psychological understanding, noting the intellectual link between Bowlby's theory and modern findings:

> One of the landmarks of contemporary developmental psychology has been its focus on parent-infant attachment (Bowlby, 1969, 1973). In fact, it was after studying associations between maternal deprivation and juvenile delinquency that John Bowlby first formulated his attachment theory, postulating a universal human need to form close affect-laden bonds, primarily between mother and infant. He also strongly argued, from an evolutionary perspective, that attachment is an innate biological system promoting proximity-seeking between an infant and a specific attachment figure. This proximity seeking then increases the likelihood of survival to a reproductive age. Because of this powerful biological instinct, Bowlby hypothesized that all human infants attach to their caregiver—even if the care is harsh or neglectful—but that these latter children manifest different patterns of attachment "security." Infants of caregivers who are available, responsive, and sensitive to their emotional and physical needs tend to manifest patterns of "secure attachment." However, if the care provided is chaotic, unpredictable, rejecting or neglectful, or if the caregiver consistently provides non-contingent responses to the child, then an anxious, insecure or disorganized pattern of attachment evolves (Shaver, Schwartz, Kirson & O'Connor, 1987). The initial pattern of attachment security was seen as a developmental pathway of major significance throughout the child's life course, with longitudinal research verifying many of these initial hypotheses (van Ljzendoorn, 1995). This underscores how important one's early environment is in shaping future behavior. Over the past decade, a diverse spectrum of research has begun to explore the neural basis of attachment—at molecular, cellular, and behavioral levels (Insel &Young, 2001; Strathearn, 2007). This research has uncovered many parallels between Bowlby's original thesis and the biological systems which may underlie attachment and stress reactivity.[22]

Among those "parallels," the authors note, are findings that maternal behavior is regulated by key neurotransmitters and hormones, and maternal behavior, in turn, stimulates neurological and hormonal responses in infants. In animals, infant cues activate these key transmitters, including oxytocin and dopamine, while long periods of mother-infant separation appear to inhibit maternal behavior, through oxytocin regulator modulation.[23] The authors stress, "Some of the same processes described in animals that require oxytocin are also present in the regulation of an array of human social behaviors and cognitions" (Kirsch et al., 2005), including social reduction of stress (Heinrichs, Baumgartner, Kirschbaum, & Ehlert, 2003) and mechanisms of trust (Kosfeld, Heinrichs, Zak, Fischbacher, & Fehr, 2005). In human studies, exposure to infant cues appears to be highly reinforcing to mothers, activating brain regions and stimulating hormones that encourage healthy maternal response and approach behavior.[24] MRIs are documenting maternal brain regions activated in response to infant cues.[25]

Many other researchers are finding confirmation of attachment theory in recent research. In an incisive article entitled *Deeper Into Attachment Theory*, Cindy Hazen of Cornell University and Phillip R. Shaver of the University of California note the significance, found in a range of studies, in an infant's bids for closeness and comfort being consistently rebuffed or consistently reinforced. They draw attention to the connection between stability of "attachment classifications" and "stability of the environment." Stability of the environment, the body of research shows, depends not just upon the stable formation of relationships, but also upon the consistent availability of a person with whom the infant can form a "primary" relationship. "Bonds that satisfy the criteria for being attachments—that is, that include proximity maintenance and safe-haven and secure-base behaviors—are commonly developed with other adults as well as with older siblings. But are these relationships of equal importance to the attached infant or child? Empirical evidence strongly suggests not." "Our views of the social world are no doubt multiply determined, but the experiences we have with the person on whom we depend for comfort and security will form the foundation of our model of the world as a place in which comfort and security can be reliably counted on or not."[26] Hazen and Shaver confirm that it is not just the responsiveness of the care giver that is important, but also the predictable availability of *the primary care giver*. They find that the quality of attachment to the primary attachment figure has a lasting and significant effect on later development and functioning. Primary attachment to mothers, they point out, appears to influence the child's representational models of self and others more than attachment to fathers.

In an article on "disinhibited attachment," Michael Rutter and other researchers from the MRC Social, Genetic and Developmental Psychiatry Center in London and the Developmental Brain-Behavior Unit at the University of Southampton document their dramatic findings. In a study of adoptees, they found that "disinhibited attachment" (lack of preferential attachment to any one care giver) was strongly related to institutional rearing, and that disinhibited attachment had a range of negative consequences. "What the findings show is that both marked and mild disinhibition (especially marked) are associated with a considerably raised rate of cognitive impairment, quasi-autism, peer relationship problems, inattention/overactivity and conduct. The rates of emotional disturbance were also somewhat raised, but not significantly so."[27]

The researchers asked whether disinhibited attachment was "simply a stylistic feature of no great importance, or rather an index of clinically significant psychopathology." They answered: "The evidence strongly pointed to the later. The majority of the children with disinhibited attachment exhibited problems in other domains of behavior and they were more likely to have received services of one kind or another than the children without social disinhibition at age 6. On those grounds, we conclude that disinhibited attachment, when seen in children from an institutional background, probably usually does reflect a clinically significant disorder." [28]

Consistently responsive care, the presence of a loved one, is essential for the child's optimal development. It is also requisite for "thriving." Babies under two years old are especially vulnerable to "separation anxiety," a dreary circumstance of modern life. Separation from a developing attachment relationship can result in an "anxiety reaction" and, according to Rutter, may affect personality development.[29] The "anxiety" the infant initially feels can cause the infant to detach from a loved one in order to avoid those "anxious" feelings. Anxiety upon separating with the loved one sometimes turns into avoidance of that person when she returns. In the researchers' terms, "insecure attachment" can result in "anxious-avoidant" behavior which means, simply, that infants respond to their mother suspiciously and hesitatingly. That anxiety is likely to have long-term consequences.

It is discouraging that such an essential work on the subject of separation anxiety as John Bowlby's *Separation* (and current research that confirms Bowlby's findings) is ignored by most au-courant observers of young children. Bowlby wrote *Separation* before day care was a mass phenomenon. His work has been criticized as irrelevant because of this.

But an honest look at his work teaches us a lot about a young child's instinctual emotional response to uncertainty and strangeness, even if it does not adequately inform us about day care per se. Bowlby dispels the myth that a child's "anxious" reaction to separation from mother is based upon a problem in the relationship to begin with and exposes separation anxiety as a normal and practically universal response to separation from mother. Bowlby explains that the former idea rests upon the erroneous assumption that fear is caused by the threat of harm. Bowlby demonstrates, with convincing evidence, that fear arises as much from the *absence* of loved ones as it does from the *presence* of danger. Indeed, when a child is with a loved one, he often feels safe, even if in actual danger. Mere strangeness provokes fear, and that fear is often intense.

Bowlby also dispels the "it will toughen them up and prepare them for the real world" rationale for allowing babies to experience separation anxiety by demonstrating that the more babies have a trustworthy base, the *less fearful* will be their personalities. "And just as we found that there is a strong case for believing that gnawing uncertainty about the accessibility and responsiveness of attachment figures is a principal condition for the development of unstable and anxious personality so is there a strong case for believing that an unthinking confidence in the unfailing accessibility and support of attachment figures is the bedrock on which stable and self-reliant personality is built."[30]

Contrary to modern rationalizations, children become over-dependent, or "anxiously attached," not because they have been taken care of too much, but because they have been taken care of too little. Studies show that babies who are permitted to depend upon one person are more, not less, ready for the confidence required in adult life. Children raised in group situations tend to be less, not more, capable of mature adulthood:

> When we come to know a person of this sort it soon becomes evident that he has no confidence that his attachment figures will be accessible and responsible to him when he wants them to be and that he has adopted a strategy of remaining in close proximity to them in order so far as possible to ensure that they will be available. To describe this as overdependency obscures the issue. Even the term separation anxiety is not ideal. A better way to describe the condition is to term it anxious attachment or insecure attachment.[31]

Bowlby found that even when separation from the mother was mitigated by a loving other trying hard to be like mother, "sadness, anger, and subsequent anxiety" occurred. "Whenever a young child who has had an opportunity to develop an attachment to a mother figure is separated from her unwillingly he shows distress; and should he also be placed in a strange environment and cared for by a succession of strange people such distress is likely to be intense." When the distress is intense, it often manifests itself in aggressive or uncivil behavior: "Some children subjected to an unpredictable regime seem to despair. Instead of developing anxious attachment; they become more or less detached, apparently neither trusting nor caring for others. Often their behavior becomes aggressive and disobedient and they are quick to retaliate."[32]

Recent research confirms what Bowlby and Winnicott discovered: that even an excellent care giver cannot replace a "good-enough" mother. The attachment to and trust in one person who loves a child, even though imperfectly, is irreplaceable. A study by Magid and McKelvey found that the effect of interrupting attachment bonds during the first two years of life can be a failure to develop a basic trust in constant human relationships and the impaired ability to form committed relationships with other people.[33] R.J. Cadnet and C. Cain find that if a child's emotional attachment to mother is disrupted during the first few years, permanent harm can be done to his capacity for emotional attachment to others. He will be less able to trust others and, throughout his life, will stay distant emotionally from others. Having many different care takers during the first few years can lead, they found, to life-long social difficulties and anti-social behavior.[34] Conversely, a 1990 study from the Institute of Human Development at the University of California found that men who were rated as dependent in childhood evolved into mature and sociable adults: "calm, warm, giving, sympathetic, insightful, undefensive, incisive, consistent across roles, comfortable with ambiguity and uncertainty and socially poised."[35]

As Winnicott taught us, such closeness makes children not only more empathetic and kind, but also more independent and authentic. Winnicott did much work on the subject of the infant's ability to "internalize" the experience of closeness, using that experience as a present and future source of confidence. By providing them with a secure base from which to explore, such closeness allows them to experience "branching out" as a desirable thing, rather than a frightening thing—for there is both the well-embedded image of mother and the actual presence of mother to fall back upon. In *Boundary and Space*, Madeleine Davis and David Wallbridge elucidate Winnicott's understanding that to be innovative one must have a traditional position to start with, so that there is a continual dialectic between the conventional and the creative. "Said Winnicott of the feeding process, for example, 'A thousand times the feeling has existed that what was wanted was created, and found to be there. From this develops a belief that the world can contain what is wanted and needed, with the result that the baby has hope that there is a live relationship between inner reality and external reality, between innate primary creativity and the world at large which is shared by all.'"[36] By realizing that he or she can affect his or her needs being met, whether that need be the need for love and comfort or the need to be fed and held, the infant develops a sense of control and a sense of self. This process of "internalization," Winnicott understood, included the "whole routine of care throughout the day and night." This was necessary for the infant to experience some sense of continuity, a "going-on-being" feeling. Winnicott found that babies needed the "holding environment" of mother in order for their "true self" to emerge. "The good-enough mother meets the omnipotence of the infant and to some extent makes sense of it. She does this repeatedly. A True Self begins to have life, through the strength given to the weak ego by the mother's implementation of the infant's omnipotent expressions."[37]

Says Simon A. Grolnick of the significance of Winnicott's findings, "The key concept in modern psycholanalytic developmentalism is internalization. The comforting, holding mother, for example, is gradually placed 'inside' and carries on her essential work, at first in an imagistic, introspective manner and later in a more abstracted 'metabolized' manner. Internalization is gradual and can be conceptualized in terms of developmental lines."[38] Within the holding environment, the infant internalizes qualities of love and stability and finds the courage to be exploratory. Winnicott demonstrated that healthy independence rises out of healthy dependence. *The steady presence of a responsive but not overbearing attachment figure goes hand in hand with the gradual capacity for self-reliance and self-motivation.* "It will now be seen why it is important that there is someone available; someone present, although present without making demands . . . The individual who has developed the capacity to be alone is constantly able to rediscover the personal impulse, and the personal impulse is not wasted because the state of being alone is something which (though paradoxically) always implies that someone else is there."[39]

The baby's development of a True Self, Winnicott added, is "immensely simplified if the infant is cared for by one person and one technique." It seems, he said, "as if the infant is designed to be cared for from birth by his own mother, or failing that by an adopted mother, and not by several nurses." Absent the holding environment, the baby "survives by means of the mind." "If the baby has a good mental apparatus this thinking becomes a substitute for maternal care and adaptation."[40] The baby learns to pretend she does not need what she really does need; in other words, to survive by means of a "False Self." When the mother is not able to provide the "most important aspect of maternal care," reliability and adaptation to basic need, warned Winnicott, the infant develops a "False Self:"

> The mother who is not good enough is not able to implement the infant's omnipotence, and so she repeatedly fails to meet the infant gesture; instead she substitutes her own gesture which is to be given sense by the compliance of the infant. This compliance on the part of the infant is the earliest stage of the False Self and belongs to the mother's inability to sense her infant's needs. Through this False Self the infant builds up a false set of relationships, and by means of introspection even attains a show of being real, so that the child may grow to be just like mother, nurse, aunt, brother, or whoever dominates the scene. The False Self has one positive and very important function: to hide the True Self, which it does by compliance with environmental demands.[41]

Bowlby reminded us that "when an individual is confident that an attachment figure will be available to him whenever he desires it, that person will be much less prone to either intense or chronic fear than will an individual who for any reason has no such confidence." As his intensive research showed, "when mother is present or her whereabouts well-known and she is willing to take part in friendly interchange, a child usually ceases to show attachment behavior and, instead, explores his environment."[42] Someone for whom life is unsafe will extend great efforts at making it safe. Someone for whom life is safe will be the more adventurous for it. *If one is putting up one's guard, one is not exploring possibilities or discovering potential.* Explained Bowlby:

> In such a situation mother can be regarded as providing her child with a secure base from which to explore and to which he can return, especially should he become tired or frightened. Throughout the rest of a person's life he is likely to show the same pattern of behavior, moving away from those he loves for ever-increasing distances and lengths of time yet always maintaining contact and sooner or later returning. The base from which he operates is likely to be either his family of origin or else a new base which he has created for himself. Anyone who has no such base is rootless.[43]

Physical and emotional closeness with mother and exploratory behavior, Bowlby understood, went hand in hand. Mother provides something to fall back upon which makes the development of the infant's own unique strengths and tendencies possible. As Victoria Hamilton puts it, she allows "a dialectic between the safe and the creative" to occur.

The connection between the formation of a strong maternal bond and formation of a strong sense of self is not just some abstract theory.

It is a connection that is confirmed over and over again. The child with a secure base is more secure. Because she is more secure, she is more capable, more resilient, and more kind. The most important aspect of continuous and stable care is that love becomes something babies expect and succumb to. Rather than developing either a hostile or a very timid, or as Winnicott warned, a "false" approach to the world, all of which would indicate that they are preparing for the worst, they are able to develop a positive approach. Being consistently loved and responded to bestows upon babies the capacity to love and relate positively to others. Babies learn how to love by soaking up love from someone they can depend upon.

It is not just the internalizing of the loved one but the "using" of the loved one which Winnicott and Bowlby recognized as important. Babies often "use" their mothers to try out aggressive behavior. If the mother is a steady presence, the baby develops a healthy sense of guilt over anti-social behavior, a sense of right and wrong. If, however, the baby is anxious over losing the mother, that anxiousness may preclude the ability to feel anxiety over the feelings of others. The more anxious the baby, the more self-centered the child and the adult. According to Professor Rolf Loeber of the University of Pittsburgh School of Medicine, "There is increasing evidence for an important critical period that occurs early in children's lives. At that time, youngsters' attachment to adult caretakers is formed. This helps them to learn prosocial skills and to unlearn any aggressive or acting out behavior."[44] Common sense and our own observations tell us this. We all know adults scarred or distorted in their behavior due to a deprivation or trauma in their childhood.

The most loving adults tend to be those who were loved well as children. Parents who expend time and energy on their children while exhibiting a generally empathetic and responsive nature, are providing their children with a standard to which to refer. Children who receive such a "good-enough" upbringing are likely to be good parents and good citizens themselves. According to Professor Mohammadreza Hojat:

> If one assumes that the primary care giver who has usually been the mother in almost all cultures, serves as a secure base for the baby to explore the world while satisfying the desire for contact comfort and other needs, then that assumption implies that unresponsiveness and unavailability of such a secure base can generate a grave frustration for the baby, which in turn leads to internally or externally directed aggression, according to the frustration-aggression theory. ... The lack of undivided attention and a loving maternal response when it is needed would generate a frustrating experience for millions of children in this country every day. Those who have not experienced love cannot offer it to others. Those who, in fact, have been abandoned early in their

lives, every day for many of their waking hours, may not develop real concepts of mercifulness and concern for others. Since more than half of the mothers in this country are employed, a great many of our children do not gain early, first-hand understanding of concepts such as maternal love, concern, responsiveness, mercifulness, dignity, respect, etc. consequently, there will be no internalized image (protype) of a nurturing mother; there will be no object of love; there will be no concept of love.[45]

The involved relationship between mother and child is mutually reinforcing on a range of emotional, neurological, molecular, and biological levels. Breaking research is confirming the fundamental age-old importance of the mother-child bond. Whether we should *need* research to confirm that babies thrive when they receive as much love and stability as they can possibly receive is another question. *How fascinating that the wisdom of the ages, which we in our modernity were so quick to discard, is coming back to us in the form of modern science.* Scientific research in a variety of disciplines is showing that animals and humans deprived of nurturing when young tend to grow to be poor nurturers themselves.

In an article entitled "Neorodevelopmental sequelae of postnatal maternal care in rodents: clinical and research implications of molecular insights," Arie Kaffman of Yale and Michael J. Meaney of the Douglass Hospital Research Centre in Montreal show that deprivation in infancy alters neural pathways that encourage nurturing behavior. Noting similar observations in non-human primates, they present data on rodents that suggest that frequent licking and grooming provided by the dam during a critical period plays an important role in modifying neurodevelopment, and that postnatal maternal care is associated with the way genes express themselves and with behavioral traits that are maintained throughout life. Offspring of dams that did not provide licking and grooming "are fearful and as adults lick their own pups infrequently, raising yet another generation of animals that are also fearful and low lickers in a pattern that propagates itself vertically across generations."[46] Kaffmann and Meany also found that rodents that have been well cared for as pups perform better in several hippocampal-dependent memory tasks and that "sensory input during early development plays an important role in brain development with long-term consequences on brain functioning in adulthood." Pointing out that similar behavioral and cognitive patterns are observed in primates and humans, they conclude that "active parenting," not just absence of abuse or neglect, appears to be required for optimal neurodevelopment and optimal development of resiliency to stress:

If similar processes occur in humans, these data suggest that interventions that seek only to eliminate neglect and abuse in maltreated children, though obviously necessary and important, may not be sufficient to promote resiliency in those children. Thus future work may need to examine more closely how parental care enhances resiliency in non-human primates and children instead of focusing almost exclusively on how childhood abuse and neglect enhance psychopathology. This is consistent with data showing that poor parental bonding, *not considered abuse or neglect*, is also associated with a significant increased risk for depression and anxiety disorders. (Canett et al., 1997) as well as with enhanced stress reactivity (Leucken &Lemery 2004; Pruessner et al., 2204) Finally, interventions that seek to enhance parental skills may not only reduce psychopathology in children of these families, but may also disrupt epigenetic transmission of these behaviors across future generations.[47]

In "Parents, Peers, and the Process of Socialization in Primates," Stephen J. Suomi discusses his own research and that of others on the consequences of disrupted mother-infant relationships in resus monkeys. When infant resus monkeys are reared away from their mothers, "the attachment relationships that these peer-reared infants develop are almost always 'anxious' in nature." [48] When peer-reared monkeys interact with their peers, "their emerging social play repertoires are usually retarded in both frequency and complexity." Peer-rearing tends to make monkeys more impulsive, especially if they are males. "Peer-reared females carry into adulthood the deprivation of their youth; they are significantly more likely to exhibit neglectful or abusive behavior toward their own offspring."[49] In addition, studies of monkeys in natural surroundings find "strong continuities" between the level and kind of attachment a female infant develops with her mother and her pattern of attachment with her own offspring. "As noted by Bowlby and other attachment theorists for the human case, the effects of inadequate early social attachments may be both life-long and cross-generational in nature. For monkeys, the type of attachment relationship an infant establishes with its mother (or mother substitute) can markedly affect its biobehavioral developmental trajectory, even after its interactions with her have ceased."[50] Disputing the "it's all nature" argument, studies that take animals from the *same* mothers and rear them differently, show very different neurological and behavioral outcomes depending on the level and kind of interaction with caretakers the young receive (see especially Dario Mestripieri's studies with macaque, 2005).

Revealing that there is a connection not just between nurturing and neurodevelopment and biobehavioral development, but also between nurturing, or the lack thereof, and hormones; Megan Gunner, Director of the Human Developmental Psychobiology Lab at the University of Minnesota, has found that social relationships control cortisol levels (an indicator of stress) in infants and young children. "The most profound discovery was that 70-80 percent of children in center-based care show ever-increasing levels of cortisol across the day, with the biggest increases occurring in toddlers. By first grade, children don't show these stress reactions to being with other children all day." Gunnar has evidence that it is not separation from parents, but the experiences young children have in childcare that produce these responses. "There is something about managing a complex peer setting for an extended time that triggers stress in young children," says Gunner.[51] She has also found that children with secure attachment levels show stable cortisol levels even when emotionally upset, while even minor emotional challenges raised cortisol levels in those with insecure attachment.

Swain et al. (above) describe "affiliative behaviors" between parents and babies as part of "an elaborate reward and stress-sensitive system that requires dopamine and oxytocin, and a host of other neurotransmitters including opiates as well as pituitary and gonadal hormones." They go on to make this notable statement:

> Altered activity of the dopaminergic system has also been associated with a wide range of human diseases and psychopathology. These include drug addiction, attention deficit disorder, obesity, compulsive gambling, and several personality traits (Blum et al., 2000; Comings & Blum, 2000) –arguably all of which involve malfunctioning motivation systems. We suggest that all of these may be associated with adverse early life events. A recent PET study showed that dopamine production in the human brain was associated with reduced self-reported maternal care in childhood. (Pruessner, Champagne, Meaney, & Dagher, 2004)[52]

Now, with so many children in day care from infancy, with so many who never had a chance to attach to their mothers in the first place and who never received consistent reliable nurturing, researchers are seeing more of the aggressive, uncivil behavior which is often the result of being insufficiently brought-up and insufficiently loved. As more and more children enter the ranks of the institutionally raised, we see more and more children who distance themselves from others and who harden themselves in order to avoid pain. This type of child, as well as the child who seems to require prescription drugs to alter his mood or behavior, is well known in today's schools. As Dr. Westman points out, the adverse consequences of interrupting the attachment bonds by separating young children from their parents are well known to clinicians. "The immediate effect is an insecure parent-child relationship. The longer term effects have consequences for society at large." He explains:

> Prior to toddlerhood, the baby enhances the mutual bonding process by smiling and by clinging to the person who embodies the essence of protection, security and survival. . . . Because the loved parent is valued above all other things, a child gradually modifies aggressive impulses and finds alternative modes of expression that are sanctioned

by love. Children and adults who did not learn how to love during infancy contribute far beyond their numbers to social disorder. They are unable to fulfill the ordinary human obligations of work, friendship, marriage and child-rearing. They contribute largely to the criminal population. The absence of human bonds leaves free 'unbound aggression to pursue its erratic course.[53]

We must ask why the many studies indicating a connection between insecure attachment to mother or inadequate nurturing by mother and later behavioral and developmental problems have been hidden from our view. The consequences of early institutionalization can be the "alienation" of teenagers from adults and even from their peers. There is a repeatedly established and observed connection between modern childrearing practices and psychosocial problems and delinquency. The less attached teenagers have been to their parents from the beginning, the more likely they are to fall prey to alcoholism, drug abuse, self-destructive or hostile behavior, and suicide. Several bodies of data confirm that infants who are institutionalized at a very young age are less likely to mature into well-adjusted, well-behaved children and adults. As Amitai Etzioni notes, "a typical finding is that infants subject to at least twenty hours a week of non-parental care are insecure in their relationship with their parents at the end of the first year and more likely to be aggressive between the ages of three and eight." Etzioni asserts, "If children age 2 or younger are too young to be institutionalized in child-care centers, a bare minimum of two years of intensive parenting is essential."[54]

Children in day care often exhibit low tolerance of frustration and elevated aggressiveness. Yale Professor Edward Zigler, in a summary of many studies on day care, concluded that children raised as such are more immature as adults and tend toward "assertiveness, aggressiveness and peer rather than adult orientation."[55] That review suggested that even children who received quality infant day care are less socially responsive, less exploratory, and less attentive than those cared for by parents.

Terrence Moore did one of the few longitudinal studies of the effects of day care. His London research resulted in his conclusion that "instability of regime introduces cumulative stresses that are likely to be detrimental to personality development." [56] Having a succession of different caregivers "unsettles" children. On the other hand, *where a mother keeps her child in her own care full time to the age of five, the child tends early to internalize adult standards of behavior, notably self-control and intellectual achievement, relative to other children of equivalent intelligence and social class."*[57] (His findings regarding social and intellectual outcomes of day care were more consistent for boys than for girls.) Indeed, teachers report that contemporary kindergartners, while appearing more "mature," are less self-controlled. They show less interest in and respect for other children and teachers.

In another compilation of research, the Rockford Institute documented the connection between unattached babyhood and adolescent difficulties. Adolescents who are not attached to parents are much more likely to use drugs and alcohol, commit delinquent acts, adopt morally permissive attitudes, engage in sexual intercourse, abort unborn children, earn lower grades, and drop out of school. They found that day care causes young children to be less responsive to adult role models and more responsive to the model provided by their peers. This, in turn, resulted in their exhibiting heightened aggressiveness and a lack of empathy for others. Thus, the potential results of insufficient attachment with parents range from shortened attention spans and impaired curiosity to aggressive and self-destructive behavior.[58]

In *The Causes of Delinquency,* sociologist Travis Hirschi reported that the number of delinquent acts committed by children is strongly influenced by the children's attachment to and level of interaction with their parents. Although in his earlier work (1969) he emphasizes the attachment itself and in his later work he emphasizes parental supervision, his overall conclusions are worth considering. Using the most advanced survey methods and analytical techniques while controlling for extraneous variables, he found that the closer the mother's supervision of the child, the greater the bond between child and parents and the better the communication between them, the less delinquency. Especially significant given our over-reliance on institutions, lack of attachment at home "is not compensated for by stronger attachments in another setting, but tends to spread from one setting to another," so that "students with weak affectional ties to parents also tend to have little concern for the opinion of teachers and tend not to like school."[59] *In other words, alienation at home becomes alienation in school and, ultimately, in society.*

Elliott Barker of Canada did a study of the upbringing of psychopaths whom he worked with for many years. He found one common illness: the lack of attachment to parents in the first three years. Doctor Barker concluded that we develop our ability to trust, empathize with others, and form affectionate relationships during these years.[60] Similarly, Professor James Q. Wilson finds that the extended absence of a working mother from her child during the early critical stages of the child's emotional development increases the risk of delinquency.[61] In *Deeper Into Attach-*

ment Theory (above) Hazen and Shaver form this powerful conclusion: "We agree with Peterson that attachment theory is potentially important not only to abstract social science but also to the solution of some of society's pressing problems, such as child abuse, domestic violence, divorce, delinquency, drug abuse, depression and teen pregnancy. A field of developmental psychopathology is emerging (e.g. Cicchetti, 1984; Sameroff & Ernde, 1989; Stroufe & Rutter, 1984), and attachment theory is influential within it."[62]

As Jacquelyn de Laveaga puts it, "research has shown over and over again that if children do not get their attachment needs met in healthy ways during the first years of life, they will seek it out in unhealthy ways." Conversely, "as they grown into adulthood, they will have a stronger sense of self-discipline and self-confidence because they were affirmed in their early years of life."[63] In effect, research confirms our gut-level, age-old knowledge that parental presence as in parental love, guidance, and limit setting, brings out the good in the child. Winnicott cut to the heart of the matter when he articulated the connection between "deprivation" and the "antisocial tendency:"

> At the root of the antisocial tendency there is always a deprivation; if it occurs at a difficult moment, it may have a lasting result because it overstrains the available defenses. Behind the antisocial tendency there is always some health and then an interruption, after which things are never the same again. The antisocial child is searching in some way or other, violently or gently, to get the world to acknowledge its debt; or is trying to make the world reform the framework that got broken up.[64]

Children learn how to be mature and responsible through the predominant influence of adult role models. Absent that dominant influence, they tend to acquire those traits which allow them to function in a chaotic world, i.e., the world of day care. Rather than developing the traits that would allow them to relate maturely to another human being, they are forced to learn about human relationships from their immature peers. If an aggressive and alienated as opposed to empathetic and sociable nature is often the result of not being permitted to attach to, depend upon, and be with one loving adult, it is no surprise that my generation, as if to confirm the consequences of its actions, have placed increased value upon teaching children to be aggressive. From competitive sports at an early age, to self-esteem and "critical thinking" agendas, to the desire to make girls "as tough as boys," to the exhausting array of activities we offer our children to ensure that they have the edge over each other, we reveal the high value we give to assertion and success, and the relatively low position we give to kindness and introspection.

Contrary to popular myth, socio-economic status has relatively little to do with whether a child will thrive, unless the child is living in poverty. The child's relationship with their parents is far more important to their development. Travis Hirschi found that the lower-class child securely attached to their parents is no more likely to be delinquent than a securely attached child from a "high-status family."[65] When society discusses the need to give support to disadvantaged children, we need to point out that there is more than one kind of "disadvantage," one having to do with not receiving enough of what money can buy and the other having to do with not receiving enough love, attention, and limit-setting. There is no greater advantage a child can have than the love and persistent presence of their parents. Notes Amitai Etzioni, "The fact is, in poor neighborhoods, one finds decent and hardworking youngsters right next to anti-social ones. Likewise, in affluent suburbs, one finds anti-social youngsters right next to decent hard-working ones. The difference is often a reflection of the homes they come from."[66]

Children who receive physical sustenance but are not sustained emotionally can whither away from neglect. The extreme but classic case of the post-WWII orphanages in France comes to mind. Some of the babies there literally died from the absence of emotional bonds. Propped up with pillows for their bottles, rarely held or talked to, these babies lacked the human contact and interaction they needed to thrive. Children learn how to love by being loved. They learn how to be sympathetic and compassionate with others by being treated sympathetically and compassionately. Most importantly, they learn how to be good parents by being the recipients of good parenting. Parents' loving presence is a gift which money cannot buy.

The ability of children to "tough it out" and "face the world" practically on their own is vastly overestimated. Because we want to believe that children can take the vicissitudes and emotional challenges which accrue when we allow hired persons and institutions to predominate in their lives, we have talked ourselves into believing that they can. Are children really so resilient? Can anyone look back honestly to their own childhood and describe him or herself as such? I remember early childhood as a time of wonder and contentment, but also as a time of anxiety and vulnerability. I was not born with the confidence and the willingness to take intellectual risks that I have today. These things were built up within me gradually and with the backdrop of my parents' presence. The trepidation I felt when my parents left me for extended hours or repeated days was real although, had I been "studied," little difference in my behavior would have been observed. No study can definitively measure the amount of security and love a child feels in life. We assess this and that social experiment by the measurable and visible behavior of our children. If we could look inside the mind of children thought to be resilient, we would find that *there is much more to a person than how they perform*. Indeed, the few times I remember hiding my true feelings from my parents as a young child were the few times that I felt deeply hurt by something they did or did not do. Children sometimes act the most strong when they are feeling the most fragile. "Putting up a front" is an age-old human defense mechanism.

We must not ignore our common sense and the tug of our hearts. If something tells us that something would probably hurt our child, it probably would. *Over-reliance* upon studies allows us to focus too much upon the persona of the child and not enough upon the person. As we have seen, statistics are distorted toward all sorts of purposes. We tell ourselves that it "must be so" because some article says it is so, even though the research does not "feel right" nor "make sense." Instead of making this assumption, we must insist upon the intrusion of reason and compassion into the debate. We have allowed ourselves to forget how childhood feels. This is by no means to say we should ignore day care studies. In addition to the studies already cited, we will explore others, including the large study by the National Institute of Child Health and Human Development. But we should beware of accepting simplistic media interpretations of studies and should ourselves interpret them *with a large concern that reason be served and good be done*. The quality of studies cannot be judged according to the number of factors "controlled for" or the sophistication of scientific method alone.

As Sharon Landesman Ramey observes, studies too often assess "stable traitlike qualities" such as intelligence and personality in children, while eliminating those test items that fluctuate in the same individual over time. This leads not only to test results that over-emphasize genetics and downplay the influence of a child's environment; it also leads to disregard for some of the most important aspects of being human. "Thus, many potentially important dimensions of a child's development—including those that are likely to fluctuate with different parenting practices (e.g. knowledge about the world; ability to generate and enact alternative, effective solutions to many real world problems; kindness toward others; health promoting behaviors; family values and spiritual belief systems; and appreciation for culture, art and citizenship) and to relate to factors classified as nongenetic biological influences (e.g. nutritional status, hormonal status during puberty) and environmental influences (e.g. school quality, neighborhood risks, presence of environmental toxins)—are not measured at all."[67] Intones Ramey, "what parents can do, actually do, and fail to do for their children encompasses a very broad spectrum and potentially influences many far-reaching aspects of a child's development."[68]

Although part of my aim is to bring to light those studies that have been hidden from our view because they challenge modern assumptions, just as important is the questioning of studies that do not stand the test of logic and the knowledge of our hearts. One of many unthoughtful and insensitive articles I encountered, for example, relied upon the results of a survey of children at two major day cares in a big city. The main point of this study was that the majority of children, when asked, said that they were "happy" at the day care and, when observed, seemed to be having a "good time." The fact that these children were questioned within the day care setting and with care providers within listening distance did not trouble the researchers. The fact that a child's stated preferences at this age are not necessarily indicative of what is good for the child was simply overlooked. A young child's preferences often will include all kinds of things not good for them—an abundance of candy, all the TV they want to watch, etc. More important than whether the children called themselves happy or appeared to be "having fun" would have been the question of whether they were being well-enough brought up and well-enough loved. (It would be simply natural for day care workers to make sure children are "having fun" when observers arrive.) That is the stuff that a deeper contentment and a steadier confidence are made of. In addition to asking the wrong questions in the wrong setting, the researchers apparently saw it as their privilege to omit the fact that this study, too, was conducted at a model day care center.

Such weak "reporting" on this issue is to be found everywhere. Another article I encountered in *Working Mother,* entitled "Day Care Detective," claimed to give mothers "who can't be there" a "glimpse of a day at child care." It proclaimed, "If you could follow your child around his center you might uncover a day like this." The center they chose was, of course a "high quality" one "near Yale University." (At least they admitted it!) They summed up by saying, "It's been a typical day at child care. Christopher played with friends, listened to stories, sang songs, talked about his life, created a book and a tower, had a game of trucks and collected sticks in a wheelbarrow. He fought some, cried some and gave and received affection from his teachers and friends." This article was apparently meant to make parents feel that a high-risk approach to childrearing was not high risk. Mothers apparently did not need to be sure what went on in their children's days; they could rather, through some sort of osmosis, assume that this article spoke for the experience of their particular child. Although parents were encouraged to drop by during their lunch hour once in a while and to discuss the day with the child, they are counseled in bold print: "Don't overreact if your child tells you something negative." Professor Linda Dunlap, quoted in the article, counsels, "Kids like to see us animated, and so sometimes they sense that we'll react more if they tell us all the bad stuff that happened at day care."[69]

I could not help contrasting these "insider" looks at high-quality day care with my own observations when visiting a friend's children at one of the best-reputed day care centers in Chicago. Babies in diapers crawled around in a large auditorium-like space. The care providers stood around the edge talking with each other like so many observers of basketball. The babies were only interacted with when there was an overt problem—one was crying; another needed a diaper change. The feeling was that of anonymity. The babies were a plurality and were treated as such even though this center was known for its individualized attention. Imagine this observation making its way into a "women's magazine." The news is simply too discouraging to publish.

Babies in day care are rewarded for hiding their true feelings and needs. Their need to be with mother, their need for calm and reassurance, their need to explore the world aggressively and selfishly, and their need for rest and quiet all must be subordinated to the needs of the group. For example, they are rewarded for not fussing when Mom drops them off, for not expecting one adult to focus upon them, and for not expecting special soothing attention when they are tired. Alice Miller warns that children who develop a "False Self" to please others can fall in love with their own image. They become expert actors, good at receiving rewards but not capable of finding a personality which feels real or right: "It is precisely because a child's feelings are so strong that they cannot be repressed without serious consequences. The stronger a prisoner is, the thicker the prison walls have to be, which impede or completely prevent later emotional growth."[70]

When we insist that a young child adjust to day care when their nature is to cry out for individual attachment, attention, and love, we insist that they become performers on the stage of modern psycho-babble, which rationalizes but does not reason about the nature of children. Even the "transitional object," much lauded for its ability to ease the transition from mother to care giver, cannot have reality for the child if the love and security which the transitional object is supposed to represent are not wholly believed in, in other words, are not experienced as "real" by the child. As Winnicott came to realize, a transitional object's usefulness depends upon the reality of the thing it symbolizes. If the mother's devotion and reliability are not real, then neither will be the efficacy of the object.

The numbers dictate that day care centers place an Orwellian emphasis upon efficiency as opposed to emotion. Too many displays of emotion, whether through tears, raucous laughter, impassioned displays of curiosity, or insistently sought out adventure are disruptive to the well-ordered group existence. In place of the "exploratory" stance toward the world, which children adopt when they have a secure base to fall back upon, children in day care centers are encouraged to be careful. In order to avoid chaos, they are taught to walk in line, to quiet down en masse, to choose activities when it is activity time and not simply when something sparks their interest, and to avoid clinging to those they love. If the care givers themselves become too emotional, i.e., too attached to certain children, it interferes with their impartial parceling out of time and attention and makes it difficult when the parents, at some inevitable point, remove the child from the center. Thus, they too must be careful—not to become too attached. The child's passionate emotional attachment to the parent is also discouraged since an emotional "scene" upon separating from parents is highly disruptive to group life and might trigger similar scenes in other children.

In day care, of necessity, the subduing of powerful emotions is rewarded; the expression of powerful emotions is discouraged. Even the passionate attachment to certain toys and all the potential that toy represents to the baby is discouraged. Sharing and waiting one's turn are obvious necessities. But babies and toddlers are not equipped to understand the notion of sharing. Ideally, sharing should not be imposed upon them much of the time. They should be able to explore the world without worrying about living up to this abstract concept, which they are developmentally unequipped to understand. Day cares drill into them the sharing behavior before it is age-appropriate. Thus, children may adopt the behavior of sharing without ever possessing the kind and considerate nature, which would enable them to *choose* to share once they are old enough to understand the concept.

Day care workers have little time for attuned and responsive relationships. As anyone who has had six children under two years old in her care knows, it is difficult just to get by. A worker in one of the most respected day care chains complained to me, "We spend most of our time dealing with necessities. With all the time spent changing diapers, preparing snacks, wiping up spills, distributing and redistributing toys, getting the children ready to go inside or outside, putting coats and mittens on and taking them off, there's no time to have fun with the kids." "We are," she said, "too busy getting by" to give these babies the "personal attention" they need. She added, "My boss wants us to be especially careful to check diapers a lot and make sure the babies are clean. Dirty babies really upset the parents." She added, "We do our best to give them some good play time and as much rest as they can grab in that noisy place, but it's just so frustrating because we know we're not giving them the love they want. It's always the ones whose parents leave them there the longest who act up the most. I know what they need is love but it's hard to give love to a child who's never fun to be around, who's always a wreck. The kids who need us the most probably get us the least. I hate to admit it. It's really a sad job." *What I took away from these comments was that the children in this esteemed day care center were well-maintained, but neither well-enough brought up nor well-enough loved.*

Dorothy Conliff, a director of community services in Madison, Wisconsin who had worked in the day care field either directly or administratively for twenty years wrote an article entitled, "Day Care: A Grand and Troubling Social Experiment." Conliff demonstrated that the amount of time day care personnel spend on physical maintenance of the babies leaves scarce little time for meaningful interaction. Because Conliff wrote from her own heartfelt experiences and not from the detached perspective of statistics, and because she provides a disturbingly real picture of the day care scenario, she is worth quoting at length:

Consider the amount of physical care and attention a baby needs—say 20 minutes for feeding every three hours or so, and 10 minutes for diapering every two hours or so, and time for the care giver to wash her hands thoroughly and sanitize the area after changing each baby. In an eight-and-a-half-hour day, then, a care giver working under the typical four-to-one ratio will have 16 diapers to change and 12 feedings to give. Four diaper changes and three feedings a piece is not an inordinate amount of care over a long day from the babies' point of view. But think about the care giver's day: Four hours to feed the babies, two hours and 40 minutes to change them. If you allow an extra two and a half minutes at each changing to put them down, clean up the area, and thoroughly wash your hands, you can get by with 40 minutes for sanitizing. (And if you think about thoroughly washing your hands 16 times a day, you may begin to understand why epidemics of diarrhea and related diseases regularly sweep through infant-care centers. That makes seven hours and 20 minutes of the day spent just on physical care—if you're lucky and the infants stay conveniently on schedule.) Since feeding and diaper changing are necessarily one-on-one activities, each infant is bound to be largely unattended during the five-plus hours that the other three babies are being attended to. So, if there's to be any stimulation at all for the child, the care giver had better chat and play up a storm while she's feeding and diapering. Obviously, such a schedule is not realistic. In group infant care based on even this four-to-one ratio, babies will not be changed every two hours and they will probably not be held when they are fed.[71]

Conliff found that the situation was "not much better" for toddlers. The "toddler line-up" is indicative of the continuing emphasis upon physical maintenance:

In many centers, even in the better ones, young unskilled staff struggle with large groups of very young children. Staff turnover rates exceed 30 percent a year, so most don't stay long enough to be trained. One common sign of staff inexperience is the Big Toddler Lineup. Inexperienced staff tend to fall back on their only model for dealing with groups of children: the elementary school. What do you do in school each time an activity changes? Line up. Not realizing that forming a line is developmentally beyond the capacity of such young children, staff struggle for long periods to get their toddlers to line up for routine events. The results are comical and predictable - babies wander off, sit down and stare into space, cry - and staff lose patience. What's not so comical is that this kind of distressingly inappropriate expectation and the impatience, disapproval and unhappiness that result are the chronic daily experience of the children. Toddlers learn through all their senses. They cannot make sense of words alone; they need to touch and   objects, move through space, put two things side by side. Without this opportunity, children become apathetic or uncontrollable - and sometimes both by turns. When children under 3 are put into impoverished or chaotic environments with inexperienced, discouraged staff who expend most of their energy just trying to maintain order, the children suffer. Some of their pain is physical, because toddlers need to move around a lot. Some is mental because of the continued frustration of basic developmental impulses. And some is emotional, because of the constant disapproval, which the child is powerless to correct.[72]

Conniff asked, And what of preschoolers ages three and up? Although they are more amenable to getting along well in group settings, the nurturing of their curiosity is unlikely:

To serve 3-year olds well, teachers somehow have to make time to answer their questions even though they have 20 or more active little ones to organize, feed, nap, and otherwise get through the day. Learning to pose questions and receive information that is satisfying is a key social as well as intellectual experience in a child's development. Children who don't have a successful experience at this stage, or whose experience is frustrated or perverted, stop participating in the learning process. They stop expressing their questions, and eventually may stop thinking them up. If their world is structured so that formulating and getting answers to questions is difficult or impossible, the developmental process is seriously damaged. And this is the most consistent drawback of day-care centers where staff are overloaded and inexperienced. Staff resort to forcing children into the same boring activity all at the same time to maintain control. The kind of repressive control that keeps them sitting down to meaningless tasks day after day hurts their self-esteem and impairs their relationship with learning.[73]

Concluded Conliff, "We have no idea how destructive a situation we have created. It is a social experiment on a grand scale with virtually no controls."

It is simply unthinking to suggest that children can "develop" just as well in day care as they would in a loving home environment. Leaving statistics aside for the moment, let us pause to think about what a day in day care is like. Probably before he or she is ready to awake, the child is awakened and rushed through a morning routine, put into the car, and driven off to the center. Because her parents must get to work on time and cannot dawdle, she is expected to make a quick transition from parent to staff personnel. If she cries upon arriving, that crying is not taken seriously, as indicative of important feelings, but as something she should not feel. Such feelings, she is implicitly taught, need to be gotten rid of. Parents and day care workers, even sympathetic ones, explain to her that she "shouldn't cry," her day will be fun, she'll see Mom at dinnertime, etc. *To the child this translates as: Your feelings for your parents are too strong. You need to control them. It is your fault that you are feeling that way; Why would anyone not enjoy such a "fun" place?*

By contrast, a toddler whose day will be spent at home will wake up when he or she is ready, (or when it is time to drive older siblings to school) perhaps stumbling into her parents' bed. She and her mother might cuddle for a while until hunger leads them, pajamas still on, to the kitchen. They have a leisurely breakfast and discuss all sorts of things—not because Mom is some sort of super-Mom always thinking of her child's betterment, but because the child's natural curiosity brings conversation out in her—even when she would prefer not to talk. As the toddler asks "why" and "what's that?" over and over again, the parent tries to answer. The mother naturally talks to her child as she moves around the kitchen; "I wonder if it will be nice enough to go to the park today;" The child is comfortably, naturally learning how to interact with another human being, although neither mother nor child would define their morning as such. After breakfast, they might cuddle up with a favorite blanket and some books. Without even knowing she is doing it, the mother kisses her child's head a hundred times as she reads. The child, in her comfort zone of love, asks questions about the story and assumes that most of them will be answered. This child has not received the message that her feelings for her mother need to be tamed, that her curiosity needs to wait its turn. Rather, those feelings and that curiosity are something which she indulges in and which, she senses, cause her mother great pride and joy.

Back at the day care center, "Sue" is not having a comfortable time. The noise and commotion are almost overwhelming, especially because she was awakened before she was ready. Many children talk and shout at once, competing for adult attention. Sue manages to wriggle onto her favorite childcare worker's lap, but another child expends his energy trying to distract the worker away from Sue. The pushing and shoving and grabbing of toys finally causes the adults to raise their voices. This worries Sue and makes her long for the quiet of her own room. Although there is a "cozy corner," the place as a whole is anything but cozy. There are toys and learning booths and cribs lined up like soldiers and colorful walls and posters but there is no escape from the public as opposed to private feel of it all. This is an institution and feels like one.

Here, each person, adult or child, is "on." Just as busy adults wait for the evenings and weekends for "down time," so too these children must wait. If Sue needs to retreat from it all, the only place to retreat is into herself. Sadly, she may have lived such a public, structured, group-oriented existence from such an early age that she has no private inner self to retreat to. From the time she was born, she was expected to be a social creature, capable of going from one adult to another, and of getting along with hordes of "peers." *For her, there may be little inner space; the demands of her outer environment have been so omnipresent.*

Weary of all the noise, frustrated that her peer will not allow her to monopolize her favorite care provider, tired from a short night's sleep, Sue lashes out at a peer by grabbing her toy and pushing her down hard. Instead of signals for interaction being read as such, she is given a "time-out" and reminded of the importance of "sharing." Once again, she learns to hide her true feelings, that the messages she gives adults will not be understood, that her need for love will not be taken seriously.

Back at home, Leslie has finished her favorite TV show and decides she wants to go outside. Her mother has a few more phone calls to make so Leslie throws a fit. Her mother makes the phone calls anyway, insisting that Leslie quiet down while she makes them, and then ventures with her toddler into the backyard. They admire the flowers and go into the garage for Leslie's tricycle. With a kiss and pat on the back, Leslie is off and riding. Her mother comments on how well she is doing and picks up the newspaper. Leslie falls and scrapes her knee, receives another kiss and hug, and continues on. At no time in her day has Leslie felt that her feelings did not matter. She knows and senses that her mother's refusal to indulge her every whim does not mean that her mother loves or understands her less.

At the day care center, Sue is being told to line up for outdoor time. The children scramble into line, competing for first place, and cannot stay still once in it. The day care worker insists that the door to the play area will not open until everyone can be still and quiet. Finally, after twenty minutes of wrangling, they venture outside. Sue mounts a bike but no one kisses her head as she does. For the first time, she gains the courage to go down the big slide, but no one notices. After a while, she realizes someone is yelling at her. The bell for inside time had rung but she had not heard it. She pulls herself together and gets back into line.

It's story time and Sue realizes that her other favorite caretaker, who usually reads the stories, hasn't been here for a while. She asks about her, but the new adult cannot understand Sue, whose language skills are just forming, so ignores her. Sue tries the question again. This time she's understood and is informed that this woman has "moved away." She never said goodbye to Sue. The children form a circle around the reader, a new face in the day care center, but some of the children form an inner circle in front of the other children. The children vie to be closest to the center. Finally, with the help of the new reader, a big circle is formed. Some of the children have a hard time keeping quiet. Others have a hard time staying still. Sue, who likes the story, asks why the bunny in the story is afraid. "Shhhhhhh!" says the reader, not because she is unkind, but because she is frustrated to the point of saying things she knows she shouldn't say. We'll have time for questions later, she sighs.

Later comes but it is time for lunch. The children sit at big tables in long rows. One child "hates" his lunch and cries hysterically. Sue tenses up as the crying gets out of control. Human beings have a natural mechanism which causes them to become tense when a child cries. Children have that same reaction and, in day care centers, are forced to feel that tensing up response to crying over and over again. Others start to cry; the crying is contagious. Sue feels like crying herself but remembers the response to her cry in the morning and tries to hold herself in check.

After lunch, it is rest time, strictly enforced. The children, twenty in a row, are told to lie down and go to sleep. They are expected to do so for one and a half hours. If they get up from their cot for anything other than the bathroom, they are punished. The care provider tucks each of them in and turns out the light. Sue does not sleep. She never does. She squirms, turns, sucks hard on her thumb, which seems less and less satisfactory, and listens to the squirming and turning of others. She can not wait until rest time is over. Although she used to succumb to an occasional sleep, she learned that another child might emit a loud shriek just as she was drifting off. In order to avoid the frightening jolt of interrupted slumber, she lies awake in her cot.

Back at home, Leslie has finished lunch and is told it is nap time. Her Mom reads her a bedtime story, sings her a bedtime song, and says good night. Leslie sings herself to sleep with a dramatic version of "Twinkle Twinkle Little Star," her favorite song. When she awakens, she babbles for a while in bed, practicing all her newest phrases, rehearsing a conversation with a friend, and taking care of her favorite animal. (Sue has learned not to talk to her doll in bed; it disturbs the other children.) After a while, with an indignant and insistent tone, Leslie calls, "Mommy!" Mom gets her out of bed, changes her damp clothes, and tells her it's time to go to the grocery store.

At the store, mother and child parade down the aisle, discussing what this and that is along the way. Many un-thought-out kisses fall on Leslie's head as Mom reaches over her to deposit groceries in the cart. After a while, Leslie is restless and starts to whine. As her whine becomes increasingly annoying, her mother loses patience and says, a little too loudly, "Leslie, that is enough!" Although Leslie intuitively knows her Mom's reproval is temporary, she cries in reaction to it. Exasperated, her mother tells her she will do a time out if she can not lower her voice. Leslie and her mother find a calming distraction in the check-out line. Leslie listens as her mother and the check-out person compare notes on two and three year olds. Leslie's mom lets her carry the bread and the cereal into the house and she feels important. After her mother has unloaded the groceries, she provides Leslie with paper and crayons. Leslie's mom tells her that her picture is so pretty, and she means it.

At 4:00, two of Mom's friends and their toddlers come over to visit. Leslie and her friends play for a while, lose interest in each other and play again. After two hours, Leslie is tired of the effort of socializing (which truly is an effort at this age) and situates herself firmly on her mother's lap. The mothers realize their children, too, have had enough, and say goodbye until next time. At the door, the children are reminded to say thank you and Leslie is told to respond, "Thank you for coming." She makes no such response, instead hiding behind her mother's leg, but she has heard what her mother thinks is appropriate. Realizing there's little time to make dinner, Leslie's mother calls Leslie's father and asks him to pick up Chinese food on the way home. She picks up a book of her own and reads it as best she can while Leslie hovers around her. When Leslie's father comes home, Leslie becomes his responsibility. Leslie's Mom needs a break. Although they all eat dinner together, Mom makes it clear that she is to direct her incessant questions toward Dad.

Back at the day care center, nap time is over, although most of the children have not slept. Tiredness and crankiness set in. The day care workers look at this as the "final stretch" and try to keep the children busy, happy, and distracted. Sue's day care is a "good" one with many opportunities for learning. Crafts, puzzles, books, games, art supplies, and reading readiness tools are all at her disposal. Sue points to a pretty picture in a book. One of the care providers, whom Sue has not seen before today, tells her it's a nice picture, asks what she likes about it, and suggests that she put it into her cubby so that she can "show mommy and daddy." At 4:00, one of the children's dads comes to pick her up. Another child cries because he wants his daddy too. Sue is exhausted. The next two hours seem long. The chairs seem too hard, the lights too bright, the voices too loud. At 6:00, Sue's dad arrives. Tears roll down her cheeks. What's the matter, asks daddy, "Aren't you happy to see me? This is said in part for the benefit of the care providers upon whom he and wife so depend. They exchange appreciative smiles with Sue's dad, thankful for the implicit complement. Once again, Sue's signals have been misunderstood.

If a child succeeds in not crying when their parent leaves this will be misinterpreted as well. Warns Dr. Westman, "The fact that crying on leaving and returning to a parent disappears often is interpreted as evidence that the child has adjusted well to day care. In fact, it may well be evidence that the child has adapted to stressful situations by entering a stage in which stress is masked or that the child has adapted by investing less in the parent. Unfortunately, the adverse effects of this kind of early life experience may not be evident in more overt ways for years."[74]

Inevitably, in day care centers, even in the best ones, there is both too much stimulation and not enough. There is too much of the stressful kind of stimulation which comes from being part of a large crowd and from partaking in a day that is constantly structured and not enough of the good kind of stimulation which comes from being one-on-one with a parent or loved one. Babies and toddlers need the steady input of trusted adults who can teach them about the world and the steady responsiveness of adults, which teaches them to respond sensitively to others. In day care, children receive too much stimulation from their peers and not enough from adults who love them. Lacking in trustworthy role models and lacking in ongoing, to-be-depended-upon intimacy with another, babies in day care centers lack the conditions for optimal development.

Receiving too much stimulation of the turbulent kind and not enough of the mature influence of an adult who can help them to make sense of the world, such babies are being honed to view the world as chaotic. Day care is the story of babies who cannot relax, who must keep going in an atmosphere that is chaotic and loud. Day care babies and children never have the time to retreat within themselves—to find out what is there.

I was part of a playgroup of babies and their mothers who met every Friday. I was continually impressed at how quickly these babies met their saturation point with each other. Inevitably, these one and two year olds would, at or before two hours of "playtime," give their mothers definite signals that they were ready to go home. We witnessed the tensing up of their facial muscles, their increased clinginess with their mothers, and their increased frustration with each other as their time together increased. Babies have neither the social knowledge nor the physical stamina to play for an extended time with other babies. After a short bit of stimulation from their peers, they reveal the clear need for comforting from their mother.

Indeed, babies are easily over-stimulated and need a loving someone to recognize the signs that the stimulation must end. That is part of the protective role of the parent. The age-old custom of singing softly to babies as we rock them, of talking sweetly and sonorously to them as we pat them, of insisting that music be turned down, and that siblings, grandparents, and friends keep their voices down for the sake of the baby reveal our natural understanding of the baby's need for rest and calm. Calmness and serenity denote the absence of agitating commotion, a physical and emotional state which cannot be found even in the best day care centers.

In a day care, the signals a baby gives as to the need for less stimulation and more comfort are, of necessity, ignored. This is not to mention that their cry is often lost in the din of other cries. *Whether they are frightened, exhausted, angry, or simply in need of quiet, it is doubtful that the care provider will look for the root cause for the baby's cry. This would only bring a sense of futility to the care provider.* For, she cannot provide the baby with quiet, nor with true love, nor with the environment that feels most safe and secure to him. She cannot provide him with rest if there is too much noise for him to sleep, nor can she provide him with true comfort if she and he are not close, affectionate, and bonded with each other. There is no way that she can provide him with the reassurance he craves. Thus, she resigns herself to attending to the non-emotional sources of a baby's cry: the dirty diaper, the hungry stomach, the need for "fresh air," or a quick hug. But the only hug that brings true comfort is the hug from someone who loves him. There is little she can do for the baby in need of love and peace if the people who love him and who can provide him with a peaceful environment are elsewhere.

Babies in day care centers lead frantic lives. They are expected to cope as adults would, to adjust as adults would to all the vicissitudes and turmoil of public as opposed to private life. There is no time in day care for daydreaming and introspection. Time in the "Learning Center" is defined *for* them: as play time, story time, art time, reading-readiness time, outside time, etc. What is missing is their own time—to define the moment as they choose, to think things over, to explore their dreams without fear of reprisal. Again, day care provides too much stimulation of the random, disorganized kind which inevitably comes from the co-habitation of large numbers of babies and toddlers, and too much of the organized kind which comes from group-centered living. It provides too little calm, quiet, space, and comfort and too little opportunity to converse and relate with a loving other.

Imagine, for example, a parent sitting down with her child for a "tea party." As she pours real tea into her own cup and milk into her child's, the "how to do things" is taken seriously. The child is encouraged to say "thank you" and to pass the cookies back to his mother and their chat begins. Although they are pretending to be two adults, the ritual is real; it occurs in a real home setting, provides the child with real food and drink, and with real opportunity for "mature" conversation. The mother says, "I'm so glad to be here for tea. How have you been?" The child, enjoying the opportunity to play the part of his mother's friend, says "Fine! Would you like another cookie?" "Oh yes, thank you," answers the mother. "These cookies are delicious! Whatever is your secret for making such good cookies?" The child is learning about civilized behavior.

Then, picture the toy tea set at the Learning Center. Two children decide to have tea. They fight over who has whom over to his house. In response to the one child asking, "How have you been?" the other loses interest and walks away. Too much of this peer-centered kind of "learning" and not enough of adult-focused learning clearly has negative implications for a child's social development. The child simply cannot learn right from wrong, proper from improper, from other children who themselves have trouble making these distinctions.

It is not simply the pretend scenarios which a child enacts with a parent but the opportunities to partake in real-life experiences under the tutelage of an adult that make being with a parent so advantageous. As

Penelope Leach puts it, "the prime learning of early childhood is about the real world and no preschool group is that:"

> It is not a family, tribe or community in which adults as well as children pursue their own ends; it is a group designed exclusively for children in which the only adults have the children themselves as their ends. Since the adults do not spend their time doing adult things, the children cannot learn adult things from them; instead the children learn from the adults how to do childish things in a more adult way. . . . But the sanitized specialness that makes the preschool suitable and safe prevents it from feeding the narrative itself: only the outside world can do that. The long childhood of human beings is not for finding the way from day care through high school, but through infancy into adulthood, and for this children need to serve an apprenticeship to parents or parent figures in the business of growing up.[75]

She adds, "schooling can only be truly educational within the context of lived learning, and in early childhood, there is a lot of living that must come first."

The evidence, mountains of research, confirms our common-sense appraisal of the beneficiality, and lack thereof, of the kind of "stimulation" babies and toddlers receive in day care. As a publication of the Rockford Institute entitled "The Family in America" observes, the negative findings on day care "continue to roll in and they are very consistent with those that have been accumulating for the past 20 years." Among the well-documented findings compiled by the Rockford Institute are these:

> Level of infant stimulation in day care is low and lacks variety.
> Day care during infancy is associated with "deviations" in the expected course of emotional development.
> Infants placed in 20 hours or more of day care avoid their mothers and are insecurely attached; sons have attachment problems with both mothers and fathers.
> Children placed in day care receive less adult attention, try to communicate less, receive and display less affection, are more aggressive, and are less responsive to adults.
> Compared with children who were cared for by their mothers as preschoolers, third-graders who were placed in day care as preschoolers are viewed more negatively by their peers, have lower academic grades, and demonstrate poorer study skills.
> Compared with children who go home to their mothers after school, suburban third-graders who are in day care after school provoke more negative reactions from peers, earn lower grades and score lower on standardized tests.[76]

In a summarization of findings on day care, T.J. Gamble and E. Ziegler conclude that children who experienced day care from infancy were rated as significantly less cooperative with adults, more physically and verbally aggressive with peers and adults, and more active; there was a tendency for them to be less tolerant of frustration.[77] Sadly, inexcusably, we Americans do not hear much about these consistently negative findings.

Of course, there are other risks of day care which, because they are physical (and therefore visible) have been difficult for the mainstream press to ignore. Attending day care increases incidence of upper respiratory tract infections (e.g. bronchitis and pneumonia), gastrointestinal infections, and "virtually all agents which cause illness in children." Chronic ear infections often lead to the need for ear tubes and to the risk of mild hearing loss. University of Michigan and Penn State researchers found chronic otitis media affected the social behavior of day care children in concerning ways; the mild hearing loss associated with it led to more solitary play, and to children initiating fewer verbal interactions.[78] A child in day care is 300 percent more likely to require hospitalization and twice as likely to die from disease as are children at home. In spite of myths to the contrary, children are at much greater risk of physical and verbal abuse at day care centers than out of them. The Rockford Institute findings also included these: "Individuals with mental illness, including sexual perversions directed toward children are sometimes drawn to the day-care setting. When parents turn their children over to strangers, there is no way to be completely sure the caregivers are not maliciously or unnaturally motivated. Day-care centers in many states have been closed because of increasingly frequent allegations of physical and sexual abuse."[79]

The negative findings in a study of sexual and physical abuse in Michigan, findings similarly found in state after state, implicate day care and make it hard, or at least unconscionable, to ignore the problem:

> Approximately one percent of all licensed (and therefore state-approved and presumed safe) day care facilities were accused of either sexual or physical abuse between 1982 and 1986. In a study of 48 children who had been sexually abused in this Michigan sample, Kathleen Faller found the following grim patterns: Day care centers accounted for 75 per cent of the sexual abuse; 25 percent came from day care homes;half of the facilities where sexual abuse occurred were state licensed! forty percent of the children had been abused by only one abuser, but over 37 percent had been abused by 4 of more abusers. Sixty-six percent of the children were 3 or 4 when sexual abuse began, but abuse began as young as 1 year of age and included children as old as age 9. Among the types of sexual abuse uncovered, the variety of perversions (disgusting even to imagine being perpetrated on children) included satanic practices in some cases. Children were threatened with death, fear and further psychological abuse if they told their parents. Of course the short-range consequences of such abuse include masturbation, sleep problems (nightmares, insomnia, etc.), physical illness, eating disorders, emotional disturbances, behavioral problems, school difficulties, and phobias. The long-term damage to such children always casts shadows on their adulthood, and some kind of intensive professional therapy (even decades after the occurrence) is usually necessary to overcome the detrimental effects of sexual abuse.[80]

Federal subsidization of and government involvement in day care does not preclude abuse. In a recent study at the Wright Institute of Berkeley, California, researcher Diane Ehrensaff investigated allegations of "sexual abuse with ritualistic elements" at the Child Development Center on the Presidio Military Base in San Francisco. Ehrensaff found considerable evidence that abuse occurred, including "vaginal discharge, genital soreness, rashes, fear of the dark, sleep disturbances, nightmares, sexually provocative language . . . and sexually inappropriate behavior." She finds that, while the focus on sexual abuse currently focuses on abuse within families, "sponsorship of a program by the government does not guarantee safety for children."[81]

Some brave souls at the *Wilmington Delaware News Journal* did a three-month investigation of day care in the state and found that "good day care is the exception." They found inadequate state supervision; centers with dismal conditions allowed to stay open; loopholes which allowed criminals to get day care jobs; child abusers who were able to exploit the system; and parents who looked hard but could not find quality care. Still, the emphasis of the report was on how to improve the system and how to find quality care. While conceding that "a stimulating environment speeds a child's self-esteem, language, pre-math and social skills" while a "dull, unstable setting stymies intellectual, physical and emotional development," the reporters never considered that the most stimulating and stable environment might be the home.[82]

As the risks of day care become manifest and as the shadows of day care on children's adulthood come to light, child development experts are increasingly concerned. One such concerned person is Professor Jay Belsky of Penn State University. Involved in day care evaluation for more than two decades, Professor Belsky moved from a neutral position to a more negative one. Although criticized for his change of stance, Belsky found the mass of evidence undeniable. He observed, "The data changed, the data looked different, and I see lots of people ignoring the data and explaining it away." The moment a researcher stumbles upon the negative effects of day care, he reports, "a host of ideologues are raising questions, criticizing methodology, mounting ad hominem attacks, or simply disregarding the data entirely in their pronouncements."[83] The distortion of data on day care and the omission of negative findings in the popular press has been discussed. To reemphasize the point, let us pause to scrutinize another example of misleading "information" on the subject.

Deborah Phillips and Carolee Howes, in a popularly referred to advocacy article, declared that the evidence shows "overwhelmingly" that "children in good quality child care show no signs of harm."[84] They cited a Clarke-Stewart and Fein article in support of this claim. Although the later article was, on the whole, positively dispositioned toward day care, Walter Peery observes that it raised important concerns, concerns which Phillips and Howes "conveniently ignored." For example, Clarke-Stewart and Fein identified "optimal" attachment patterns in infants as depending upon secure attachment to parents characterized by "trust and enjoyment in the interaction" and acknowledged considerable evidence that day care "disrupts" this optimal pattern. They acknowledged that children in day care "are more likely than children at home to position themselves farther away from mother, to spend less time close to or in physical contact with mother, and to ignore or avoid mother after a brief separation."[85] As Peery's analysis reveals, no more reassurance comes from the second article cited by Phillips and Howes; one by Michael Rutter, which concluded that "it would be misleading to conclude that it is without risks or effects" and that "much depends on the quality of the day care and on the age, characteristics, and family circumstances of the child."[86]

Another source cited by Phillips and Howes (*Day Care: Scientific and Social Policy Issues* by Ziegler and Gordon) is an especially inappropriate example of the "harmlessness of day care." The two articles in this compilation that deal particularly with the effects of day care, one by Rutter and another by E.A. Farber and B. England, are anything but reassuring. Rutter found, for example, that:

> Children who experienced day care from infancy were rated as significantly less co-operative with adults, more physically and verbally aggressive with peers and adults, and more active; there was a tendency for them to be less tolerant of frustration . . . Day care results in some social inhibition with adults rather than social facilitation as might have been expected . . . Negative interactions with other children decreased and negative interactions with teachers increased between three and five; this tendency was marginally greater in those with the greatest nursery school experience prior to starting school.[87]

For teenage boys, Rutter found "diffused mothering" tended to result in "fearless aggressive nonconformity" and "peer-group orientation." Farber and England found that "50 to 70 percent of the infants (they studied) placed in day care demonstrated insecure attachments to their mothers" and that "by two years of age, children placed in day care in earliest infancy displayed less enthusiasm, were less compliant, and less persistent on task and had higher negative affect than infants who had been cared for by non-working mothers."[88]

Peery laments, "Exactly how any day-care advocates can read this research, let alone cite it as proof that 'children in good quality child care show no signs of harm' is almost beyond comprehension." He asks, "Why do day-care proponents use such misleading tactics?" and concludes:

> It appears most day-care advocates are so convinced of proposition #1 (women must work outside the home) and proposition #2 (day care is necessary for the children of working mothers) that they are completely converted to day care as a "necessity" to alleviate perceived adult problems. Consequently, they become intellectually dishonest and distort the research findings. Why else would day-care advocates continually ignore the consistently negative effects and conditions of risk inherent in day care, while disseminating disinformation?[89]

Peery correctly observes that day care is all too often viewed as a solution to an adult problem. This allows the question of whether day care is optimal for children to be ignored. Although almost no one contends that day care is actually beneficial, the question becomes whether we can positively prove that day care is harmful. Peery insists that this is the wrong question. *We must consider the optimal conditions for raising our children. To do otherwise is to permit an appalling lowering of standards.*

Especially disturbing was the spate of one-sided publicity and lopsided analysis given in 2001 to the release of a National Institute of Child Health and Human Development study claiming to disprove that day care disrupts the "attachment" between mother and child. The press's unquestioning promotion of this preliminary study and the lack of attention to the negative findings buried within the study is truly alarming. This study of more than one thousand children up to the age of four and a half, "measured" the children's "sense of trust" in their mother and found that "sensitivity and responsiveness" of the mother is not affected by particular childcare arrangements. Although the study did find that children who attended childcare centers had "somewhat more behavior problems" than children who experienced other non-maternal care arrangements, the major reported claim of the study (although there was not consensus upon this claim among the researchers) was that day care was not harmful; a mother's responsiveness, not the hours spent with her child, was said to be the important determinant of attachment. In order to make this claim, researchers and their promoters in the press had to keep their focus selective in these ways:

1.   This study included more types of childcare than previous studies (including care by fathers, grandparents, or other relatives in the home) and greater variability in the numbers of hours of care than some

studies (some children only receiving a few hours of care a week). Inevitably, this skews the study toward more favorable results. *Most children were not in full-time non-maternal care, and most were not in day care centers during the first two years of life.* In fact, within the NICH report, we discover that "the average child spent 27 hours a week in non-maternal care over the first 4 1/2 years of life." "During the children's first 2 years of life, most child care took place in family homes with relatives or in child care homes; as children got older, more were in center based care."[90] This in a study widely touted as proving that "day care" is not harmful!

2.   Attachment was measured by the extent to which children would go to their mother and be comforted by her upon seeing her after separation. The researchers relied upon the Ainsworth Strange Situation that measures attachment security in terms of proximity seeking, crying, contact maintenance, and strength of greeting on reunion. Although preferring the comfort of mother to others is widely acknowledged as a sign of attachment, a child in need of a hug going up to someone likely to give that hug and being happy to get it is not in itself enough to measure attachment in this situation. For, if it is notable that there were not big differences in attachment behavior between those in care and those at home, it also notable that there were not less signs of separation anxiety among those *accustomed* to separation from their mothers than among those children *unaccustomed* to day care. We must remember that day care advocates advise working mothers in reassuring books that, if they simply ignore the fussing and crying of infants upon their initial placement in daycare, the fussing and crying will eventually subside, as babies "get used to it." It is then notable that even infants that were experienced with lots of daycare *did show distress* during separations. While this is interpreted as meaning they are securely attached, we should also be concerned about the distress itself. Why would we want to skip over their distress and rejoice at signs of their relief upon seeing their mothers? Moreover, given the variability in the hours in care and the kinds of care, the varying extent to which babies felt the *need* for comfort or showed *signs* of stress before reuniting with their mothers should have been taken into account. Even the claim that attachment was not impaired is clouded by the study's own description of its very mixed findings. If we read the study's own words with hearts and minds alive, we certainly do not come to the simple conclusion that day care has no effect on attachment:

Infants with extensive childcare experience did not differ in the distress they exhibited during separations from mother in the Strange Situation or in the confidence with which trained coders assigned them attachment classifications. There were no significant main effects of child-care experience (quality, amount, age of entry, stability, or type of care) on attachment security or avoidance. There were, however, significant main effects of maternal sensitivity and responsiveness. Significant inter-action effects revealed that infants were less likely to be secure when low maternal sensitivity/responsiveness was combined with poorer quality child care; more than minimal amounts of child care, or more than one care arrangement. In addition, boys experiencing many hours in care and girls in minimal amounts of care were somewhat less likely to be securely attached.[91]

Indeed, the study found that "child care was a small but significant predictor of maternal engagement" and that, even for children in high quality care, "more child care hours predicted less child engagement." This is important, for the study also found that "maternal sensitivity was the strongest predictor of preschool attachment classification."[92]

3.   While the study announced a relationship between small cognitive advances and quality childcare, within the study the "primary indica-tor of quality care" is said to be "positive caregiving." This, in turn, is said to include qualities such as showing a positive attitude and having physical contact, responding to vocalizations, asking questions, praising and encouraging, reading, encouraging development, and teaching (all of which mothers are known to do!). Indeed, the study admitted that most centers were not high quality and that "the highest level of positive caregiving was provided by in home caregivers, including fathers and grandparents, caring for only 1 child; closely followed by home based arrangements with relatively few children per adult." In the study's own words, "The least positive care was found in center based care with higher rations of children to adults."[93] Moreover, what the study actually says is that cognitive advances are not related to the amount of care, but to the quality and that "language stimulation predicted subsequent cognitive and language performance 9 to 12 months later."[94] In other words, it was the language stimulation and the positive individualized attention, not being in day care that made the difference.

4.   In order to emphasize their findings at all, the fact that the study was only in its preliminary stages had to be downplayed. As Scott Richart pointed out in an article for *Chronicles: A Magazine of American Culture*: "The fix is in. By releasing the 'preliminary' results with great fanfare two or more years before the final results will be in, the researchers have laid the groundwork for dismissing any findings which might not serve the needs of government and big business. Why should it matter if your daughter suffers from recurrent middle-ear infections, has trouble mak-ing herself understood, and acts like a barbarian? At least her sense of trust in you is intact."[95] Long-term findings, Richart believed, would inevitably reveal that day care children are "far more aggressive, have lower grades and poorer study skills," and have "trouble interacting with their peers."

5.   Most reports on the study, in making exaggerated claims about the benefits of "quality care," ignored the study's own internal findings on the relation between the *quantity* of day care and negative outcomes.

Here are the findings on quantity in the words of the NICHD report itself:

For children whose mothers showed low levels of sensitivity during mother-child interactions, more than 10 hours of care each week increase the risk of insecure attachment to their mothers.

Children who spent more time in child care were somewhat less cooperative, more disobedient, and more aggressive at age 2 and age 41/2, and in kindergarten, but not at age 3. These findings were based on reports from caregivers, mothers, and/or teachers about children's behavior.

Children who averaged 30 hours of child care or more each week during their first 41/2 years of life were somewhat more likely to show problem behaviors at age 4 and in kindergarten, based on caregiver reports. But child care quantity did not predict problem behaviors in the home environment as reported by mothers.

Time spent in child care did not predict clinical levels (behaviors that may require special attention) of behavior problems or psychopathology.

Once again, family features were stronger predictors of children's social behavior and development that was quantity of child care.[96]

In addition to all these weaknesses in the presentation of the report, there is this one—it ignores what the great majority of mothers who stay home with their babies would tell researchers, if only they asked: their attachment seems to grow more intense the more time they spend together; with each day they are more attuned to each other's signals and nuances; their babies shows clear signs of frustration when separated from them; the continual building-up of closeness depends upon the baby's deep and subtle as well as immediate and specific responses to mother. Too often, in the picture we are given, the meaning that lies beyond statistics does not count for much.

It is very hard to see how these NICHD findings could be interpreted as vindication of full-time day care, especially given that the report itself stated "even minor differences [in outcomes for those in day care] may be important from different perspectives, especially if they are consistent over time and if they increase or decrease as children develop."[97] But that is just how the findings were presented and interpreted.

All limitations, all negative findings, and all studies with contrary conclusions were ignored by the press. "Good Morning America," *The New York Times,* and the many shows and magazines that followed their lead treated this preliminary study as conclusive and downplayed the negative findings included within the study. Just listen to these authoritatively presented words of confidence in *Parents Magazine*: "(The) National Institute of Child Health and Human Development recently released important research that lets everybody off the hook: Even when they're in less than ideal child-care settings, babies bond just as well with their mothers as do infants who are without their moms all day long. What really matters is how sensitive a working mom is to her baby's need when they are together." And, the most disturbing statement: "A working mother's loving attention can offset the negative impact of poor-quality child care."[98] It is difficult to see how a child's willingness to be comforted by and desire to be with mother after separation translates into the position that a mother "offsets" the negative impact of poor-quality childcare! Richart intones, "what are we to make of such a statement? That it is OK for a child's day to be miserable, for her to be treated negligently and carelessly—even harshly, so long as she is treated kindly and affectionately at night? Such nonsense hardly deserves a response."

Well, Richart was mostly right: In 2006, NICHD came out with the results of the long term study and reluctantly, it seems, found that poor behavior was linked to time in day care. Sharon Landesman Ramey, one of the co-authors of the study and director of the Georgetown University Center on Health and Education, was publicly quoted as saying, "I have accused the study authors of doing everything they could to make this negative finding go away, but they couldn't do it. —They knew this would be disturbing news for parents, but at some point, if that's what you're finding, then you have to report it." [99] Although this study found that genes and parental guidance were the most important influences in how children behaved, it also found that children with experience in day care centers had a higher incidence of problem behavior such as aggression, bullying, and disobedience. These findings held up regardless of the child's sex or family income and regardless of the quality of the day care center.

In addition, the study found that even after controlling for a host of background factors distinguishing families and children and even after taking into consideration the observed quality of day care that children experienced at six, fifteen, thirty-six, and fifty-four months of age, the quantity of care itself was associated with a host of developmental outcomes. These included less engaged and close interaction between mother and child and more "externalizing" behavior on the part of the child. In other words, while it was found that center-based care had greater deleterious behavioral effects, the amount of care also had an effect. Noted Jay Belsky, also a co-author, "This study makes it clear that it is not just quality that matters."

In an article for the *Journal of Developmental & Behavioral Pediatrics* entitled "Quantity Counts: Amount of Child Care and Children's Socioemotional Development," Belsky recounts the difficult road he has traveled in stating the connection between quantity and adverse outcomes and points to the steady flow of "disconcerting evidence" pertaining to the effects of full-time or near-full-time non-maternal care in the early years of life. In the mid 1980s Belsky created controversy and angered many of his colleagues when, based on the evidence he was seeing, he moved away from his former position that quality was what mattered.

> Belsky's (1-3) analysis of child care research produced the conclusion that early and extensive nonmaternal care carried risks in terms of increasing the probability of insecure infant-parent attachment relationships and promoting aggression and non-compliance during the toddler, preschool, and early primary school years. Widespread critiques of Belsky's analysis called attention to much of the research cited by Belsky and its failure to take into consideration child-care quality and control for background factors likely to make children with varying child care experiences developmentally different in the first place.[100]

In the fifteen years since this controversy erupted, much more re-search has been done controlling for quality of care and pre-existing family differences (see this article for references to a wide range of studies). Along with the NICHD study, these studies conclude that even after these factors are controlled for, "quantity or dosage of child care predicts a host of developmental outcomes" and typically does so "in a manner consistent with Belsky's original risk factor conclusion and/or subsequent observation that it is cumulative history of lots of time in child care that carries developmental risks."[101] Security of attachment, socioemotional development, and behavior are all negatively affected by increasing hours of day care.

The truth is that *even high quality day care centers* cannot provide the optimal conditions for development. A 1985 study by Ron Haskins in the journal *Child Development* found that those children who had spent more time in day care exhibited proportionately more negative effects *regardless of the quality of care*. Teachers were more likely to rate these children as having "aggressiveness as a serious deficit of social behavior." Elementary teachers I interviewed confided that they, similarly, saw a significant difference between the learning styles and abilities of those children who spent more time with parents than with care givers and those children who, conversely, spent more time with care givers than with parents. A recent University of California-Irvine study confirms this distinction. An analysis of 105 middle class six-year-olds indicated that the more hours mothers work, "the lower the children's grades and the poorer their work habits and efforts." The study also showed that "as mothers worked more hours . . . the children displayed less resilience, resourcefulness and adaptability in the classroom."[102]

Again, it is important to remember the variability in the hours the children in the NICHD study spent in day care and the later age at which most of the children in this study moved from in-home to institutional care. If anything, this makes the negative findings more compelling. Although this study was high profile, we need to acknowledge (and create) other studies that focus on the effects of placing babies (not toddlers) into day care centers full time. Since the child's day is part of their upbringing, or lack thereof, we simply must be concerned about the nature of day care itself.

Day care is by its nature impermanent and unstable, un-nurturing, and unrelaxing. The NICHD study found that one-fourth of the children in a regular childcare arrangement had had that arrangement changed at least once in the twelve months preceding the study interviews. As Richard Gill adduces, "This, of course, is quite apart from the change of caregivers within any given arrangement, and also the change of caregivers as the child moves from one age group to another. If one is looking for enduring and stable relationships they will be hard to find in the context of out-of-home-care."[103] The personnel come and go at an average rate of 41 percent per year at the average day care center.[104]

Attempts to make paid workers as loving and committed as parents are doomed from the start. One highly touted solution to day care workers' lack of commitment is higher pay. But this would require increasing the ratio of children to workers in order to pay for the salary increase. Indeed, researchers Victor R. Fuchs and Mary Coleman found it highly improbable that income of child-care workers could be raised without violating that other criterion of quality care: low ratio of children to childcare workers. Fuchs and Coleman trace the low pay of childcare workers to the following:

> 1) their individual qualifications would command less in other jobs as well; 2) the positive features of child care attract some women even though they could earn more doing other work 3) parents and others who buy child care are apparently unwilling or unable to pay for more highly educated workers of for those with more work experience, 4) a low child-worker ratio.[105]

Even if higher salaries were possible, there seems to be little relation between how much money a worker receives and how much they will love and commit themselves to a particular child. The above-mentioned RAND investigation marveled at the fact that "families with more resources (high earnings, more education, more income, intact families) do not typically obtain higher quality care for their children than families with lower resources."[106]

Thus, those childcare advocates who insist that the "child care crisis" can be solved by more government money miss the point that love and commitment cannot be bought. Certainly, the experiences of my relatively well-off friends and acquaintances bear this out. Urie Bronfenbrenner, from Cornell, wisely reminded us that it is impossible to pay someone enough to get them to do for children what parents will do for free. Dr. Burton White, a nationally known expert on parent education, believes the childcare industry is a "total disaster area" with "no feasible way of turning it into a model industry."[107] He feels there is an "unbridgeable gap" between the way children should be raised and the possibilities provided by day care centers.

Even a paid care provider whose actions and words are loving cannot substitute for a parent who really loves the child. Even if the parent's words and actions are not as perfectly scripted as the (illusive) perfect care provider's are, the parents "being-there" kind of love will have a powerful effect upon the child. I have always been impressed by the special ability of parents' love to shine through actions and words which are not in themselves loving. This is tremendously comforting to a child. It tells the child that even when limits are being set and reprimands are being issued, the motive is an appreciation as opposed to a depreciation of the child. One often hears parents complain about their children only to realize that underneath the complaint lies praise, even for the child's "shortcomings." A parent might express dismay at the two-year-old who is into everything and testing every limit, and yet the parent's facial expression reveals pride rather than exasperation. A mother might complain that her son is just like his father—unable to sit still—and on her face is amusement rather than dismay. When parents speak of a child's stubbornness, rambunctiousness, or restlessness we see in their faces and hear in their tone that what might to the care giver be a tiresome trait making her job more difficult is, in some curious and deep-seated way, a source of pleasure for the parent. Underneath parents' complaints about their children often lies a brag.

The parents' love shines through to the child as well as to outside observers. I am continually impressed by the tone of love which slips through when my friends discipline their children. Love for a child by a parent is so strong that it tends to reveal itself. "That is it—I've had it—time out—now" translates into "You deserve punishment but I still love you." More often than not when a care giver emits the same words, they translate as just that: "That's it—I've had it." One rarely hears care givers discuss the difficult aspects of the children in their charge with affection and pride. What is difficult is just that—difficult. If parents are exhausted, frustrated, even exasperated by certain aspects of their children's behavior, what emotions does that behavior inspire in a care giver for whom the children are much less important? When the parents' love "shows through" their anger or frustration, the child's self-image is less likely to be damaged.

When growing up, I had a friend whose mother had quite a temper and certainly would not have passed muster with most child development experts. I remember marveling that my friend did not often take her mother's outbursts to heart, but, rather, seemed completely confident of her mother's affections. Looking back on it, I see that the mother's love shone through. Her personality was not ideally suited to mothering but her love was. More than a few times, I noticed the slight twinkle of amusement in her eyes when she reprimanded her daughter for some bit of mischief or another.

A parent cannot help but notice the difference in how they respond to the foibles and misdeeds of their own children and how they feel about the foibles and misdeeds of other children. As much as I might like and enjoy my children's friends, I do not love many of them. If the friend falls and cuts their knee, I might respond the same way as I would to my own child, but I do not feel the same way and the friend is not comforted as much as if the comforting were provided by a parent. If the friend breaks a vase, I might actually respond more sympathetically than I would to my own child and yet I would likely feel less sympathetic. This is the illogic of love. Children know and feel the big difference between duty and obligation and love. If I read to my child and his friend while sitting between them, there is, of course, a completely different kind of communication occurring on my right side and on my left. The same words are experienced differently when they are given to or received by someone you love. When children are happy or sad, parents naturally absorb those feelings. Children are emboldened to explore the world knowing that a person who feels their pain and their joy as they encounter the peaks and valleys to which their explorations take them is right there by their side.

It is important to note that included in the *studies that confirm our innate knowledge about what children need, but which never come into public view*, are recent studies from Canada, Australia, England, and New Zealand. The large Canadian study, published in 2006, found that children raised in day care were seventeen times more hostile than children raised at home and almost three times more anxious. Although it found that preschool for toddlers could hold cognitive advantages, it found negative cognitive outcomes emerging by age five for children who had been in day care as babies. It also found negative effects on parents.[108] An Australian study, published in 2006, confirmed prior research finding that day care seems to harm babies' brain chemistry and negatively affect their social-emotional development.[109] A British (EPPE) study published in 2005 found "high levels of group care" before age three was associated with higher levels of anti-social behavior at age three, but it also found that this effect appeared to decrease if the child continued to attend "high quality care." It found that children whose mothers returned to work shortly after giving birth "are more likely to be slower developers." (However, it found cognitive advantages to preschool for toddlers.)[110] Another English study, heralded by Penelope Leach, found that toddlers looked after by their mothers do significantly better in developmental tests than those looked after in nurseries.[111] A recent New Zealand study is one more (of many) that found that experiences in childhood and adolescence had significant effect upon the parenting styles of mothers.[112] The child lives on in the adult.

Particularly disturbing to mothers who have been misled into thinking that day care is OK must be recent evidence linking the development of the brain to one-on-one stimulation between mother and child. When a mother's love is constant and present, and when mother and child engage in the normal chitchat of being together, the benefits that child reaps are not only emotional but also intellectual and neurological. Scientific and psychiatric research now back up the gut-level urge to nurture and protect our offspring as something which the child suffers not only socially and emotionally, but also intellectually without. Recent science tells us that those babies who receive the steady security of maternal love and the steadily evolving verbal stimulation and responsiveness that tend to go with it turn out to be better thinkers than those who do not. Those who lack the steady evolution of conversation lack the nourishing diet of language and the reasoning abilities, which accompany it. For lack of this intellectual nourishment, they are less conversant, less affectionate, and actually develop differently neurologically. Science now supports the age-old wisdom that "mothering" makes a huge difference in a child's life—so huge that it affects the neurological "wiring" in a child's brain. That this viewpoint is unliberated in no way makes it less true.

One of the researchers in this field, Jane Healy, wrote a book entitled *Endangered Minds: Why Children Don't Think and What We Can Do About It*. What triggered her interest in the growth of children's brains was the mass of reports by teachers and psychologists that an alarming number of today's children are, in some way, emotionally and intellectually impaired. Children today, teachers report, are less able to think abstractly or deeply, less able to converse clearly, less able to comprehend what they have read, less imaginative, and less capable of solving their problems with other children in a reasonable non-violent manner. "Teachers of the youngest children, claiming they see more pronounced changes each year, warned that we haven't seen anything yet!" Healy developed a questionnaire requesting anecdotal information on cognitive changes observed in students. In the three hundred responses she received, she found an "amazing" degree of unanimity: "Yes, attention spans are noticeably shorter. Yes, reading, writing, and oral language skills seem to be declining—even in the 'best' neighborhoods. Yes, no matter how 'bright,' students are less able to bend their minds around difficult problems in math, science, and other subjects. Yes, teachers feel frustrated and would like to do a better job."[113] The "provocative" results of her questionnaire encouraged Healy to search further. The answers Healy found as she spoke to experts in neurological development are deeply disturbing: She found that we are raising a generation of "different brains" and that many students' faltering academic skills—at every socioeconomic level—reflect subtle but significant changes in their physical foundations for learning.

Recent research indicates that the optimal wiring of neurons in a baby's brain depends in part upon how much of the (good kind of) stimulation a baby's brain receives. The brain is plastic in that the area that is stimulated the most grows the most, not in size, but in the sense that it makes the most neural connections. The newborn brain is a mass of brain cells with the potential to form a mass of connections. Healy cites one of the experts in neuroanatomy, Dr. Marian Diamond of the University of California, Berkeley:

> To those of us in the field, there is absolutely no doubt that culture changes brains, and there's no doubt in my mind that children's brains are changing. As long as stimuli come in to a certain area, you get more branching. It is the pattern of the branching that differentiates among us. The cortex is changing all the time—I call it the dance of the neurons. This is true of the brains of cats, dogs, rats, monkeys or man.[114]

According to Dr. Kenneth A Klivington of the Salk Institute of California, whom Healy interviewed: "Structure and function are inseparable. We know that environments shape brains; all sorts of experiments have demonstrated that it happens. There are some studies currently being done that show profound differences in the structure of the brain depend-

ing on what is taken in by the senses."[115] Perhaps helping to explain the
inordinate numbers of children having difficulty in reading comprehension and in the formulation and expression of ideas is the fact that "association areas, critically important for planning, reasoning, and using
language to express ideas are the most plastic of all; their development
depends on the way the child uses his or her brain at different stages of
development."[116]

It turns out that the natural chatter between a child and a trusted and
loving adult as they discuss, plan, and reason their way through their days
is critical not only to language development but also to the development
of reason. According to Healy:

> Language shapes culture, language shapes thinking and language shapes brains.
> The verbal bath in which a society soaks its children arranges their synapses and the
> intellects; it helps them learn to reason, reflect, and respond to the world. . . . Severe
> deprivation of language during early years guarantees lasting neural changes that
> noticeably affect speech and understanding. More subtle forms of language depri-
> vation do not show up in such dramatic ways, but may ultimately affect abilities to
> think abstractly, plan ahead and defer gratification, control attention, and perform
> higher-order analysis and problem-solving—the very skills so much at issue in
> American schools today.[117]

Day care is precisely that "subtle form of language deprivation," for,
in day care, children are deprived of the optimal conditions for language
development. Again, in day care, there is both too much stimulation and
not enough. There is too much stimulation of the loud, turbulent, unintel-
ligible kind and not enough of the calm, attuned, intelligible kind that
comes when one adult speaks with one child. Studies across different
cultures and different times show that mothers have a special ability to
engender language development in their children and a natural tendency
to tailor their speech according to the child's language needs. Recent
research published in the magazine *Science* indicates that the affectionate cooing and babbling which mothers naturally do with their children
facilitates language development. Researchers found that mothers in
the three countries studied, the United States, Sweden, and Russia, automatically exaggerated word pronunciation and spoke in a voice about
an octave higher than normal. They did this automatically and without
any prompting. The scientists found that the heightened pitch attracts the
babies' attention and stimulates their verbal response.[118] Notes Healy,

> Studies show that mothers instinctively shape and expand their child's language, tai-
> loring their own responses precisely to each child's developmental need. They seem
> to know just how to pull the youngster's language up a notch by using forms in their
> own speech that are just one degree above the child's current level. Simply exposing

children to adult language does not automatically make the learning "take," because youngsters can't repeat speech patterns that are much more complicated than those they are already using (another reason, incidentally, why most TV—even Sesame Street—is a flop as a language model.)[119]

Clearly, in day care centers, children receive *lots of noise but little conversation*. It is of little help that day care centers have dubbed themselves Learning Centers. For, the kind of growth young children need is verbal and emotional. The combination of a loving person and lots of being talked to and read to is what stimulates their brains most. It has been proven, for example, that gentle caressing changes the chemistry of the newborn brain and that deprivation of a loving touch can translate into a deprivation in the functioning of the brain. If day care centers, lacking the ability to cuddle and converse with each child, focus instead upon "skills" such as early reading and writing, this is putting the cart before the horse. It is not age-appropriate, for babies' and toddlers' brains are not designed to read and write but rather to listen and chatter. We might with great effort be able to force the technique of reading upon a young child who has not had the proper verbal stimulation, but that child will likely lack the comprehension of what he has read which makes reading a pleasure. Early reading programs can instill a dislike of reading whereas the natural verbal interplay of mother and child prepares a child, at the appropriate age, to enter the world of reading with his brain fully attuned to the adventure.

Indeed, studies tell us what we know at heart: Some stimulation is good, but too much is bad. A little bit of excitement in a safe environment and the receptors of the brain can open. But too much excitement, stress, or fear and the receptors for learning can actually close. As one neuro-biologist I interviewed who preferred to remain anonymous put it, "Nurturing is an important part of the stimulation package."

In day care centers the baby who "talks" all too often is not listened to or not heard. It takes a lot of listening to and "translating" to understand what a one- to two-year-old is saying. Someone familiar with that baby's accent and code words will understand her best. What must it do to her language development when her efforts at communicating are, often as not, misunderstood or ignored? Indeed, in day care centers, children are rewarded for being quiet more often than they are rewarded for being vocal. Group activities require that they "quiet down." According to Healy, studies demonstrate that even the best centers cannot and do not provide adequate opportunity for language development:

The children spent most of their time in teacher-directed large-group activities, and . . . most of their language behavior was receptive, such as listening to and following teachers' directions. Although teachers provided adequate oral language models, they were not active listeners, did not encourage curiosity about language, and did not spontaneously expand on children's vocabulary or concepts. . . . In other settings the situation is even worse. Basic concerns for physical needs and safety predominate; even teacher talk is minimized. In some centers children watch video for substantial portions of the day.[120]

It is no wonder that Healy asks, "Who's minding the children's brains?" and concludes that "as mothers pull away from babies, babies are not getting the challenge they need."

Even the best day care centers cannot provide the kind of one-on-one interaction babies and toddlers need if their brains are to "thrive." University of London psychologists compared the language used by eighteen-month-old children cared for at home with the language used by "advantaged" children of the same age cared for in day care or "nursery:"

The British researchers found that when compared to children cared for at home, children in group care or day-care centers were "less likely to have language records indicative of advanced language development, in that a significantly smaller proportion showed high numbers of word combinations" The psychologists considered their findings "particularly striking" since the parents of the children in day care enjoyed notable advantages in income, occupational status, and education over the parents of the children cared for at home. "More advantaged groups would be expected to show better language development that less advantaged groups," remark the researchers. But then perhaps the meaning of this study is precisely that children cared for by their mothers do enjoy a major advantage over children whose more highly educated mothers leave them in day care centers.[121]

More recently, a study from the University of London and the Institute of Psychiatry showed that children in institutional care had reading levels an average of six months lower than children reared in family foster care, and that the disadvantage remained into school years. "Our study showed that institutional group rearing, typified by a lack of continuity and individualized care, was less likely to prepare young 'looked after' children for the cognitively challenging activities at primary schools than home-centered rearing where continuity of 'parenting' was high."[122]

Disappointingly, but not surprisingly, the press has misinterpreted the breaking research on brain development. Instead of heeding its message about the importance of the *combination* of nurturing and verbal stimulation to a baby's brain, the press has latched onto the need for stimulation and ignored the need for a nurturer. Instead of respecting the true conclusion of the research: that what attentive mothers by nature do—making their babies a part of their days and talking with them as they do—is just what babies brains need, the press has drawn its own conclusions, apparently deciding that if babies' brains need more stimulation they surely need more "lessons," "learning activities," and "head start" programs. A February 1996 *Newsweek* article entitled "Your Child's Brain" is typical. Stated the writer, "The implications of this new understanding are at once promising and disturbing. They suggest that, with the right input at the right time, almost anything is possible. But they imply, too, that if you miss the window you're playing with a handicap. They offer an explanation of why the gains a toddler makes in Head Start are so often evanescent: this intensive instruction begins too late to fundamentally rewire the brain."[123] Columnist Joan Beck drew similar conclusions. She saw the latest research in neurobiology as evidence that Head Start programs needed to start even earlier and that instructional types of learning did as well.

This is a blatant misinterpretation of the research. Trying to force-feed young minds with academic learning and "skills" may actually inhibit the proper growth of the brain by preventing the development of the creative and thinking skills which are best developed by free play. Sigel's 1986 study found that early didactic, authoritarian approaches with younger children actually relate negatively to intellectual achievement. Reports Healy in *Your Child's Growing Mind*:

> Studies show that children who are heavily managed by caregivers may lack both initiative and thinking skills. When adults are overly restrictive in controlling and limiting activities, children show up with poorer problem-solving and mental organizational activities. . . . It is possible to force skills by intensive instruction, but this may cause the child to use immature, inappropriate neural networks and distort the natural growth process. Trying to speed learning over unfinished neuron systems might be akin to racing a limousine over a narrow path in the woods. You can do it, but neither the car nor the path ends up in very good shape.[124]

It is true that there is an "advantage" to early exposure to foreign languages (in elementary school) and to music and pre-math skills (achieved for example, by counting how many crackers are on a plate or making a pattern out of sliced oranges.) As Dr. Harry Chugani's research demonstrates, there are "windows of opportunity" for learning certain things and within which the plastic brain can lose some of its neural connections if not properly stimulated.[125] But it is not true that there is an "advantage" to very early academic instruction and a very early emphasis upon skill learning. It simply is not so. Teachers concerns regarding the increasing numbers of students "unable to use language—oral or written—with the types of precision that might reasonably be expected at any given age or supposed 'ability level' should be a wake up call to us, the parents. We need to think hard about just what our responsibilities are in regard to our children's "early childhood development."

All too often this phrase conjures up images of "learning centers," instilling in our little ones all kinds of techniques for facing a competitive world. Day care centers in the Atlanta area are called "Creme de la Creme." In my area, "Bright Horizons" and "Bright Beginnings" are but two of the names for day care that lure us in. Common designations given to day care centers for infants and toddlers are "academy," "educational center," "school," and "enrichment center." The Goddard School for Early Childhood Development, which advertises "the difference a Goddard primary education makes" enrolls *infants* through preschool age children. Apparently, we are to believe that primary education begins at infancy, not kindergarten. Many day care centers claim to make a difference in a child's academic life. But infancy and toddlerhood are not appropriate times for academia. The real difference in an infant's and toddler's development is that between having someone who loves her and converses with her there on a continual basis and not having that steady presence and interaction. In spite of the masterful job advocacy groups have done at making "early childhood programs" appear to be an advantage, the very young children in these programs are deprived of the most essential ingredients for developing optimally. Warns Healy, "Language changes the way your brain sets up the categories it works with. For these students the whole thought process just isn't there; the linkages between ideas that language provides are missing."[126]

This and much more are missing when a child is institutionalized at a young age. Missing is the intimacy with someone he trusts, which allows him to care for others and to be trustworthy. Missing is the nurturing and peaceful environment which allows him to daydream, think and come up with ideas. Missing is the steady input of grown-up as opposed to immature ideas regarding socially acceptable behavior and right and wrong. Missing is the "secure base" provided by the "good-enough," "being-there" kind of mother, which gives him the confidence to explore the world and to discover the possibilities within himself. Perhaps most disturbing to me is my conviction that something will be missing in his humanness. For, to be human is to have the capacity for intimate attachments based upon love, which grow more intimate because of the possibilities for delving into another soul that language provides; it is to reason about things and to have a moral sense of things; it is to be capable of spontaneity that stems not just from instinct but also from original thought, from the intellect. It is the ability to take control of one's life and to find and define one's individuality. These human qualities, it seems to me, are not best nurtured by institutions but by an environment that combines a high degree of stability with a high degree of love.

If we as adults have these human qualities, if we are capable of being at once strong and independent and generous and sensitive to the needs of others, especially to the young and vulnerable, then we must place the discussion of day care on a higher plane. So far the question has been, How can we provide the best day care for children at the most convenience to parents? The question needs to become, What are the optimal conditions for rearing a child?

If being with parents is best for young children, then government should facilitate the parent-child relationship. Surely, government should not actively discourage that relationship. Rather than subsidizing day care with tax dollars that obligate mothers who choose to bring up their children to subsidize more prosperous mothers who do not, and rather than giving preferential tax breaks to working mothers, tax breaks should be given to families to do with what they will. When government aid is provided for day care, it should not encourage group-based care while discouraging family-based or in-home care. Moreover, lawmakers who would take this position must be courageous enough to face the crossfire. They must express their refusal to view "children's issues" as concomitant with support of institutional "child care." The issues which children face today, clearly, cannot be solved primarily by government. No amount of government funding can produce time and love. Nor can any institution substitute for it.

It is time to confront and scrutinize those reassuring reports that tell us day care is OK. When children are put into day care, the attachment process is not permitted to occur. There is much less opportunity for one-on-one interaction. It is much less likely that the baby will be the recipient of ongoing love. The development of a kind and trusting approach to others and of a confidently exploratory approach to the world are less likely. Anti-social tendencies and learning difficulties are more likely. Optimal development of the growing brain is less likely. And it is much more likely that the baby will contract dangerous diseases and be the recipient of abuse. At a minimum, we must pay attention to those studies showing that day care is not OK. In the end, however, it is difficult to "study" the state of a child's soul. It is only by thinking hard and clearly that we will develop resiliency to rationalizations ungrounded in reason, and recommendations made for our children by people who know nothing about our particular child. For the sake of our children, there must be a private realm wherein no official, no professional, no politician, and no statistician doth tread.

Notes

1. Penelope Leach, *Children First: What Our Society Must Do-and is not Doing- for Our Children Today.* New York: Knopf, 1994: 85.
2. Edward Z. Tronick, "Emotions and Emotional Communication in Infants," *American Psychologist* 44:2. (February, 1989): 115.
3. Daniel N. Stern, *The Interpersonal World of the Infant: A View from Psychoanalysis and Developmental Psychology.* New York: Basic Books, 1985: 21.
4. Stern, *The Interpersonal World of the Infant.* 34.
5. Amanda Woodward, "Psychologist Provides New View on Infant Intelligence," *The Division of the Social Sciences Reports:University of Chicago* 14. (Spring 1994): 3.
6. Stern, *The Interpersonal World of the Infant.* 10.
7. Ruth Heldman, *The Journal of Child Psychology and Psychiatry* (March/April, 2007): 333.
8. *Ibid.,* 346-347.
9. T. B. Brazelton et al., "Early Mother-Infant Reciprocity," Ciba Foundation Symposium 33. (1975):137-154.
10. Victoria Hamilton, "John Bowlby: An Ethologist Basis for Psychoanalysis," in *Beyond Freud: A Study of Modern Psychoanalytic Theorists,* edited by J. Pepper. New York: Analytic Press, 1985: 15.
11. John Bowlby, "The Making and Breaking of Affectional Bonds," *British Journal of Psychiatry* (1997): 203.
12. Alice Sterling Honig, "Parents Do It Best," *The Family in America :New Research.* (December, 1993): 1.
13. Jack Westman, M.D., "The Risks of Day Care," *Day Care: Child Psychology & Adult Economics,* edited by Bryce Christensen. Rockford: Rockford Institute, 1989: 21.
14. *Ibid.,* 21.
15. David Elkind, *Miseducation.* New York: Knopf, 1993: 95-96.
16. *Ibid.,* 98.
17. *Ibid.,* 98.
18. *Ibid.,* 99.
19. Leach, *Children First.* 85.
20. *Ibid.,* 83-84.
21. *Ibid.,* 84.
22. James E. Swain et al. "Brain Basis of Early Parent-Infant Interactions: Psychology, Physiology, and In Vivo Functional Neuroimaging Studies," *Journal Of Child Psychology and Psychiatry* 48. (March/April, 2007): 263-264.
23. *Ibid.,* 266.
24. *Ibid.,* 266-270.
25. *Ibid.,* 277-278.
26. Cindy Hazan and Phillip Shaver, "Deeper into Attachment Theory," *Psychological Inquiry* 5:1. (1994): 68-79.
27. Michael Rutter et al., "Early Adolescent Outcomes for Institutionally-Deprived and Non-deprived Adoptees. I: Disinhibited Attachment," *Journal of Child Psychology and Psychiatry* 48:1. (January, 2007): 26.

28.   *Ibid.*, 28.
29.   Michael.Rutter, "Social-Emotional Consequences of Day Care for Preschool Children," *American Journal of Orthopsychiatry*, 51(1). (January, 1981).
30.   John Bowlby, *Separation:Anxiety and Anger.* New York: Basic Books, 1973: 322.
31.   *Ibid.*, 213.
32.   *Ibid.*,
33.   Ken Magid and Carole Kelvey, *High Risk: Children Without a Conscience.* New York: Bantam Books, 1988.
34.   Cadnet and Cain.
35.   Leach, *Children First.* 92.
36.   Madeline Davis and David Wallbridge, *Boundary and Space: An Introduction to the Works of D.W. Winnicott.* New York: Brunner/Mazel, 1981: 41.
37.   *Ibid.*, 48.
38.   Simon A. Grolnick, *The Work and Play of Winnicott.* Norvak, NJ: Jason Aronson, Inc., 1990: 28.
39.   Winnicott, "The Capacity to Be Alone," based on a paper read at an Extra Scientific Meeting of the British Psycho-Analytical Society. (July 24, 1957); and first published in *Int. Journal of Psycho-Anal.* 39, 410:6-20.
40.   Davis and Wallbridge, *The Work and Play of Winnicott.* 42.
41.   *Ibid.*, 48.
42.   Bowlby, *Separtion.* 202.
43.   Bowlby,"The Making and Breaking of Affectional Bonds." 204.
44.   Rolf Loeber, "Development and Risk Factors of Juvenile Antisocial Behavior and Delinquency," cited in "The Real Root Causes of Violent Crime: The Breakdown of Marriage, Family, and Community," *Heritage Foundation Backgrounder.* (March 17, 1995): 12.
45.   Mohammadreza Hojat, "A Mother's Love: What Children Will Not Receive in Day-Care Centers," Rockford Institute Center, *The Family in America* 8:12. (December 1993): 4.
46.   Arie Kaffman and Michael J. Meany, "Neurodevelopmental Sequelae of Postnatal Maternal Care in Rodents:Clinical and Reasearch Implications of Molecular Insights," *Journal of Child Psychology and Psychiatry* 48:3/4. (March/April, 2007): 235.
47.   *Ibid.*, 238.
48.   Stephen J. Suomi, "Parents, Peers, and the Process of Socialization in Primates," *Parenting and the Child's World* edited by J. Borkowski, S. Landesman Ramey, and Marie Bristol-Power. Mahwah, New Jersey: Lawrence Erlbaum Assoc., 2002: 274.
49.   *Ibid.*, 274-275.
50.   *Ibid.*, 276.
51.   Megan Gunnar, "How Young Children Manage Stress" *Office of the Vice President of Research, University of Minnesota.* (June 30, 2005; February 13, 2007): http://www.research.emn.edu/spotlight/*gunnar*.html.
52.   Swain, "Brain Basis of Early Parent Interaction." 270.
53.   Westman, "The Risks of Day Care." 21-22.
54.   Amitai Etzioni, "Children of the Universe," *Utne Reader*, 57, (May/June 1993): 60.
55.   Edward Zigler, "Effects of Infant Day Care: Another Look at the Evidence." (1988).
56.   Terrence Moore, noted in "Is Day Care Good for Kids?" *National Review.* (May 13, 1988): 30.

57.   *Ibid.*, 30.
58.   Jacquelyn deLaveaga, interview entitled "The Need for Nurturing," *The Family in America,* Rockford Institute 7:6. (June, 1993).
59.   Travis Hirschi, *Causes of Delinquency.* New Brunswick: Transaction Publishers, 2006: 131.
60.   "The Need for Nurturing," *The Family in America.* (June, 1993).
61.   James Q. Wilson, *Crime and Public Policy.* San Francisco: Institute for Contemporary Studies Press, 1983: 53-68.
62.   Hazen and Shaver, "Deeper into Attachment Theory." 77.
63.   "The Need for Nurturing," *The Family in America.* (June, 1993).
64.   D. W. Winnicott, *The Family and Individual Development.* London: Tavistok, 1965. See "Adolescence: Struggling through the Doldrums."
65.   Hirschi, *Causes of Delinquency.* 108.
66.   Amitai Etzioni, "Children of the Universe," *Utne Reader* 57. (May/June, 1993): 60.
67.   Sharon Landesman Ramey, "The Science and Art of Parenting," *Parenting and the Child's World* edited by J. Borkowski, S. Landesman Ramey, and Marie Bristol-Power. (Mahwah, New Jersey: Lawrence Erlbaum Assoc., 2002): 57.
68.   *Ibid.*, 58.
69.   Sandi Kahn Shelton, "Day Care Detective," *Working Mother.* (June, 1995): 40-47.
70.   Alice Miller, *The Drama of the Gifted Child.* New York: Basic Books, 1981: 54.
71.   Dorothy Conniff, "Day Care: A Grand and Troubling Social Experiment," *Utne Reader* 57. (May/June, 1993): 66-67.
72.   *Ibid.*, 67.
73.   *Ibid.*, 67.
74.   Westman, "The Risks of Day Care." 23.
75.   Leach, *Children First.* 144.
76.   *Day Care: Child Psychology & Adult Economics,* edited by Bryce Christensen. Rockford: Rockford Institute, 1989.
77.   T.J. Gamble and E. Ziegler, "Effects of Infant Day Care: Another Look at the Evidence," *American Journal of Orthopsychiatry* 56: 26-42.
78.   Lynne Vernon-Feagans, Elizabeth E. Manlove, and Brenda L. Volling, "Otitis Media and the Social Behavior of Day-Care-Attending Children," *Child Development* 67. (1996): 1528-1539.
79.   J. Craig Peery, "Children At Risk: The Case Against Day Care," *The Family in America,* Rockford Institute 5:2. (February, 1991): 6.
80.   *Ibid.*, 6.
81.   Diane Ehransaff, "Preschool Child Sex Abuse: The Aftermath of the Presidio Case," *American Journal of Orthopsychiatry* 62. (1992): 234-244.
82.   Cris Barrish and Stacey Tiedge, ""System Puts Kids at Risk," *Delaware News Journal,* (June 8-10): 1997.
83.   Jay Belsky, participant in "Risks of Day Care," Consultation held on December 6, 1988, summarized in *Day Care*: 42-67.
84.   Deborah Phillips and Carolee Howes, *Quality in Child Care Research.* Washington, D.C.: Research Monographs of the National Association of the Education of Young Children, 1987: 1.
85.   K.A.Clarke- Stewart and G.Fein, "Early Childhood Programs," in M. M. Haith and J. J. Campos, editors (P.H. Mussen, series editor), *Handbook of Child Pyschology: Vol.2, Infancy and Developmental Psychobiology.* New York: Wiley, 1983: 980.
86.   Peery," Children at Risk." 3.

87. Rutter, "Social-Emotional Consequences of Day Care for Preschool Children," *American Journal of Orthopsychiatry* 51. (1981): 9-11.
88. Peery, "Children at Risk." 4.
89. *Ibid.*, 4.
90. "The NICHD Study of Early Child Care and Youth Development: Findings for Children up to Age 4 ½ years" *National Institute of Child Health and Human Development.* (January, 2006): 1.
91. *Ibid.*, "The NICHD Study of Early Child Care and Youth Development." 1-47.
92. *Ibid.*, "The NICHD Study of Early Child Care and Youth Development." 1-47.
93. Ibid., "The NICHD Study of Early Child Care and Youth Development." 1-47.
94. *Ibid.*, "The NICHD Study of Early Child Care and Youth Development." 1-47.
95. Scott Richart, *Chronicles: A Magazine of American Culture.*
96. "The NICHD Study of Early Child Care and Youth Development." 1-47.
97. *Ibid.*
98. *Parents Magazine.*
99. Ramey, see *New York Times.* (March 26, 2007).
100. J. Belsky, "Quantity Counts: Amount of Child Care and Children's Socio-emotional Development," *Journal of Developmental and Behavioral Pediatrics.* (June, 2002).
101. *Ibid.*
102. UC Irvine study.
103. Richard T Gill, "Day Care or Parental Care?" *The Public Interest* 105. (Fall, 1991): 3-16.
104. Etzioni,"Children of the Universe," *Utne Reader* 54.
105. Victor R. Fuch and Mary Coleman, "Small Children, Small Pay: Why Child Care Pays So Little," *The American Prospect.* (Winter, 1991): 75-79.
106. Linda J. Waite, Arleen Leibowitz, and Christina Witsberger, "What Parents Pay For: Child Care Characteristics, Quality, and Costs," *Journal of Social Issues* 47:2. (1991): 33-48.
107. Karl Zinsmeister, "Day Care: The Problem with Day Care," *The American Enterprise.* (May/June, 1998): 13.
108. Pierre Lefebvre, Philip Merrigan, and Mattieu Verstraete, "Impact of Early Childhood Care and the Education on Children's Preschool Cognitive Development: Canadian Results from a Large Quasi-experiment," *CIRPEE.* (October, 2006).
109. "Daycare Increases Risk of Mental Disorder: Study," *The Canadian Sentinel.* (March 29, 2007; April 30, 2007): <http://thecanadiansentinel.blogspot.com/2007/03daycare-increases-risks-of-mental.html>.
110. "Preschool Better than Staying at Home," *Telegraph.* 26. (November, 2004; January 30, 2007): <http://www.literacytrust.org.uk/Research/pressearly.html>
111. Richard Gardner, "Toddlers Looked After by Mothers 'Develop Better,'" *The Independent Online Edition.* (October 3, 2005; October 3, 2005): <http://news.independent.co.uk/uk/health_medical/article316677.ece.>
112. Jay Belsky, et al., "Intergenerational Transmission of Warm-Sensitive-Stimulating Parenting: A Prospective Study of Mothers and Fathers of 3-Year-olds" *Child Development* 76:2. (March, 2005).
113. Jane Healy, Ph.D., *Endangered Minds: Why Children Don't Think and What We Can Do About It?* New York: Touchstone Books, 1990: 15-16.
114. *Ibid.*, 49.
115. *Ibid.*, 51.
116. *Ibid.*, 56.
117. *Ibid.*, 86.

118. "Cross-Language Analysis of Phonetic Units in Language Addressed to Infants,"
      Science. (August, 1997): 684-6.
119. *Ibid.*, 94.
120. *Ibid.*, 95.
121. E.C. Melhuish, et al., "Type of Childcare at 18 months-II. Relations with Cogni-
      tive and Language Development," *Journal of Child Psychology and Psychiatry*
      31. (1990): 861-869.
122. P. Roy and M.Rutter, "Institutional Care: Associations Between Inattention and
      Early Reading Performance," *Child Pyschiatry* 47:5. (May, 2006): 480-7.
123. Sharon Begley, "Your Child's Brain," *Newsweek.* (February 19, 1996): 56.
124. Healy, *Your Child's Growing Mind.* New York: Doubleday, 1994: 21.
125. Harry T.Chugani, M.D., "Neuroimaging of Developmental Non-Linearity and
      Developmental Pathlogies," in *Developmental Neuroimaging: Mapping the De-
      velopment of Brain and Behavior*, edited by Thatcher et al.
126. Healy, *Endangered Minds.* 100.

3

Moral Relativism and its Influence upon Modern Parents

Tell me not, in mournful numbers,
Life is but an empty dream!
For the soul is dead that slumbers,
And things are not what they seem.

————

Lives of great men all remind us
We can make our lives sublime,
And, departing, leave behind us
Footprints on the sand of time;

Footprints, that perhaps another,
Sailing o'er life's solemn main,
A forlorn and shipwrecked brother
Seeing, shall take heart again. . . .

—Henry Wadsworth Longfellow

Whereas, once, the goal of the good parent was to nurture and protect and to instill virtue, good manners, and diligence, today's parenting goals are nebulous and confused. Although ideas about how much discipline and how much "attention" is appropriate for children changed, constants throughout most societies and most times were the ideas that parents had both to protect their children from evil and to teach their children right from wrong. "Bringing up" a child meant bringing them closer to the good. In a time when the very idea of the good is thought by many to signify nothing more meaningful than any individual's idea of it, one idea being as valid as another, it is difficult for parents to latch onto "goodness" as a goal. In its place, are materialism, consumerism, abstract political goals that have nothing to do with how we treat each other on a day to day basis, and celebrities that show us how to be free of all moral concern.

Relativism as a philosophy has permeated the nation's soul, leaving its indelible mark on the children we raise. If there really is no high and low, better and worse, good or bad, beyond each person's definition of these things—if moral questions are not only indeterminate but also pointless, then what really matters is power as society defines it at the moment. Moreover, if there really is no such thing as virtue, it follows that nothing is corrupting; and, if nothing is corrupting, we no longer value a child's innocence. The devaluing of innocence has taken its toll on our children and our society.

Although, as a country, we relentlessly knock down the idea that one person might really have a better understanding of "the good" than another, no one denies that some people have more power. No wonder, then, that the goal of many American parents seems to be nothing higher than "achieving" in the workplace and giving their children "the edge" in everything from sports, to reading, to mathematics so that their children may be high achievers themselves. The emphasis upon achieving is an emphasis upon doing rather than being and says little about the character of the person who achieves. That it is better to *be* certain ways than certain other ways seems to be old thinking.

Usually absent is consideration of the quality of a person's soul, call it what you will. "As long as you work hard and believe in yourself, you can be whatever you want to be" is a constant refrain in schools, children's books, and children's television. The theme is a good one insofar as it attempts to restore the work ethic so badly damaged by the politics of resentment. Underprivileged children who have received the demoralizing message that society's deck is stacked against them, try as they might to "achieve," need to believe hard work can result in dreams coming true. But the challenge to work hard toward personal goals is inadequate, for it is based upon the ethos of self-fulfillment and not upon a striving toward greater virtue. Too often absent is the message from society: *Strive toward something greater than yourself;* and from parents: *I know something about being good. Let me teach you what I know.* An optimistic spirit and disciplined work habits, while important, derive their import from the character of the person possessing those qualities. One can work hard at being a thief. One can be optimistic about the lucrative potential of inside secrets of the stock market. The "work ethic," if it really is to have a positive effect upon American children, must have a higher purpose. It is not enough to tell children that they can be whatever they feel like being. Children need to believe in something other than the power of their own whims.

Four interspersed and confused philosophical trends lie beneath the bustling society in which modern parenting is rooted. The first is relativism in all its mutated forms and particularly in the form of "self-fulfillment." The second is individualism and majoritarianism as they have come to be defined in modern American society. The third is the alliance of historicism and feminism in the rewriting of history. And, finally, we cannot discount the influence of Marx and Nietzsche on parents whose formative years occurred in the sixties and seventies. (We underestimate the subtle but powerful influence their ideas continue to have.) Let us pause to examine these trends, for, to leave out a discussion of the philosophical currents of the times in a discussion of childrearing trends would be like trying to study a tree without studying the roots. A deficiency in many discussions of "children's issues" is the focus on that which can be seen: accomplishments, grades, and behavior. If we focus more upon the invisible inner foundations of the parents, we will pay more respect to the inner foundation of the child.

I would argue that underlying all of the major changes in American life is the socialist current, which we imported and ingested—without first studying the source. Thus, I will begin with the socialist influence on American life and return to it at the end of the chapter.

We trend-setting Americans were not the first to change our minds regarding the relative importance of children and material, sexual rewards. Fascinatingly, it was the Soviet Union that set the trend and laid out new modes and orders for us. One of the most interesting books I have read is one by H. Kent Geiger, Professor of Sociology at the University of Wisconsin and expert on Soviet society, called *The Family in Soviet Society*. This thorough and scholarly work is immune to the culture wars because it was written in 1968, just *before* social change swept over the U.S. In fact, in a forward explaining why such a study had not been undertaken in the U.S., Alex Inkeles declared, "Our cultural tradition emphasized the individual's right to privacy and sharply limited the rights of society to interfere in the sphere of family life. And our values of individualism and the pursuit of happiness legitimated a conception of family life as mainly a means for pursuing individual happiness rather than for fulfilling society's purpose."[1]

With Lenin and Communism, guided by the thought of Marx and Engels, came not just political change but radical changes in the Soviet family, in Soviet morals, and in Soviet childrearing. Among the beliefs swallowed whole by the revolutionaries were the ideas that the family was an instrument of bourgeoisie petty values; that the family threatened the bold, superior design of the state; that children did not need their parents and would become better "world citizens" if brought up in state-run institutions; and that the old-world ideas of parents were a threat to the new progressive order communists were trying to install. Proclaimed Alexandra M. Kollantai, one of the leading advocates of the new feminism, "the family deprives the worker of revolutionary consciousness." "She, like many of her colleagues, fulminated against the 'small, isolated, closed-in family' and awaited the time when first loyalty would be to society, while family, love, all of personal life would come second."[2] According to the revolutionaries, focus upon one's spouse, parents, or children was inappropriate. It interfered with the path to true fulfillment defined as work in and for socialist-internationalist society. Work was to take foremost form in peoples' minds; religion, family, and the small community were modes of backwardness.

So too, in the brave new world the communists were creating, sex was to be "free;" its purpose was physical pleasure. That pleasure was said to be akin to any material pleasure, such as eating and drinking, and was deprived of its connection with love. It was postulated that love itself was merely a bourgeoisie construct, a fantasy. It was firmly asserted that fidelity was a form of private property, and therefore harmful rather than desirable. Ironically, sex was declared a "private" matter of indifference to the state—so long as sex did not mingle with *commitment* to family. Commitment was a word and a way of being that was to be reserved for the new Marxist-Leninist-internationalist society; *any other commitments were counter-revolutionary*. Women were to be "liberated" from their commitment to family so that they could put proper emphasis upon material growth and productive work. Divorce was made "free" and, in fact, encouraged as a path to sexual liberation. Geiger describes the Soviet plan for a new social order in the 1920s as follows:

> To summarize, the family will eventually die out, is in fact starting to do so now, but nonetheless will be needed for the duration of the transition period, and the party and its followers should take an active role in helping things along, mainly by setting a good example. Preconditions for the new social ordering of the relations between the sexes were required. The most crucial was the entrance of woman into social production, which would give her economic independence and hence social equality. Her work in social production would then have to be balanced by society's assumption of the responsibilities of childrearing, supplying and preparing food, washing clothing, and so on. All such patterns—the entry of women into the labor market, the socialization of household chores, the assumption of public responsibility for childrearing—were originally subsidiary links in the causal chain leading to the end of the family, and to the equality and freedom for the individual, but in early Soviet writing they tended to

assume the status of end-goals in themselves, and to be justified in their own terms. Lenin himself elaborated slightly the position of Marx and Engels on social equality for women. He was as strongly opposed as they, perhaps even more so, to the individual household with its "stinking kitchen," and, like them, asserted that only socialism and an end to small households could "save woman from housewifery."[3]

Geiger goes on, "As a corollary to such information, the liberation of women in itself was seen as a condition for economic development. Thereby the family became by implication a direct obstacle to the 'development of the base.'—The rearing of children by society was hailed by all not only because it saved time and released the mother for outside work, but because it would be more scientific, more rational, more organized than rearing within the individual family."[4]

As a result, A. V. Lunacharski, Commissar of Education could write in the early 1930s: Our problem now is to do away with the household and to free women from the care of children. It would be idiotic to separate children from their parents by force. But when, in our communal houses, we have well-organized quarters for children—there is no doubt that the parents will, of their own free will, send their children to these quarters, where they will be supervised by trained pedagogical and medical personnel.—Soviet writer L. M. Sabosvich argued, however that "since the child was the property of the state, not the individual family, the state therefore had the right to compel parents to surrender their children to special 'children's towns', to be built 'at a distance from the family.'"[5]

Soviet women did indeed enter the work force en masse, although not universally as planned, and did enroll their children in state-run day care and boarding schools. Families did fall apart, and couples did see marriage as optional, if desirable at all. Of fascinating import: As early as the late 1930s, Soviet leaders themselves were rethinking these policies, for they were beginning to see the "problems" of lower birthrates, irresponsible adult behavior, and children with such poor emotional and intellectual outcomes that they could barely function in society. The newly prevalent problem of juvenile delinquency had to be faced as well. Even more severe were the problems of child abandonment and of overwrought care givers, who could not cope with the strain of fostering large numbers of troubled children.[6] Thus, as early as the 1930s, the Soviets did begin to tone down their emphasis on family disintegration to the point that they were actively encouraging women to "marry young" so as to increase the birthrate. They even declared that sex was not a private matter after all if it led to a dissolute and unproductive society. Lenin now wrote that the society could not withstand "orgiastic conditions" and the "weakening" and "waste" that went with it.[7]

By the 1940s, influential writer Anton S. Makarenko was advocating families as "small collectives" and promoting "responsible" parenting as the only method that seemed to work in creating un-troubled, un-trouble-some children! Families were now to be held liable under criminal law for the delinquent acts of their children.[8] (Delinquency had become a common, vexing problem among children who had had little parental influence.) But the Soviets would never re-embrace the family or what are in our country call "family values." They wanted the productivity which well brought up children could bring to society and the numbers of new workers that families could breed, *but they feared and despised family structure and family morals as a bane to revolutionary ideals and progress.* This unresolved conflict between Soviet priorities remained until Glasnost and still haunts Soviet society today. These conflicts are beautifully portrayed in Francine du Plessix Gray's *Soviet Women: Walking the Tightrope.*[9]

I believe that the travails of Soviet social engineering contain such important warnings for modern Americans and provide such important insights into the modern American family that, henceforth in this chapter, I will insert excerpts from Geiger's book when they seem powerfully to pertain to our own problems.

* * *

The self-fulfillment ethos predominates in our society whether that fulfillment be sought in the workplace, through artistic pursuits, or through identification with an interest group or ideological cause, which seeks power and authority through the assertion of large numbers. What is remarkable about today's self-fulfillment ethos is that it has virtually nothing to do with love. The giving and receiving of love, which traditionally has been thought to be the most fulfilling of all things for most people, has little to do with today's definition of fulfillment. When women are extolled to break away from the "shackles of home," they are told that true fulfillment lies away from the ones they love. When it becomes normal for college students to "hook up" *rather than* getting to know each other and when every piece of popular culture glorifies sexiness, the body for its own sake, and quick surrender to physical attraction, we have devalued commitment and love. For many students, from middle school to graduate school, the age-appropriate search for love, meaning, and companionship has been replaced by quick pleasure, getting ahead, and living up to media ideals of attraction and attractiveness.

American society tells children to accept themselves, but does not urge them to be better human beings with a large capacity for love. Instead, it urges them toward "accomplishments," which will impress future college admissions counselors or future employers and provides them with "escapes" which will ease the strain of that process. The calling to responsibility, kindness, moderation, and decency is diluted, when it *is* made, due to the concern that pointing out attributes in which they are deficient might damage the adolescent self-image or interfere with the tireless energy required for goal-oriented "activities." The idea is to *feel* good and to move upward, not to *be* good. Never mind that it is a struggle to achieve anything if one lacks purpose, the loving support of family, and role models for adult behavior.

Children's view of life as aimless and selfish is reinforced by parents' casual approach to marriage and commitment, by the view that extra-marital affairs are normal, by the ever-changing face of their care givers, and by the widely varying behavior patterns and beliefs of the adults who surround them. When the parents of young children pursue fleeting pleasures at the expense of family solidarity, they give their children a message about the value they place upon self-fulfillment—their own. In the summer of 2006, newsmakers cheerfully reported that affairs are now the norm, with women catching up to men in the percentages having affairs (about 40 percent of women, 60 percent of men.) When society accepts divorce as a practical solution to growing tired of one's spouse; when disloyal behavior toward wife, husband, and children are viewed as commonplace; and when disproportionate numbers of children give birth out of wedlock and view the child they have brought into the world less as a responsibility than as an extension of their egos, we have edged toward that atomization Hobbes envisioned in the *State of Nature* wherein life is nasty and brutish (if not short).

The phenomenal increase in divorce and illegitimacy rates is testimony to the new "modes and orders" Americans have embraced. We modern Americans love labels that cast people in ethnic/economic terms. But, whether they are labeled "advantaged," "disadvantaged," or somewhere in between ("middle class"), American children often have a big disadvantage in common: the lack of two parents devoted to them and each other and the lack of a stable home life that includes the steady presence and moral guidance of those they love. The census bureau estimated that only 39 percent of children born in 1988 would live with both parents until their eighteenth birthday. There was also a sharp trend away from marrying at all for the sake of children. The U.S. Department of Health and Human Services reported that white illegitimacy rates *doubled* during the1980s so that one out of five white children in the 1990s was born to an unmarried mother.[10]

Those numbers continued to increase and are indicative of social change of astronomical proportions. They represent a watershed change in how babies are conceived and reared. A study by the General Social Survey of the National Opinion Research Center at the University of Chicago demonstrates that the percentage of children who live with both biological parents who remain married dropped precipitously from 73 percent in 1972 to 51.7 percent in 1998. Twenty-eight years ago, 45 percent of households consisted of married couples with children. In 1998, the percentage had fallen to 26 percent. In 1970, 11 percent of all births were to unmarried mothers. By 2004, that percent had jumped to 34.[11] By the turn of the century, 53 percent of all *first births* occurred outside of marriage.[12] Today, at least one baby in three is born out of wedlock and at least half of marriages fail. *This means that a decisive majority of American children are either children of divorce or children whose parents never married in the first place.*

In an article entitled "Nonmarriage trend is threatening generations," columnist William Rasberry referred to statistics showing that "in 1975, nearly 77 percent of black women in their late 20s had been married at some time in their lives. By 1990, the corresponding figure was 45 percent—a drop of over 30 points in 15 years." Lamented Raspberry, "Children of never-married parents are more likely to become unwed parents themselves, continuing the disaster yet another generation."[13] Rasberry correctly foresaw that the nonmarriage trend would increasingly cross racial lines, for it reflected fundamental societal shifts. Indeed, as Andrew Peyton Thomas shows, illegitimacy is not a "black thing" but an American thing.[14]

Observes Nicholas Eberstadt, "High rates of nonmarriage, of course, can no longer be interpreted as signifying high rates of childlessness. Paralleling the breakup of two-parent families is the rise of families that never formed. Over the past four decades, our country has experienced a veritable explosion of out-of wedlock births."[15]

The word drastic accurately describes the changes in the American child's family structure. These changes have precipitously reinforced themselves. It behooves us to slow down and to step back, away from the charging thrust of "progress," in order to scrutinize our priorities and their effects.

Many factors have contributed to these stunning changes in American society which leave children with only one parent to raise them, the most important of which is this: Society decided that divorce and single parenting were OK even when the reasons were not compelling. Sometimes divorce is a necessary solution to unremitting family stress. It is good that we now show understanding toward those couples who have to get out of a bad situation; sympathy toward men and women who have been rejected, mistreated, or abandoned by their spouses; and respect for those who did what they could to make the relationship work. It is harmful to children, however, when we go so far as to make divorce a *cultural norm*. The idea of life-long fidelity runs contrary to sexual liberation, moral relativism and the self-fulfillment ethos, all of which glorify freedom from traditional restraints."Doing your own thing" ultimately includes freedom from commitment to wife, husband, parents, and children. No wonder the legal system made divorce much easier. The great majority of states have adopted no-fault divorce statutes, thereby paving a smooth road out of marriage. Whether no-fault divorce in itself is a problem is open to debate. Reformers deserve rightful credit for promoting legal redress for women in mentally or verbally abusive marriages and for making divorce a viable solution for irredeemable marriages. My focus is not on the legal apparatus of divorce, but on the way the divorce trend fits into larger trends in childrearing.

Divorce and out-of-wedlock births create the family-without-a-father syndrome, which almost everyone who has taken an open look at the research now concurs, is damaging to children. The feminist idea that gender differences are a myth perpetuated by men to keep women down (that the only true differences are physical) leads to the idea that fathers are really not needed; they provide nothing that mother cannot also provide. If men's and women's differences are the product of "social conditioning" what possible advantage can a father offer? Lest children feel the need for Dad, many forward thinking Americans disagree. They decry the idea that children need a father so that they can support the unwed woman who "chooses" to build a family through artificial insemination or deliberate pregnancy out of wedlock and so that they can legitimate and justify the wayward father. The thoroughly documented evidence that children do need a father and that divorce is hard on children has not deterred them. Indeed, feminism has evolved to *promote* the woman who *consciously* chooses to start a family without a man in the picture (except insofar as he is needed for conception). That woman then finds someone to look after her children while she is at work.

> As increasing numbers of fathers were absent and mothers employed, upbringing became problematic—In an official apologia published in 1936 it was argued that the idea of state rearing of children now identified as "Kollantai's theory," was harmful because it "unwittingly" vindicated parents who did not wish to trouble with their children.[16] (Geiger)

The unraveling of old concepts of loyalty and maturity allows parent-hood to be undertaken without the criterion which used to accompany it—that it was time to "settle down." The idea that it is not necessarily the parents' responsibility to be with and bring up the child provides a disincentive for the two-parent family. If children are perfectly fine in day care centers, why encourage two parents so that one parent has the option to stay home with the child? Why do we need fathers at all? "One suspects, however, that the Soviet husbandly masses were as a rule little inclined to take over duties that in other Bolshevik speeches were described as trivial and properly social rather than familial functions."[17]

The ridicule sustained by Dan Quayle for criticizing Murphy Brown's prime-time decision to give birth out of wedlock was, of course, an example of such a subtext at work. Murphy Brown had declared, "One parent is not uncommon. . . . There's no one right way to raise a child." She responded to Quayle's criticism on the 1992 premier, saying, "Perhaps it's time for the Vice President to expand his definition and recognize that, either by choice or circumstance, families come in all shapes and sizes." Observed the Media Research Center:

> A very disturbing trend is the small screen's insistence that single-parent homes are as healthy as nuclear families. . . . Murphy's lower-profile predecessor was the daughter of a Golden Girls character who conceived artificially. Murphy paved the way for a financially untroubled main character on Empty Nest who decided to raise here illegitimate child herself last fall. This season, on Roseanne, a main character became pregnant during a one-night stand and claimed over the course of several episodes that her baby would be just fine without a father's financial and emotional help. Not until the father threatened to sue for custody did she finally accept his offer to be a part of the baby's life.[18]

The firestorm reaction to Quayle's criticism of the promotion of such a concept showed that the concept of the traditional family was, indeed, nearly ruined as far as American popular culture was concerned. Since then, there have been some signs of an attempt to resurrect the goal of cohesive and close families responsible for each other as well as themselves. (The data on the emotional and societal consequences of divorce is too pervasive and conclusive to deny.) A few brave souls in the media have been willing to give those attempting this resurrection a voice.

> A writer presented this vignette of the situation: As has been rightfully indicated already in the press, there exists among our youth a licentiousness, an irresponsible, attitude to woman and the consequences of marriage. He marries several times and produces babies, but who is going to rear them and what will happen to them—about that who cares, for we are "growing into the future," for we are communists, and in the communist society there is no family.[19] (Geiger)

Research confirms what common sense and our hearts should have told us all along. Children of divorce or of single parents usually suffer, many never fully recovering from the trauma of their parents' separation, or from the void caused by their own permanent separation from one of their parents. Children do, after all, need a father, and children do derive different but essential benefits from mothers and fathers. A year after the Murphy Brown debate, *Atlantic Monthly* came out with an article by Barbara Defoe Whitehead entitled "Dan Quayle was Right."[20] The author demonstrated that two-parent biological families bestow upon children the best economic, emotional, and spiritual benefits. A May 1988 issue of *Demography* showed that the presence of fathers in the home is vital to adolescent emotional well being, educational attainment, and subsequent economic success.[21] A University of Maryland School of Medicine study found that American children in poor inner city families who had fathers around them had greater feelings of competence and were less likely to be depressed.[22] Rutgers University research found that boys from broken homes were significantly more like to exhibit "depression, uncommunicative behavior, hyperactivity, aggression and delinquent behavior."[23] Judith Wallerstein's twenty-five-year study, documented in *The Unexpected Consequences of Divorce*[24] and Elizabeth Marquardt's survey of hundreds of adults who grew up in divorced families, documented in *Between Two Worlds,*[25] both found that children of divorce have an emotional disadvantage to their peers—and that that disadvantage persists in adulthood. Of course, there are exceptions to this rule, but the findings are compelling and consistent enough to require taking them seriously.

Now, even the mainstream press is weighing the risks of bringing up children without a father. Defoe Whitehead's book *The Divorce Culture* received a mostly positive review in the *New York Times*. Intoned columnist Mona Charin, "The crisis of father absence—a joke to the chattering class just three years ago when Vice President Dan Quayle first mentioned it—has been transformed into conventional wisdom so fast is almost makes your head spin." Charin gave as an example researcher Sarah McLanahan, featured on "Frontline." McLanahan set out several years ago to prove that children raised by single parents were just as well off as those raised by two parents. The data "stopped her cold." "Instead, she found that children raised by only one parent were twice as likely to drop out of high school, get pregnant before marriage, have drinking problems and experience a host of other difficulties (including getting divorced themselves) than were children raised by two married parents."[26]

In another article, columnist William Rasberry lamented:

Father absence is the bane of the black community, pre-disposing its children (boys especially, but increasingly girls as well) to school failure, criminal behavior and economic hardship—and to intergenerational repetition of the grim cycle. —Fatherless boys as a general rule become ineligible as husbands—though no less likely to become fathers—and their children fall into the pattern that render them ineligible as husbands. The absence of fathers means, as well, that girls lack both the pattern against which to measure the boys who pursue them and an example of sacrificial love between a man and a woman.[27]

Rasberry is on to something. In a joint study, researchers from Duke, Indiana, and Auburn universities and in New Zealand found that "the absence of fathers in early life appears to be a more significant risk factor for girls' early sexual activity and adolescent pregnancy than previously believed." Remarked Duke researcher Kenneth A. Dodge, "We knew that a number of studies had identified the link between absent fathers and risk for daughters' early sexual activity, but the risk had been ascribed to more generalized family problems, such as poverty and stress. Our research shows clearly that father absence itself during the first five years of life is a unique risk factor."[28]

As more evidence of American society's new willingness to assess its children-without-fathers syndrome, John Stossel documented the unique, complementary attributes that fathers and mothers bring to a child's life: We have evidence that fathers behave differently than mothers; mothers tending to be more solicitous and comforting, fathers tending to be more playful and action oriented. (One might question why we need evidence of this—simply *having* a father should have told us as much.) Fathers are more likely to encourage their children to take risks, while mothers are more likely to teach their children common-sense precautions. Mothers are more likely to educate their children, while fathers are more likely to "have fun" with them. Children, it turns out, need both approaches. Explained David Blankenhorn of the National Fatherhood Initiative:

The best mother in the world cannot be a father. Children with the best mothers in the world want and need their fathers. A boy needs to figure out what it means to be a man. Boys who don't get that from their father tend to develop what the researchers call protest masculinity or hyper masculinity. They're the kids who are much more likely to say I'm going to hurt you if you look at me the wrong way. I've got that swagger and that kind of extreme masculine behavior. . . . Father is like the gatekeeper for the son into the world of feeling like he's a good man. [29]

As infidelity, childbirth out of wedlock, and divorce have become more acceptable, so, of course, have the economic difficulties associated with single parenting. A study by researchers at Vanderbilt, Georgia State, and the University of Delaware shows that it is not just teen motherhood that contributes to poverty; it is *unwed* motherhood. In numerous statistical studies, the researchers established that unwed mothers *age twenty and over* are "faring poorly." In fact, roughly two in five are "poor." After giving birth, nearly 60 percent of these women rely on food stamps or Aid to Families with Dependent Children (AFDC). Possible reasons for this alarming trend, the researchers speculate, are "changing societal values" and "dreary economic prospects for potential husbands."[30] Patrick Fagan confirms the connection between "single parenting" and poverty. He points to a Census Bureau report showing that more than half of all children in female-headed families live in poverty. He observes that *married* black America is doing very well, now close to the poverty rate for white families, while blacks from broken families are increasingly impoverished. Fagan reminds us that it is not that "Black America" is in poverty but that single-parent America is in poverty.[31]

Again, we are reminded that the sad epidemic of undernurtured children cuts across ethnic lines and that it is unfair to attribute it to race. Children are children, and we must confess that they are all vulnerable. They all have fundamental needs that no one other than their parents are in an ideal position to fulfill.

In an article in *Pediatrics*, Arthur B. Elsters demonstrates that lack of married parents is also a much bigger factor than race or poverty in the crime rate. A major 1988 study of 11,000 individuals found that "the percentage of single-parent households with children between the ages of 12 and 20 is associated significantly with rates of violent crime and burglary." The study upends the widespread assumption that race and crime are related.[32] Illegitimacy, the absence of marriage, and the absence of close families are the key factors. Compiling a large body of research from diverse sources to support his claim, Patrick Fagan states: "The evidence is overwhelming: teenage criminal behavior has its roots in habitual deprivation of parental love and affection going back to early infancy. Future delinquents invariably have a chaotic, disintegrating family life. This frequently leads to aggression and hostility toward others outside the family. —By way of contrast, normal children enjoy a sense of personal security derived from their natural attachment to their mother. The future criminal is often denied that natural attachment." In addition, "most delinquents are children who have been abandoned by their fathers."[33] Here is just some of the evidence Fagan compiles on fatherless sons:

A father's attention to his son has enormous positive effects on a boy's emotional and social development. But a boy abandoned by his father is deprived of a deep sense of personal security. According to Rolf Loeber, Professor Psychiatry, Psychology and Epidemiology at the Western psychiatric Institute in the University of Pittsburg Schools of Medicine, "A close and intense relationship between a boy and his father prevents hostility and inappropriate aggressiveness." This inappropriate aggressiveness is an early indication of potential delinquency later on, particularly in boys. Furthermore, such bad behavior is a barrier to the child's finding a place among his more normal peers, and aggressiveness usually is the precursor of a hostile and violent 'street' attitude. Elijah Anderson, Professor of Sociology at the University of Pennsylvania, observes that these young men, very sensitive in their demands for 'respect,' display a demeanor which communicates "deterrent aggression" not un-like the behavior that causes normal peers to reject and isolate aggressive boys in grade school. The message of this body language, of course, triggers rejection by the normal adult community. The dominant role of fathers in preventing delinquency is well-established. Over forty years ago, this phenomenon was highlighted in the classic studies of the causes of delinquency by Sheldon and Eleanor Glueck of Harvard University. They described in academic terms what many children hear their mothers often say: "Wait till your father gets home!" In a well-functioning family, the very presence of father embodies authority, an authority conveyed through his daily involvement in family life. This paternal authority is critical to the prevention of psychopathology and delinquency.[34]

The above-cited article in *Demography* confirms that fathers in the home help keep children away from delinquent behavior.

Crime is often directly related to the absence of father and, more broadly, to the absence of love, nurture, guidance, and stability in a person's life.

Furthermore, in spite of all their efforts many Soviet women have been unable to provide proper supervision and guidance for their children. The substantial amount of juvenile crime in postwar Russia can be traced partly to this. Soviet research investigations invariably point to fatherless and functionally motherless families as a social problem.[35] (Geiger)

Nor is crime simply a law enforcement problem. Although clear and inevitable punishments provide disincentives to crime, we must take a look at what inspires a person toward crime in the first place. In a review of John DiIulio Jr.'s book on black crime, Charen puts it succinctly:

Criminals, especially the pathological variety our family-less culture has been producing in the last generation or so, cannot be rehabilitated, reformed or saved, DiIulio believes. They are the bitter fruit of loveless, abusive unions of unsocialized people. Having received nothing, they are without human compassion. They kill and rape without mercy or remorse. They can only be incapacitated by prison. . . . The plain fact is that of the most vicious criminals we produce, nearly all come from the same kind of environments: no father, an incompetent, abusive and frequently drug-addicted mother, and a chaotic, violent neighborhood. [36]

There is another interesting and significant byproduct of "single parenting:" The economic pressures of single parenting have been largely responsible for the increase in mothers working out of "economic necessity." Forty-five percent of all working women are without husbands, and at least two-thirds of all single mothers work. Women with husbands, however, are almost as likely to work when their husbands earn at least $35,000 as when they earn less than $25,000 a year.[37] Thus, while divorce and single parenting contribute to the numbers of mothers working because of "economic necessity," those who are not single parents are likely to work for other reasons. When white *married* women seek employment today their decision usually reflects a preference for a higher standard of living. As Jack Westman puts it, "The perception of having to work, therefore, varies considerably and often depends less on straightforward economic pressures than on personal and societal definitions of success, self-fulfillment, family obligations and material desires."[38] A 1993 Gallop Poll indicated that two-thirds of working mothers declared that only economic necessity prevented them from staying home with their children. Other studies, such as one by the *New York Times,* show the percentage working out of economic necessity to be much lower. What is certain is that changes in marriage patterns and changes in tastes have *both* contributed greatly to the increased number of mothers of very young children in the workforce.

What is also certain is that our definition of what is "necessary" has changed. No longer are the early childhood years viewed as a time for cutting back, sacrificing, and saving by the parents. Current generations of parents are much more prone to wanting to have it all, and right now. Families tend to consider at least one car, at least one TV, a computer, a washer, a dryer, and a dishwasher as "necessary"—as part of the bottom line for suitable living. Moreover, families are less likely to view the birth of their child as cause for scaling back on previous amenities. Penn State researchers observed that, in the workforce of the 1950's, "providing basic necessities for the family appeared to be the predominant economic motive: by 1980 standard-of-living preferences dominated the economic motive." In the 1950s, they show, it was considered normal and acceptable even for highly educated families to live in a sparsely furnished apartment with few appliances during their children's early years.[39] They were, after all, "just getting started." There were certain things that a family *worked toward* and did not need from the beginning. Unless they had received an early inheritance, young couples with children were expected to lack the luxuries and conveniences of older couples with higher salaries. Excited by the fast rush of our own expectations, accustomed to a technology that creates and satisfies those expectations at an ever accelerated pace, we modern Americans live in an instant society.

The desire for convenient, easy technological solutions to our physical needs runs parallel to the wish that our own and our children's emotional needs can be taken care of with similar efficiency. Unburdensome relationships with husbands and wives, sons and daughters, mothers and fathers—"free sex" and a "guilt-free" life—have been promoted by many academicians, social reformers, and media personalities. Most of us Americans are tempted, in one way or another, to find an easy way out of commitment and a fast solution to emotional pain. Quick-fix drugs which mask the symptoms of our damaged relationships are now the norm. A study in the Journal of the American Medical Association finds that the rate at which *preschoolers* were given stimulants like Ritalin and anti-depressants like Prozac had doubled, perhaps even tripled, between 1991 and 1995. (Doctor Joseph Coyle, Chairman of Psychiatry at Harvard Medical School, warns that even the diagnosis of ADD/ADHD in very young children is considered unreliable, and that negative effects of the drugs on the growing brain have not been ruled out.[40]) What is clear is that larger and larger numbers of children, young and adolescent, are being perceived as *needing* these drugs by parents and teachers. Teachers who have been around for a long time continue to report upon young children who have no capacity for listening, who have no respect for each other or for adults, and upon boys who exhibit behavior which is much more symptomatic than the boyish restlessness that boys used to exhibit.

These dual trends—the ever-accelerated dispensing of mood and behavior altering prescription drugs to children, and the ever-increasing numbers of children perceived to be *in need* of these drugs simply must give us pause. We must sympathize with and respect those families whose children have learning and behavior difficulties in spite of their stellar upbringing. We must also acknowledge the evidence that attention problems often have a genetic component. Given the drastic increase in reported learning and behavioral "difficulties," however, it would be frivolous to discount the possibility that the environment is interacting with genetic predisposition to increase the attention and behavior problems that teachers and parents find.

Socially engineered solutions do not solve the problem of children brought up in fragmented and inattentive families but are often part of the problem. For, they form an alternative to the individual responsibility for children and the mutual commitment of couples toward which parenthood and marriage used to be intended. *Underlying the casualness with which we bear children and with which we disband the child's family unit is the idea that much of the job of bringing up the child really is not the family's anyway.* It is easier to be casual about sex and irresponsible about birth control if society not only helps raise our children, but also helps pay for them. Society skips over the social-emotional needs of the child and instead emphasizes the need for the divorced or single mother to "get back on her feet." Work-fare programs and government-sponsored education programs which provide day care for babies while their mothers study for careers make it clear that social agencies will bear some of the responsibility for childrearing. There is a thoroughly documented circular relationship between the family without a father syndrome and dependency upon the state. The state sponsorship of day care and the idea that sex is "free," i.e., without obligation, lures fathers and mothers away from their children, and parents away from their dependence upon each other.

Once again, however, things are not as easy as they might seem. Women are often the ones left "picking up the pieces," "trying to make ends meet," struggling to balance motherhood and work, or straining to cope with the bureaucratic maze of federal assistance.

> In fact, the parallel between the individual freedom and sexual exploitation of the female of these times and the individual freedom and economic exploitation of the proletarian worker described in classical Marxism is quite striking. Both freedoms were purely formal. —It was mainly men who wanted sexual variety, or at least sexual gratification, whereas the women tended much more to be interested in love. Thus, the double standard continued to prevail, and writers began to stress that "the girl is the person who suffers."[41] (Geiger)

Government dependency, in turn, is a very difficult problem to tackle from an ethical standpoint. I certainly do not have the answer. I do know that of foremost concern must be the people themselves and that we must exert emotional and intellectual energy toward *really helping* the most vulnerable—the children. We must beware policies that claim to do good while actually doing harm to the vulnerable in our society. It is an indelicate balance. As decent human beings, we must care about unwed mothers and their children. As a society, we must work hard to alleviate poverty and the plight of the poor. On the other hand, there is no question that welfare can create a dependency at once demeaning and enervating to those who receive it. Making matters more complicated, when *reform* of welfare rests upon providing mothers with the education and childcare they need to get a job, it instills another kind of dependency—dependency upon the state to rear children. We cannot solve the problem of babies irresponsibly brought into the world and neither well-enough brought up nor well-enough loved by welfare reform alone. For, welfare reform addresses the mother's self-esteem and pocketbook, but does not address the moral obligation of each and every parent toward their children. Recognizing that the more irresponsible parents there are, the more suffering children there are—the more children who will not themselves have the skills or the confidence to move out of poverty, or the emotional strength to rear their own children well—we must care about the concepts of responsibility and love.

Those who buy into welfare reform as a *sufficient* solution to broken, troubled families buy into a sterile, state-run vision of parenting. This solution values the parent's financial obligation to their children but not the time they spend with their children. If we emphasize the financial relationship without also emphasizing the emotional relationship, we make the same mistake as when we emphasize "achievement" while ignoring the character of those who achieve. Moreover, we provide fathers with the excuse to abandon the women they impregnate, so long as they contribute to the child financially. When the American press focuses on do-nothing fathers, it invariably refers to fathers who neglect child-support *payments*. We should abandon the term child support insofar as it refers to money, perhaps calling it instead "child payment." Children need so much more "support" than money can buy.

The disappointing truth is that, if subsidized day care takes the mother away from the child, welfare and welfare-reform programs too often encourage out-of-wedlock births in the first place. Despite media claims to the contrary, the overwhelming majority of scholarly studies in the last fifteen years show that state sponsorship encourages illegitimacy and discourages marriage. Among these studies are the following: In a recent study, Texas A&M University and Arizona State University sociologists Mark A. Fossett and K. Jill Kiecolt found that high levels of public assistance were associated with "lower prevalence of marriage for black men and black women, lower prevalence of husband-wife families, lower percentages of marital births for black women and lower percentages of black children living in husband-wife families." They found that "public assistance provides a degree of economic independence for women and reduces pressures to rely on marriage for financial support."[42]

Well-meaning social programs can discourage the intensity of familial bonds by providing an alternative to familial relationships. Research by former Director of the Congressional Budget Office Dr. June O'Neill found, holding constant a wide range of other variables such as income, parental education, and urban and neighborhood setting, that a 50 percent increase in the monthly value of AFDC and food stamp benefits led to a 43 percent increase in the number of out-of-wedlock births.[43] Research by Dr. C. R. Winegarden of the University of Toledo found that half of the increases in black illegitimacy could be attributed to the effects of welfare.[44] Recent research presented at a meeting at the National Academy of Sciences by Mark Rosenzweig of the University of Pennsylvania showed a reduction of AFDC payment of $130 a month could lead to a 40 percent drop in out-of-wedlock births among low-income women under age twenty-two.[45] State funding is, then, a clearly documented incentive for illegitimacy.

As Washington Post Reporter Leon Dash has demonstrated in *When Children Want Children*, most unwed teen mothers conceive their babies knowingly rather than accidentally.[46] They are aware of the role the state will play in supporting them and their child. If the state sponsors day care, it cannot be bad. If the state sponsors illegitimacy, it cannot be bad. Thus is the fear of being deemed irresponsible removed; thus is the seriousness of the childrearing endeavor removed. Thus are children brought into this world with too little thought and too little love. *If we really have the interests of children in mind, we must not suspend thought for the sake of appearances. We must ask if legislation which seems child-friendly really is so.*

I am reminded of a social worker friend's experience in Chicago. She worked at a center for unwed teens that cared for the babies and subsidized the mothers as they completed high school or underwent vocational training. Many of the babies, she told me, would cry and resist when their mothers came to get them—so abusive and negligent were the mothers or so unattached were they to them. It was not, she said, that the care they were receiving at the center was so good; indeed, by any informed standard it was barely adequate. It was that their home environment was so bad. When these mothers were interviewed about why they had not used contraceptives, their answers included the fact that they knew "someone" would support them and their baby. Their answers revealed the absence of any feeling that their child was primarily *their* responsibility. In other words, these young women might have been less likely to give birth as teens had they not been so sure that the child could be passed on to the state. Thus, the sad and circular reality that when the state assumes the burden of raising its citizens' children, it also encourages the irresponsible and unimpassioned giving of birth. This, in turn, results in children who are neglected or mistreated. Children neglected or mistreated by their parents, in turn, serve as "evidence" that the state-run rearing of children is a "good," i.e., a beneficial thing.

There are no easy solutions to the rearing of children's children, but my friend's experience points to the incomplete nature of the reports we have heard on the subject. The "success" of such programs in "getting unwed mothers off of welfare" conceals the child's need for the mother herself. These solutions *are* helpful economically, and the economic side of family life *is* important. Some studies have shown that unwed mothers in poverty are more susceptible to depression and more likely to mistreat their children than unwed mothers in less desperate conditions. Not for this reason alone, it is a reasonable and a good thing to seek ways to help women and children out of poverty. But that cannot be the whole *solution* to family crisis because that is not the whole *cause* of family crisis. So far, the "solution," as Mona Charen points out, has been a spate of reports and initiatives full of politically sensitive wording like "low-income non-custodial fathers, partners and co-parenting" but *absent* the language of "husband wife, commitment and abandonment:"

> No doubt they would find such talk overly judgmental. But the alternative they seem to be offering (and I would love to be proved wrong about this)—more social workers, more jobs programs for "non-custodial fathers," more "establishment of paternity at birth" and so on—is like treating a cut to the jugular with Band-Aids. . . . The aim of strengthening fatherhood is laudatory. But unless all of those now getting interested in the problem recognize that fatherhood cannot be fortified without simultaneously fortifying the traditional family, they will be spinning their wheels.[47]

I should note that I do not agree with those that advocate a return to the stigmatizing of unwed parents and their children as an alternative solution. I do believe in a return to the *valuing* of fathers' essential role in the family, of the intact family, of responsible parenting, and of firmly founded mother-child attachment. We can appreciate strong families without stereotyping single mothers or condemning all divorces. Families, schools, churches, synagogues, and mosques can play a central role in emphasizing the *positive* role parents play in children's lives. It would be a positive step if schools stopped interfering with that effort. For example, when the National Education Association dictates that schools teach sex education in the context of choices, life-style options, and methods for safe sex but *absent* the language of responsibility, commitment, and love, that only provides yet another disincentive for our growing children and teenagers to take the matter seriously. Our educational decisions need to take into account the larger social context and the actual result of messages that, although perhaps well meaning, have not worked out well. Hindsight, foresight, and a willingness to examine the consequences of our recent policies and to learn from communist mistakes are essential:

First, national statistics of interest to marriage and family life are now being published. —(For another example, in a 1960 article on "Unusual Children," reporter Kotovshchikova divulged facts of explosive potential for Soviet family policy. A sociologist finds that they "have the significance of the most convincing social experiment." —The author refrains carefully from overgeneralizing or overstating her case, but the message is indeed clear: some factor in institutional homes for infants and young children resulted in retardation of development. Regarding speech retardation, for instance, "in the infants' homes there are extremely few conversations with grown-ups, and for the most part they do not have an individual make-up, but a group one (in which the attention of the listener is always more spread out than individual interaction.")[48]——"An authoritative example of current doubts is given by the Director of the Laboratory of Higher Nervous Activity in the Child, Pavlov Institute of Physiology, USSR Academy of Sciences: 'The question of the rearing of children in infants' homes and crèches has tremendous significance to the state. It is a matter of the formation of a generation which is full-valued in the neuro-psychological sense. By the way, it has been shown by numerous observations that the retardation of the development of children in infants' homes and partly in crèches (especially in the 24-hour a day groups) is compensated for in later years with difficulty and incompletely.'"[49]

The more we try to define family issues as government issues the more we try to fit a square peg into a round hole. No matter what the programs, the underlying issue is the kind of behavior society encourages and the kind of upbringing children receive. When children are told one hundred times to "believe in themselves" for every one time they are reminded of the importance of being a kind and loyal husband or wife, father or mother, daughter or son, this has an inevitable effect. Moreover, they cannot believe in themselves if they lack the steady love and guidance of their parents. Ultimately, children's issues are much more than public policy issues. We as a society and as parents need to decide what our moral priorities are. Barbara Defoe Whitehead puts it bluntly:

The family has weakened because, quite simply, many Americans have changed their minds. They changed their minds about staying together for the sake of the children; about the necessity of putting children's needs before their own; about marriage as a lifelong commitment; and about what it means to be unmarried and pregnant. And many Americans changed their minds about the obligations of a father and husband.[50]

We must ask: How good are the intentions of those whose prescriptions for a better society ignore the need of each and every child for parents who love them and who take seriously the task of rearing them? How good are their prescriptions if they give no thought to sheltering children from the threatening storm of "popular culture" with all its negative implications for children?

As Americans have become less dependable, they have come to depend upon each other less. Many Americans look to the workplace for the loyal and devoted treatment they used to expect at home. Ironically, the glamorization of the work place has turned labor into a source of resentment. When expectations of work are so high as to supersede expectations of family, children, and friends, a job is no longer just a job but a place where one seeks perfect circumstances, perfect feelings, and spiritual rewards. As work displaces family as a source of "fulfillment," work is also expected to provide the "good feelings" and the comfortable environment that family and home used to provide. No wonder, then, that the eighties and nineties have witnessed a spate of lawsuits of employees against employers. Employers are expected not only to provide us with a paycheck but also to make us happy! We have imbibed in the image of the workplace as inherently rewarding and in the image of childrearing as inherently demoralizing.

As virtuous behavior of individuals within families has become less important and self-fulfillment and personal success have become more important, American society has moved toward a moral precipice wherein doing what one wills to do is more important than doing what is right. A popularized and distorted version of Nietzsche will to power is alive and well in America. However, it is proving to be a spur not to the passionate creativity that Nietzsche envisioned, but to relentless mediocrity wherein everyone is expected to think and act as the majority thinks and acts. Although each person is expected to determine their own destiny, the respect for meaning beyond the individual which inspires people to go beyond impulse and toward greater aspirations is too often missing. The herd mentality which Nietzsche so dreaded has infected much of the nation. There is a powerful connection between the American version of relativism and the conformism and dearth of meaning that pervade American life.

Let no one doubt the influence of American relativism upon American parents. The very idea that one way of parenting is better than another is met with indignation. Methods of parenting are not decisions with consequences; they are life-style choices. Whether one leaves a baby all day in child care or not; whether one marries for the sake of children or not; whether one is faithful to one's spouse and devoted to one's children or not; whether one protects and respects a child's innocence or not—is not, it has been said, indicative of a good or less good way of bringing up a child. The indignation with which one is still met when suggesting that, perhaps, children are better off if the parents are married, stay together, spend as much time as possible with the young, and place firm limits on children's exposure to media influence is of the irrational kind that does not allow for discussion. Such suggestions are dismissed as sexist and irrelevant to the modern world. Trepidations about the effect upon children of the modern choices of modern parents are relegated to oblivion before they are given a hearing. Those harboring such concerns are dismissed for their inability to appreciate that the traditional family is obsolete and that innocence should be as well; after all, "it's just sex." In its place is an openness to every form of relationship between children and their parents, which is closed only to the idea that some family structures and decisions are better, or at least work out better, than others. Anyone suggesting that all children have certain fundamental needs is condemned for their insensitivity to parents. Insensitivity is the closest thing we modern Americans have to sin.

Underneath our openness is a closedness to the clear and simple reality of which child psychologists, psychiatrists, educators, and neuro-biological researchers are starting to confess: that children are more likely to thrive when they part of an intact family and the recipients of steady parental love and prevalent maternal care and, that for children who lack these things, life is a struggle—a struggle which leaves its blueprint on their character, their emotional and intellectual makeup, and their future. Denying this is to be closed to the truth. Still, the use of labels instead of reasons stings those who admit to this reality and causes most to keep quiet.

Nevertheless, questions must be raised because, if anything is apparent, it is that we are witnessing a crisis of character and community which has its roots in children who are neither well-enough brought up nor well-enough loved. Although we have abandoned the past for the sake of the current, the current will not help us to find a way out of this morass—a morass now engulfing and alarming teachers who have had the opportunity to compare today's child with the child of twenty years ago.

What happens when self-assertion is emphasized to such an extent that the end of our assertions is thought about relatively little? I believe that then freedom comes to mean nothing higher than doing what one prefers. While the end, for example, might be "liberation"—that liberation, upon examination, means nothing higher than "doing anything." It has to do with what one *does*, not with what one *is* as a human being. We are liberated from something (i.e., male domination) but not for something. The goal of what Plato called "the good" is severed from the goal of freedom. Leo Strauss foresaw the consequences of the modern understanding of "choice:"

According to our social science, we can be or become wise in all matters of secondary importance, but we have to be resigned to utter ignorance in the most important respect: we cannot have any knowledge regarding the ultimate principles of our choices, i.e. regarding their soundness or unsoundness; our ultimate principles have no other support than our arbitrary and hence blind preferences. We are then in the position of beings who are sane and sober when engaged in trivial business and who gamble like madmen when confronted with serious issues—retail sanity and wholesale madness. . . . Once we realize that the principles of our actions have no other support than our blind choice, we really do not believe in them any more. We cannot wholeheartedly act upon them any more. We cannot live any more as responsible beings. [51]

One woman I know placed her children in full-time day care at three weeks of age. She described this decision to return to work "earlier than she had to" as a "choice" no more significant than deciding whether to have beef or chicken for dinner. She remarked that the important thing was "having the choice," explaining that *which* choice women made "doesn't matter." She will, she says, accept all women's childrearing choices as "equally valid." The "equal validity" concept *is* appealing. It conjures up a vision of women in solidarity making free choices and enjoying each other's freedom. It cheats us, however, of our intellectual integrity. *Why think laboriously and independently about a choice that does not mean anything?* "Having the choice" *is* vital to a woman's rightful equality and freedom. But the connection between freedom and equality and information and ideas must not be forgotten. Civil rights leaders of the 60s, for example, understood that voting rights had to be supplemented by a quality education.

Freedom is toward self-fulfillment, but self-fulfillment turns out to be elusive. The catch-22 is that if one does not believe in the goodness of one's choices, or if they are merely selfish, they are less "fulfilling." The doing is less rewarding if it seeks ends which have no intrinsic worth. Every act cancels out every other act in that each act is merely a preparation for the next act, which is itself ill defined. This helps to explain the devaluing of mothering. "Mothering" is a kind of activity in which, if one allows oneself to be "liberated" from society's definition of fulfillment, one can find joy in the moment. The simple moment is full of meaning precisely because it is not a means toward achievement but rather contains its own meaning. The meaning of a child's hand in a mother's, of a parent and child perusing a book, wandering together through a garden, or simply window-shopping on a city street does not require explanation. All who have experienced it know it to be there. As Max Horkheimer foresaw, however, the emphasis upon productiveness and the doctrine that insists upon seeing truth as relative to each person's needs and choices threatens to ruin the meaningfulness of such quiet moments:

Less and less is anything done for its own sake. A hike that takes a man out of the city to the banks of a river or a mountain top would be irrational and idiotic, judged by utilitarian standards; he is devoting himself to a silly, or destructive pastime. In the view of formalized reason, an activity is reasonable only if it serves another purpose, e. g. health or relaxation which helps to replenish his working power. . . . Productive work, manual or intellectual, has become respectable, indeed the only accepted way of spending one's life, and any occupation, the pursuit of any end that eventually yields an income, is called productive.[52]

Children today are expected to be as "productive" as their parents. But to emphasize productivity without also emphasizing or even believing in virtue is to lead children and society down a path of mindless busyness. Perhaps mindless is the wrong word. For, today's children are expected to generate endless mental and physical energy toward an endless series of tasks whose end is the child's intellectual, athletic, dramatic, and musical advancement. Rather than being mindless, the busyness is foundationless. It is based on a forward reaching surge, not on an underlying purpose. The surrender to media images and the extreme focus on our children's image spring from the same relativist well—that does not believe in meaning beneath the surface in the first place.

I do believe the political and social movements of the sixties had something to do with a belief that the mechanization of society had gone too far—that there was a sameness which underlay our diversity and that that sameness stemmed in part from, as Horkheimer put it, an "image of reality as structured by man's intellectual and physical tools of domination."[53] But the vague theories we latched onto as alternatives to a mechanized society in the end exacerbated that mechanization. For, the leftist, Freudian, and relativist philosophies in vogue in universities at the time and, which seemed to provide alternatives, had in common a diminution of concepts of virtue. Virtue was seen as a lie perpetuated by those in power to get those not in power to go along with their way of doing things. *Virtue was abandoned with abandon—rejected as a giving-in to the powers that be.* The problem is that without goodness as a goal, life rapidly loses meaning. If "anything goes," meaning tends to go with it. If we deny that there is a moral reality and deny that there are any lessons in history, if we instead use history to invent "norms," we cannot reasonably claim insight into how things are or should be. We can only claim knowledge of our current preferences. The media society in which we found ourselves residing encouraged and stimulated those preferences—placing satisfaction and sensation over substance.

Thus, we come around full circle. For, a society which becomes a bundle of individual preferences or a manifestation of physiological "impulses" is impersonal and atomized. At the same time, it is more prone to "group think." For, people who believe it their right simply to prefer things rather than to inquire about them are prone to that mechanized sameness which the rebellion of the sixties and seventies supposedly sought to avoid. As we have come to value spontaneity more and more, we have become less and less capable of individualism: the emphasis upon impulse and action which, on the surface of it, looks so individualistic defeats the introspection required of the true individual. *Random individuality and conformity tend to go hand in hand because they are both unthoughtful approaches to life. It should be noted that one need not be self-effacing in order to reject selfishness as a guiding creed. Indeed, self-respect and non-conformism are required of the person who insists upon listening to her conscience.*

Existentialist, behaviorist, and Freudian explanations of human inclinations, all popularized in the 1950s and 1960s, contributed even more to the philosophy of randomness than the pragmatic, evolutionist, and empiricist movements which preceded them. Sartre, the European existentialist, declared that "hope lies only in action, and that the only thing that allows man to live is action." Man "commits himself to his life, and thereby draws his image, beyond which there is nothing." The idea that "appearance becomes essence" was highly appealing to students ready to refashion the world in a less capitalistic image. Indeed, Sartre argued that existentialism was essential for confronting the problems created by the Cold War and the United States' response to Communism. Sartre did, then, believe in a kind of "free will." But he rejected its connection to immutable laws of nature and man's innate rationality.[54]

B. F. Skinner, the American behaviorist, dismissed human nature as of little consequence—as "what a person . . . would have been like if we had seen him before his behavior was subjected to the action of the human environment." The inescapable and continual impact of the environment upon the human being meant that ideas of a natural impulse toward the good were vain and that "responsibility" was impossible.[55] Mechanistic explanations of human behavior allowed for the development of a powerful alliance between modern psychology and modern science. While William James and John Dewey paved the way for this synthesis, their philosophies are moderate in comparison with the behaviorists' application of a biological, material approach to every facet of mental and emotional life. The American behaviorist John B. Watson declared in *Behavior*, "Psychology, as the behaviorist views it, is a purely objective, experimental branch of natural science which needs consciousness as little as do the sciences of chemistry and physics. . . . This suggested elimination of states of consciousness as proper objects of investigation in themselves will remove the barrier which exists between psychology and the other sciences. The findings of psychology become the functional correlates of structure and lend themselves to explanation in physio-chemical terms."[56]

As behaviorism emerged on the American landscape, an American version of Freudianism did as well. Disciples of Freud discovered the irrational basis of human action; many viewed human beings as bundles of physiological impulses and instincts which were only vaguely conscious to the individual. In the 1960s, one of those disciples, Herbert Marcuse, titillated American students with the promise that the overcoming of capitalism would lead to the uninhibited expression of those impulses and instincts; especially, he promised, it would lead to free sex. Allan Bloom described well the connection between American Freudianism and nihilism:

> Once Americans have become convinced that there is indeed a basement to which psychiatrists have the key, their orientation became that of the self, the mysterious, free, unlimited center of our being. All our beliefs issue from it and have no other validation. There is a whole arsenal of terms for talking about nothing—caring, self-fulfillment, expanding consciousness, and so on, almost indefinitely. . . . Nothing determinate, nothing that has a referent . . . The inner seems to have no relation to the outer. The outer is dissolved and becomes formless in the light of the inner, and the inner is a will-o'-the-wisp, or pure emptiness.[57]

The idea of social conditioning that arose from seeing man as an all-physical specimen, and the idea of the inevitability of action that sprang from seeing man as all-emotional impulse often succumbed to intellectual confusion. For example, people were sometimes viewed as *determined* by emotional impulse, at other times, as *liberated* by their emotional natures to express their creativity. People were sometimes viewed as *determined* by their physical environment; on the other hand, behaviorists seemed to believe in *their own power to determine behavior* through Skinnerian experiments in "positive and negative reinforcement." Simplified ideas of emotional compulsion and of mechanical programming *both* led human beings away from the burden and opportunity of choice (the "anxiety of true freedom") and away from ideas of right and wrong. These ideas also, of course, contributed to the nature/nurture dichotomy by seeing much of man's behavior as inescapable.

Human nature being what it is, however, ideas regarding right and wrong and better and worse *will* come out. Thus, what emerged from this intellectual upheaval were new ideas regarding right and wrong which were more insidious than the old ideas because they did not admit to requiring conformity. Underneath the terminology of liberation, an oppressive conformity arose. Historical determinism, which had such an influence on American students of the 1960s and 1970s, was a powerful tool in the depiction of liberated ideas as ineluctable and inevitable. Traditional American ideas were caricatured as not only wrong but stupid in that they went against the inevitable march of progress that no individual was powerful enough to stop. American individualism was anathema to "structuralists" such as Claude Levi-Strauss who saw social change as the result of underlying social structures, not as the result of moral conviction or individual assertion. Many structuralists believed that society was governed by natural laws in the same way as nature. It was up to the social "scientist" to "discover" those laws and to make prescriptions for society accordingly.

Indeed, in the guise of "progress" all sorts of new social strictures and rules sprang up and, in a deception many have succumbed to, the person who questioned these strictures was not "immoral" but "unliberated." Thus, the ironic end result of the rebellion against the powers that be is that the "what is" is glorified as never before. Anyone concerned with what should be and who defines the term in non-modern terms is labeled reactionary and thought to be naive. In truth, the surrendering of ourselves to the drumbeat of progress as, for example, evidenced by the domination of "popular culture" in our lives, is an abdication of reason.

Horkheimer foresaw the ever-increasing influence of relativism upon American life and knew that the result would be the domination of "subjective reason," which is concerned with reason not as a means to the truth but as a means to personal objectives. Warned Horkheimer, "The idea that an aim can be reasonable for its own sake—on the basis of virtues that insight reveals it to have in itself—without reference to some kind of subjective advantage is utterly alien to subjective reason even where it rises above the consideration of immediate utilitarian values and elevates itself to reflections about the social order as a whole." [58] In the subjective view, even ends are means to further ends. There is no objective end nor are there objective beginnings for there is no truth—there is only each person's idea of it. If the validity of ends cannot be determined, then what matters is choice and predilection—not the superiority or inferiority of a given choice. Reason becomes not a source of insight into what it true, but simply, a way of a choosing and achieving preferences. Says Horkheimer, reason "has finally renounced even the task of passing judgment on man's actions and way of life." It has "turned them over for ultimate sanction to the conflicting interests to which our world actually seems abandoned."[59]

The result of all this is two-fold and contradictory. First, we are open to anything and everything and, second, we are closed to opposing viewpoints, no matter how reasonable, because each viewpoint is perceived to be nothing higher than an assertion of will and cannot possibly have reality to back it up. To succumb to another's reasons is to succumb to their will and to diminish one's own "assertiveness." On the one hand, all opinion is just that, opinion, and is therefore relative; to be "reasonable" no longer means to use one's mind well, but to be "open." Since truth regarding the big questions is not possible, reasoning regarding the big questions is not worth listening to and can reveal nothing worth knowing. Thus, the other side of an openness to all opinions is a disrespect for reason. With no hope of a common moral-rational ground, what is left in the place of rational discourse is the assertion of will. To acknowledge the reasonableness of another's opinion is to lessen the power of oneself or one's group.

We see both trends firmly embedded in modern American life. If one's position is not underlain by truth but by opinion, then it is easily knocked down and one must guard it carefully. Moreover, if the preferences of others threaten to assert themselves forcefully, then one must with even greater forcefulness assert one's own. The constant concern for the assertion of will is concomitant with a defensiveness which causes different ideas to be viewed as threatening. I believe that this helps to explain why so little reason has been allowed into the discussion of how American children are (not) being brought up. We have willed it to be so that children do not need a strong moral compass and a strong and present family to guide them. So, we ignore good reasons and solid evidence that children do indeed need these things.

As we pay less attention to reason, we pay more attention to slogans and labels. When language is no longer an avenue to the truth, it is easily manipulated as a means toward social-political ends. Since the sixties and seventies, slogans such as racist, imperialist, reactionary, and sexist have been effectively used to silence those who do not have a racist, imperialist, or sexist bone in their body, but who simply want to enter the discussion. Instead of being something that helps us unravel some of the mysteries of life, language frequently becomes a tool in the pursuit of goals and desires. With words being used as weapons, it becomes au-courant to scrutinize the language of others for signs that they are not "open enough" to the modern viewpoint. Horkheimer foresaw this trend as well:

As in the days of magic, each word is regarded as a dangerous force that might destroy society and for which the speaker must be held responsible. Correspondingly, the pursuit of truth, under social control, is curtailed. The difference between thinking and acting is held void. Thus, every thought is regarded as an act, every reflection as a thesis, and every thesis is a watchword. Everyone is called on the carpet for what he says and does not say. Everything and everybody is classified and labeled.[60]

When language is a tool, it requires less thought and less care. Words can be "used" and detached from their original meaning:

As soon as a thought or a word becomes a tool, one can dispense with actually "thinking" it, that is, with going through the logical acts involved in verbal formulation of it. . . . What are the consequences of the formalization of reason? Justice, equality, happiness, tolerance, all the concepts that, as mentioned, were in preceding centuries supposed to be inherent in or sanctioned by reason, have lost their intellectual roots.[61]

In this intellectual climate, many things can be assumed to be good without subjection to logic and for no better reason than that we would like them to be good. For example, because of the diminution of the idea of truth, theories that maternal tendencies are solely the product of "socialization" do not need to be proven to be true—they need only to be advantageous. (Again, power for the individual or group is more important than reason or goodness. Although we modern Americans deny that one person can actually have a better understanding of "the good" than another, few of us would deny that some people have more power.) Great leaps of faith are made in defense of causes and beliefs, which themselves are not clearly examined. Anyone who doubts this need only look at the number of things that have become unspeakable in our time. And yet, the very idea of the politically correct and politically incorrect, an idea whose tremendous influence upon our society cannot be denied, points to our inability to get away from the idea of right and wrong. The same people who insist upon seeing morality as opinion and truth as conjecture also insist upon vilifying those who are not open to these conflicting 'truths:' that nothing is true and that their particular perspective "should" be adopted by everyone. Their openness is underlain by the assumption that the only openness worth having is openness to this viewpoint.

Underlying this trend, which sees "truth" as too threatening a subject for discussion, is the tendency to simplify ideas in order to categorize or dismiss them. This tendency allows us to see moral/philosophical questions in terms of neat dichotomies. A persistent dichotomy in modern thinking is that between facts and values—between the real or "objective" and the idealistic or "subjective." In our high-tech, results-driven society, realists are said to be those who appreciate the "facts"—facts being objectively valid, i.e., scientifically verifiable. Idealists are those who formulate "mere opinions" regarding the unscientifically verifiable, i.e., regarding goodness and justice. Those who adhere to this dichotomy, which denigrates "idealism," are often only willing to discuss goodness or justice insofar as they treat them as "facts," not values. For example, it can be "objectively" observed that this country has this particular view of justice, this country another. It is a "fact" that country A defines justice as B. These people are willing to *describe* society but, being tied to the "scientific method," are unable to make *judgments regarding* society.

Those who believe that only facts, and not values, are "true" sometimes nevertheless accept "values" as things which society "needs." But if the good is "need" why is it good to fulfill needs? Moreover, if there is no such thing as better and worse, what makes the scientific method (often the one concession to "truth" which relativists make) better than others? By what criterion does one judge the scientific method itself? As much as relativists try, they simply cannot escape the notions of better and worse, right and wrong.

Objectivists, who are in this case relativists, tend to see the fact that there are so many different opinions regarding "abstract" concepts such as justice and responsibility as evidence that there is no way to determine which opinion is true or better. And yet, the fact that people do not agree on the truth need not mean that there is no truth. It could mean that we humans have a true understanding of some things, but not of all things. It could mean that some people are more capable of grasping the truth regarding certain things than other people. Too frequently, we mistake the universal for the true.

Related to all of this is the distinction frequently made in the analysis of politics and "culture" between what we "have" to do and what we "ought" to do, between the necessary and the valuable. "Realists" are said to be those who look at the "facts" and "see" what *has* to be done, as if facts could speak for themselves in the absence of ideas. (The emphasis is upon the scientific method of observation.) "Idealists" are said to be those who think in terms of "ideals"—not in terms of what has to be done, but in terms of what *should be*. Although it is obvious, it is helpful to point out that *all* political and cultural activity rests upon ideas. For, then the distinction is not between what we have to do and what we ought to do, but rather between those who have the best ideas about what we ought to do and those who do not. Who has the best ideas, in turn, can be evaluated based on *both* prudence and principle, in terms of both what is practical and what is right. Our understanding of what is practical and what is right, in turn, certainly must be grounded in our understanding of reality.

We as a nation need to return to the understanding that people should consider both the moral worth *and* the practical consequences of their actions and that the prudent and the good are often intricately intertwined. The tendency to see human action in terms of simplistic dichotomies leaves too little room for reason in our lives. For, if we are fact-gatherers who fail to realize the importance of ideas, we will be all too vulnerable to a statistical and sterile interpretation of our own life and the lives of our children. We will be all too prone to following the herd without thinking about where the herd is going. And, if we believe in ideology, without believing in the relevance of common sense or historical lessons or verifiable facts, we will be all too prone to accepting the reporting of statistics and media stories unthinkingly, so long as those statistics and stories serve our "higher" purposes.

Take the idea of the maternal. The labeling, the dichotomizing, the attempt to be value-neutral and the attempt to make facts "fit" an ideological scheme are all evident in our discussion of this subject. Those who suggest that ideas of a maternal instinct have validity are rejected as sexist and myopic, in other words, as wrong. On the other hand, those who express concern about children who lack prevalent maternal care are called to task for not being neutral regarding the subject of what is "best" for children. Those who suggest that motherhood is not a construct of exploitation but a real feature of nature are met with disregard. But in place of these disposed-of-concepts are new ones—that maternal feelings are a product of chauvinist fantasies and that men and women are the same except for physical appearance. Those who fail to accept this new vision of reality are dismissed as "irrelevant" to modern times. Those impressed by reality's refusal to live up to this vision are made to believe that they just have not tried hard enough to achieve it. They are presented with "studies" which are supposed to supplant true thought and true feelings. (Of course, recent brain research and recent anthropological findings of a maternal reality across human cultures and across the animal kingdom have made it very difficult for those who claim that science is on the side of gender-neutrality. See Chapters 1 and 2.)

Thus, a mother's longing to be with her baby most of the time is not "real" but rather is a sign of inauthenticity and insufficient self-seeking. Thus, a girl's confusion when she is taught that girls are the same in nature as boys while, at the same time, popular images demand that she acquire the most exaggerated feminine looks is something we overlook. Thus, a boy's inevitable confusion when he is expected to be more girl-like in the classroom, but to crush his opponent on the football field, is another thing we overlook. And so we are taught to overcome the real.

In a scenario that provides endless opportunities for Freudian analysis, it seems that the more we repress the idea of male/female differences, the more those differences emerge in exaggerated displays of "sexiness." This is evident in our obsession with plastic surgery, in the way the entertainment industry sells the "looks" and the sex appeal of its stars, and in the stunning popularity of pornography. As Lloyd E. Sandelands perceived, "The repressed returns in fantasy images of exaggerated sex differences and lusty attractions. In the movies, male actors become more improbably muscled while female actors become more impossibly buxom. —Behind these (movies) and innumerable other returns of the repressed in public are daily returns of the repressed in private, particularly in the growing appetite for sex on the phone, on the Internet, on cable television, in magazines, and in rentals of videotapes. For all of the fear and reluctance about sex, there is a lot of it being watched these days, most of it un-progressive in its portrait of sex differences and sex roles."[62]

Underlying the "openness" of gender-neutrality is a closedness to what nature, history, biology, neurobiology, and our everyday lives all suggest—that there is such a thing as masculine and feminine, and that the differences between boys and girls are latent. What on the surface suggests to girls that they be whatever they want to be, in reality, prohibits them from being feminine and from believing in any such thing. As for boys, the evidence is now cold and hard that being brought up in the age of girl power, to the extent that implicit social-educational and media messages taught them to feel shame just for being male, led to an alarming decline in male adolescent motivation. Also de-motivating was the message that men are no longer needed as providers and fathers. Sandelands points to a 1981 *New York Times* article by art critic John Russell entitled, "The Retreat of Manhood as Mirrored in the Arts." In plays, movies, painting, sculpture, and opera, Russell traced a hundred-year decline of man from powerful hero to whining baby. Not coincidentally, this decline came with the emergence of a triumphal, freestanding woman."[63] The way we teach boys is now being widely reviewed, due to startling statistics on declining numbers of boys doing well in high school or even graduating from high school and on steadily declining male enrollment numbers in colleges (see Chapter 4).

If the disparaging of the masculine leads to male confusion, frustration, and insecurity, the disparaging of femininity often means forsaking complexity for the sake of hard matter-of-factness. Hard matter-of-factness is the means to progress defined as liberation from childrearing. One has to be tough to hand a beloved infant over to childcare workers. But is tough matter-of-factness really better than subtlety and sensitivity to the feelings of others? The answer, in terms of the outcome for our children, is a resounding no. As society spirals away from all vestiges of civility, one longs for the civilizing influence which women can have and have had upon society in general. As society becomes more uniformly masculine and as masculinity as a male quality is denied and so emerges in distorted, exaggerated forms, society becomes more base and raw. Society suffers because increasing numbers of men lack character and confidence—and because men are no longer taught to be gentlemen because they *are* men (with much to offer but with certain qualities that need to be tamed). The increase in violence and the decrease in good manners, the increase in simplistic solutions to difficult problems, and the trivialization in the way we define our humanness are all related to the gender-neutralization of American society.

Our attempt to be gender-neutral and to put openness to all forms of self-seeking in front of a study of what young children need, relates to our larger societal attempt to be neutral or open in regard to "culture." As Allan Bloom famously argued in *The Closing of the American Mind*, it has become anathema in many academic circles to argue that certain cultures have better ideas about the human condition (and into freedom and justice) than others. Bloom argued that the openness of Americans to anything and everything has, in reality, been a closing of the mind to nature, to history, and to beliefs that have been held to be "truths" across virtually all other cultures and all other times. Bloom argued that although multiculturalism is, on the surface, an "openness" to all cultures, the relativistic idea that all cultures are valid but none are superior which often underlies it, means that nothing can be learned from other cultures other than an "openness" to their peculiarities. The study of history and philosophy are debased because past cultures and books are not treated as sources of important ideas but rather as "validation" of our already-there opinion that cultures are relative. Any differences between cultures is taken as evidence that truth is cultural rather than objective, and that it is our best recourse simply to be "open" to all differences.

As Bloom pointed out, a truthful examination of "cultures" throughout history shows that most cultures do believe in certain moral truths and do not believe in moral relativism. They do not believe in mere randomness; on the contrary, they believe it society's role to instill in its citizenry a sense of responsibility. Most cultures have, in one fashion or another, emphasized loyalty to family, community, and country and the obligations of mother, father, and citizen. There are, of course, vast differences between regimes, and these differences are based upon different definitions of human society and politics and of what is fair, just, and prudent. That there are differences in no way proves that all regimes are equal. Do we believe that governments which do not allow women the right to vote or even to take part in public life have as clear an idea of freedom as does the U.S.?

If we insist upon seeing culture as relative we close ourselves not only to the possibility of really *learning* about other places and times but also to the possibility of a better understanding of human nature and to the improvement of life. This, of course, has ramifications for our children's future. If we are going to "create a *better* world for our children," we will need to study the world. Without this study students are left, in Bloom's words, "exhausted and flaccid, capable of calculating but not of passionate insight."[64] Bloom observed the contradiction between declaring oneself "open" to all cultures and hostility to tradition so great that it closes one off from intellectually worthwhile ideas. If openness is limited to the new and the current, it is not openness after all:

> To deny the possibility of knowing good and bad is to suppress true openness. . . .
> There are two kinds of openness, the openness of indifference—promoted with the twin purposes of humbling our intellectual pride and letting us be whatever we want to be—just as long as we don't want to be knowers—and the openness that invites us to the quest for knowledge and certitude, for which history and the various cultures provide a brilliant array of examples for examination.[65]

Bloom's mentor Leo Strauss insisted that such an examination of human history and historical ideas reveals that restraint is just as "natural" as freedom:

> By virtue of his rationality, man has a latitude of alternatives such as no other earthly being has. The sense of this latitude, of this freedom, is accompanied by a sense that the full and unrestrained exercise of that freedom is not right. Man's freedom is accompanied by a sacred awe, by a kind of divination that not everything is permitted. We may call this awe-inspired fear "man's natural conscience." Restraint is therefore as natural or as primeval as freedom. [66]

Not only restraint but also the giving and receiving of love is natural to humankind. Rabbi Joshua L. Liebman, who saw modern psychology and psychiatry as a potential avenue into the best within us, argued that within every healthy person lay a conscience and a compulsion toward "love, sympathy and relatedness."

> Dynamic psychology indicates today that in the very nature of man there is not only an unconquerable urge to receive love from others, an inability to live with serenity and joy when deprived of affection from our fellows, but what is more important, there is an inner necessity to give love and to bestow affection upon the outer world. . . . The parent is driven by the irresistible desire to add something to live, no longer to receive something from life. Man's restless yearning to give something of himself, whether it be a physical child or a spiritual child—the child of his mind—a bridge, a poem, a song, an invention, a cure for disease—is the true answer to all cynics and pessimists who maintain that man is total selfishness. [67]

Even the most horrible dictators have recognized the need to justify and misrepresent their actions as somehow satisfying "man's natural conscience." Hitler knew that in order to achieve his will-to-power objectives he had to define his objectives as logical and just. It is only those who are willing to acknowledge the existence of a better and a worse, a good and a bad, beyond the individual definition of it who can refute a person like Hitler. It is, of course, not enough to say that Hitler was not open enough to other races and ideas. (The one "value" many relativists insist upon is "toleration.") For, this begs the question of why we should not be open to (i.e., "tolerant" of) Hitler. In the end, we must be able to say that his ideas were intellectually and morally, horribly wrong and to defend this assertion in non-relativist (i.e., rational and moral) terms. Moral and cultural relativists are especially prone to intellectual contradictions due to their inability to escape from the notions of right and wrong from which they claim to be exempt.

Relativists are prone to other intellectual contradictions as well. In denying a truth beneath or above the randomness of individual will, our society emphasizes self-expression and self-fulfillment. It is up to the individual to find oneself, create oneself, and express oneself as imaginatively as possible. The creed is not "God created man in his image," but rather "people create themselves in their own image." And yet, the very same people for whom this creed is an underlying fact of their existence often describe people as products of their environment. "Social conditioning" is blamed by them for anything occurring in nature which does not bolster their particular agenda. Thus, the modern American who sees it as the job of every female to find and express her individuality will, at the same time, blame any expression of individuality which emphasizes familial love and motherhood as, in fact, not an expression of individuality but a byproduct of social conditioning. Women who focus on their young children have surely been "conditioned" by a white male society to do so.

A bastardized form of the modern philosophic concept of the "authentic" allows modern Americans to bridge the contradiction between the randomness of self-assertion and the determinism of social conditioning. There is, according to this creed, an authentic expression of self and an inauthentic, the inauthentic being the traditional. Again, however, the rationalization falls short. For, what do the concepts of authentic and inauthentic indicate if not a concern for the true as opposed to the false? The concepts of right and wrong are inescapable.

Looking further into the question of how the same persons who believe in the creed of self-creation can also believe in the creed of social conditioning, we find this common sub-structure: both creeds are underlain by the view that there is no human nature. Rather, we are born with a blank slate upon which (a) we make our own random impression or (b) society impresses upon us its image. Whether we look at the self as something which the self creates or as something which society creates, the idea is that the inner being is malleable; indeed, there is no human "being" in any universal and unchanging sense of the term. *All is change and flux. It behooves us, then, to ride the waves of change rather than allowing the waves to roll over us, passing us by, as it were.* Drastic (as opposed to moderate and reasoned) changes in society and in childhood are defined are inevitable currents, ineluctable waves of progress. Indeed, those waves are riding in, crashing loudly upon the shore. The sound of those beneath the waves (not a part of them) is, so far, too muffled to be heard.

Of course, infinite details of life point to the inadequacy of the view of life which allows neither for an innate human nature nor for a human understanding of the good. Where does an original thought come from? Why do almost all cultures across all times and places have certain fundamental beliefs in common? Why do concepts of the good, the just, the fair, and the reasonable rear their heads in any discussion, indeed, in any conduct of human affairs as much as we might try to disguise those concepts with such notions as the authentic? Why do some ideas turn out to be better than others? Why are children born so full of yearning for knowledge of right and wrong? *Children have an innate and natural belief in better and worse, right and wrong. Many adults spend much time prodding children away from these natural beliefs.* Children are taught methods of "critical thinking," but they are taught to suppress their desire to know the truth. Children today are indoctrinated into a cynicism so heavy that it removes from their lives the potential for moral and historical knowledge, for which they so long. Asked Rabbi Liebman, "Why should we continue to interpret the universe in terms of the lowest that we know rather than in terms of the highest that we experience? Intelligence, purpose, and personality, the will to love, the need to love, the yearning to be related—these are as important clues to reality as atoms and electrons. . . . Why should we not believe that that which is highest in ourselves is a reflection of that which is deepest in the universe—that we are children of a Power who makes possible the growing achievement of relatedness, fulfillment, goodness?"[68]

Rabbi Liebman also understood that objective science, insofar as it denied the world of emotions, was a pipe dream which set the stage for the exploitation of those emotions because they are real even if we deny their existence. "No wonder life began to be more shallow and humanity began to be more callous and insensitive! . . . Man became half human while worshiping at the shrine of pure reason; the result was that the emotions were captured by perverts and tyrants. The dictators of our age, recognizing that human beings become moral and spiritual invalids on a diet of abstract science, invaded the sphere of emotions with their death dances and blood symbols."[69]

The desire for good and the need for love are as true a part of being human as bodily functions. We live in a world which has tried to discard these vital human ingredients and the consequences are devastating. Movies and modern culture now emphasize the bodily functions of human beings at the expense of his and her moral concerns. They emphasize the need for sex, satisfaction, and power and de-emphasize the need for love and a well-ordered inner life. The consequence is that, almost overnight, we as a nation have lost our innocence. The almost unbelievable change in our standards which has occurred in the last twenty-five years is enough to make one's head spin.

To watch adult-focused TV shows from the fifties is to enter a world which, by today's standards, is child-like in the extreme. The cynicism, skepticism, and "sophistication" which have overtaken us like a tidal wave make innocence anachronistic and outmoded. The other night I was reminded that the train of lost innocence is accelerating ever faster as I came upon a rerun of "Hill Street Blues." Only fifteen years old, a show known for its guttural portrayal of urban life, now seems tame and naive. The crimes are not decadent enough, the criminals are not hardened enough, and the cops not cool and worldly enough for today's standards. The contrast between this show and "NYPD Blue," which came later, is striking. In turn, the contrast between "NYPD Blue" and more recent crime shows, such as "Missing" and "CSI," is striking. All of these shows are tame compared to many of Hollywood's popular movies.

And, of course, the more exposure we have to Hollywood shock-value tactics, the less easily we are shocked. Our loss of innocence is a continually self-reinforcing phenomenon. This loss affects the innocent—our children—most of all. (See Chapter 4 for a discussion of media worship and media influence.)

Relativism leads to a void in adult's lives and in the lives of the children they raise. The vacuum created by the discarding of moral concepts is filled, as I have said, with pleasure seeking, achievement, and power. Politics becomes the realm not of maximum justice and freedom according to the limitations of human nature but, as many of my generation have been taught, "who gets what, when, where, and how." Power-seeking individuals and groups reveal their belief that the betterment of human beings is less important than their assertion of will. Into the arena of power-to-me are American children born. Being the creatures we are, that are in need of moral guidance, reformers fill this void by giving us "causes" that are assumed to be right without having to stand the test of reason or nature. But what fills the void most is majority opinion.

Relativists who latch onto causes run into problems trying to "prove" their cause is better than another, which is often why they abandoned traditional morality in the first place; it could not be "proven." Majority opinion is a convenient way out. *In the absence of tradition (which contains ideas of right and wrong evolved and refined over many years) what majority opinion provides is the opinion with the most power.* If one opinion is not truer than another is in a moral and rational sense, then it behooves us, and especially behooves politicians, to discover not which opinions are true but rather which opinions are held by the most people. We grasp onto the only acceptable interpretation of meaning available—the opinion of the majority. Knowledge of majority opinion becomes the path to power and to acceptance. *For, although majority opinion will not inform us regarding what is right, it does inform us regarding current society's definition of the socially admirable.* Awareness of majority opinion is the path to self-fulfillment defined as the confident assertion of self within society. It is the way to "feeling good" as it is modernly defined.

We who had children in the 1980s and 1990s were repeatedly told, for example, that working in a professional office and wearing business attire was the preference of the majority of mothers. The media's portrayal of this as the situation preferred by the vast majority was an essential part of the promotion of the idea. *Telling us that most women prefer such and such is a way of telling us that we should as well.* The influence of the press's portrayal of majority opinion upon modern parents is enormous and relentlessly pursued by those that have the power to exert that influence (see Chapter 1). When statistics on how many women work are exaggerated and when polltakers fail to mention the great numbers of women working part time, and when the intelligent mother who takes time off from her career for the sake of her young children disappears completely from view, the reasons are not innocent. By portraying the full-time working mother as the self-satisfied majority, those who struggled to find alternatives were made to feel outdated oddities. They were un-empowered.

On the other hand, we should remember that once industrial, modern life separated men's work from home and separated work at home from work which earned an income, so that women were often called "housewives"—women's contentment with that role was exaggerated and over-estimated. Women were expected to be more narrow in their intellectual and emotional life than they actually were. (Today, it is not that women are *expected* to be narrow; it is that they are often *assumed* to be narrow. Women today who are described as housewives have "home offices," work part time, and carve out intellectual and creative adventures.) Even as more young women decide to stay home with their very young children or to work only part time when their children are young, (as appears likely) it is important to respect mothers of young children who have chosen the alternative of going back to work or who must work because of financial pressure. (This is not the same as saying the choice is "only" a choice, with no consequences.) We must not do away with one unkind portrayal of women only to replace it with another. The press likes to stir up the "mommy wars." *Isn't it so current to think that this is about us—about which adult "viewpoint" wins?* Let's make room for an honest, respectful discussion about children—their needs, their problems, and their potential. Let's also rediscover the lost art of disagreeing in a respectful way.

The more we are deprived of alternatives to the current, the more we will cater to the crowd. Thus, ironically, being a liberated person can preclude liberation from the here and now and can pertain only to previous social strictures. Horkheimer foresaw this trend as well:

Today the idea of the majority, deprived of its rational foundations has assumed a completely irrational aspect. Every philosophical ethical and political idea—its lifeline connecting it with its historical origins having been severed—has a tendency to become the nucleus of a new mythology, and this is one of the reasons why the advance of enlightenment tends at certain points to revert to superstition and paranoia. The majority principle in the form of popular verdicts on each and every matter, implemented by all kinds of polls and modern techniques of communication, has become the sovereign force to which thought must cater.[70]

As majority opinion becomes a substitute for careful thought it becomes increasingly void of that moderation which, through checks and balances in politics and a serious education in private life, the founders intended majority opinion to have.

Majority opinion is fast becoming an excuse for abandoning ideas we have not taken the time to understand. As Horkheimer foresaw, public opinion is fast becoming a "substitute" for reason. *Theories of childhood and of human nature itself are adopted and abandoned with appalling ease; as if childrearing were no more than some social experiment, and as if our common humanity were nothing more than a disposable option.* We Americans are like ships passing in the night, moving with the tide but unable to see where we are going; we are moving in the same waters but without any common moral-philosophical ground. No wonder Alan Bloom proscribed the need for a counterpoise to the "merely current:"

> The active presence of a tradition in a man's soul gives him a resource against the ephemeral, the kind of resource that only the wise can find simply within themselves. . . . This is the really dangerous form of the tyranny of the majority, not the kind that actively persecutes minorities but the kind that breaks the inner will to resist because there is no qualified source of nonconforming principles and no sense of superior right. [71]

Closer attention to our moral-philosophical roots would both prevent us from being unknowingly appropriated by the past *and* remind us of that which is noble in it. It would give a frame of reference to the principles, and lack thereof, which we bequeath to our children. It would bring to the foreground a consideration of our "foundations," a consideration essential to taking seriously the proposition of "bringing up" a child. Our current foundations, I believe, are to be found in the ideas regarding liberty and equality which played so great a part in the American founding and in their intertwining with European relativism which, in the twentieth century, left its mark upon our nation's soul. Let us look briefly at these historical American undercurrents of American modernity.

Being Americans, we are, of course, influenced by social contract theory. The American experiment in democracy arose, in part, out of Hobbes' view of the "state of nature" as "nasty, brutish and short." The state of nature, according to Hobbes, was a state of extreme selfishness wherein each person fended for themselves and all suffered the harsh consequences. In order to have a probability of success, civil society had to be based upon an understanding of natural human shortcomings. Any civil society based upon notions of man's perfectibility was doomed to failure. What society *could* achieve was to allow each person the maximum amount of freedom consistent with doing others no harm. Through an elaborate system of checks and balances and the separation of powers, the founders aimed to create a body politic wherein no one person or group of person would be permitted to harm others or to have an inordinate degree of power. Locke's notion of consent and Montesquieu's concept of the republic were combined to create "new government" with "new guards."

While people's basest impulses would be curbed, their freedom would be maximized because government would be based upon consent. The Constitution of 1787 combined the belief in man's imperfectability with the belief in each person's right to freedom and equality under the law. Moreover, the founders saw humankind more fully than Hobbes: People are "naturally" equal in that they are born with freedom of choice and in that, as distinguished from the beasts, they have the capacity to make rational and moral decisions. People are equal not only in their desire for existence and subsistence but also in their desire for "happiness," which reaches beyond the scope of the mere satisfaction of physical needs. Thus, the assertion of each person's right to life, liberty, and the pursuit of happiness was not just a practical solution to political problems but also an assertion of principle. Even if in contradistinction, the founders believed both in man's imperfectability and in the dignity of which all men were deserving.

It cannot truthfully be said that America has been untrue to the principle of freedom. That principle has been the steady and driving force in our nation's history, causing a continual self-examination as to how well we have lived up to our own creed. From the time of Washington to the time of Lincoln, Wilson, Truman, Johnson, and Reagan this principle has had political punch and has been used by Americans to evaluate American policy and to check American extremes. Of huge value to the antislavery movement was the demonstration that it violated in the most egregious way our founding ideals (see Chapter 4). What *can* be said is that the American regime has emphasized the "principle" of freedom without prescribing for us the virtues which might tell us what to do with our freedom. Although fervent beliefs in the possibilities of improving the lot of mankind lay behind the formation of the American democracy, the regime itself was decisively practical. Each person was to see the advantage to themselves in the social contract in that it allowed them to pursue their interests to the maximum extent possible in a civilized society. The regime sanctioned self-interest and, some have argued, did so at the expense of virtue.

The founders avoided a "subjective" stance toward religion, philosophy, and morality so that those things could be protected and private, and so that the government would be rational rather than arbitrary. All too often, they realized, in the political sphere one person's "morality" meant another's misfortune. All too often, those in the highest political positions do not have the highest moral sense. The fact that men, and not God, run government made the individual's freedom from government—to the extent possible—a Federalist goal. Said the Federalists, "If men were angels, no government would be necessary. If angels were to govern men, neither external nor internal controls would be necessary."

In a regime decisively practical in form but founded upon the bedrock of democratic principles, the founders hoped that virtuous ideas and actions would readily appear. Along with the emphasis upon the low in each man was an emphasis on the dignity each deserved and the magnanimity of which some were capable. The possibilities of great people with great minds, privately educated and brought up with a sense of duty toward the public sphere, and making great contributions, was a possibility the founders counted upon and believed in.

Moreover, the religious roots of Americans combined with the Lockean idea of not harming others to produce an overall valuing of kindness and generosity. We must remember that while the Constitutional prescriptions for government were Lockean, the country as a whole had deep moral-philosophical roots stemming, in part, from the Puritans. The founders expected those roots to influence the American body politic and they did have influence as evidenced, for example, in the formation of the nineteenth-century Whig Party and, more generally, in the religiosity of the American people which many foreigners observed.

The regime, we must remember, is more than the government per se. If we are to blame our politics for our current moral impasse, we must also blame the ethical, religious, and academic leaders who, because they do have great "liberty," greatly influence our social milieu. *We must view the American regime partly in terms of the moral and intellectual ground in which the government resides.*

Still, the people are members of the regime (even if the regime gives them tremendous liberty) and so have characters influenced by it. A danger inherent in our regime is that the people, as part of a regime which itself avoids a subjective stance toward "virtue," themselves become less virtuous. It is especially important in such a regime that the moral *sur-*

roundings of the government remain strong. If the government cannot and should not prescribe moral behavior for its citizens, it is important that the ground in which it resides is strongly concerned with good character. Families, churches, synagogues, and schools are then responsible for seeing to it that freedom does not degenerate into randomness. With the impact of relativism and, concomitantly, cynicism and skepticism, that degeneration into randomness is here. The moral-rational ground in which the regime resides, our ground, is crumbling.

The regime's emphasis upon freedom as opposed to virtue combined with the seeping into American religious and educational institutions of the leftist idea that "virtues" were just capitalism's method of enforcing itself made us vulnerable to European relativism when it pounded upon our shores. Said Leo Strauss:

> The notion of a return to the state of nature on the level of humanity was the ideal basis for claiming a freedom from society which is not a freedom for something. It was the ideal basis for an appeal from society to something indefinite and indefinable, to an ultimate sanctity of the individual, unredeemed and unjustified.[72]

I would submit that it was not just the practical nature of our regime that made us vulnerable to relativism but also the fact that we were beginning to forget the principled underpinnings of our regime. By the 1960s, our forgetting was beginning to overshadow our remembering. Rather than viewing transgressions from our principles as transgressions from our roots, many began to view such transgressions as endemic to democratic capitalism. Without remembering our foundation in principle and with growing disbelief in America, we were susceptible to disbelief in general. European relativism and Marxist analysis succeeded in severing American individualism from its principled roots and its moral-religious surroundings. When the dust settled, we were left with individualism without the concept of virtue, creativity without the burden of responsibility, and social causes for the sake of which unvirtuous behavior was justified.

It is true, however, that there is a relativistic component of the American regime itself. To examine our foundations further, we need to examine this irony: Our government does not impose upon us concepts of virtue but allows us to pursue our own concepts; it, indeed, relies upon the ingenuity and integrity of man. And yet, a very reason for the formation of the social contract is that, when left to their own devices, people often seek selfish rather than virtuous ends. Truly private life, then, is inherently unvirtuous. Thus, there is an inherent tension in the American founding. The idea that one person or group must not impose their will upon another is underlain by the idea that individual will is the predominant feature of human life. When the idea of individual will is severed from the principles which it served and from the moral-religious tradition which surrounded and mitigated it throughout most of American history, we are left with freedom which is valued for its own sake and not for any good that may come from it.

When American individualism, leftist cynicism toward Western tradition, and European relativism merge, the results are nothing short of anarchic. The result is nothing short of catastrophic as far as the upbringing of children is concerned. For, if we forget that which is noble and principled in our history, we deprive children not only of an understanding of the ground on which they stand, but also of respect for it. We leave them with nothing to stand upon. If we deprive them of the concept of right and wrong we, again, deprive them of a ground to stand upon and leave them skimming across the surface of their days without direction and without equilibrium. Without anything to look up to or to look back to, children are adrift, lost in the cynical and relativist waters in which we bathe them.

Due to the influence of Marxist interpretations of the American regime, history all too often has been defined for the American child not in terms of constant opportunities for improvement but as an inevitable and deterministic process in which real change could only be brought about by revolutionary upheaval. Whereas, previously, most Americans were influenced by the moral-religious belief in the free will and the accountability and responsibility of each individual toward God and country, the creed of social conditioning began to upset the delicate balance between American self-assertiveness and American principle. *If we were "determined" by forces detrimental to us, it behooved us to assert ourselves more forcefully, to throw off the restraints that were keeping us down.* Thus, determinism ironically fed into the cult of the self.

While our individualism was too ingrained in us for us to let go of, our morals and political principles were apparently not so steadfast. What the influx of leftist-relativist thought has meant for Americans is not the abandonment of capitalism, but the abandonment of virtuous democracy. Americanized socialism, like philosophical relativism, undercuts the concepts of individual and civic responsibility. Cynics in the extreme regarding our own politics, suspicious regarding the very concepts of right and wrong, we have also become cynics regarding our own capacity for virtue.

Again, however, children need to believe in something more than the power of their own whims. I have observed that the same advocacy groups that have led us toward group-centered childrearing for infants and toddlers and a relativistic and cynical teaching of history, politics, and ethics for school-age children are the same ones shouting out the "work toward your dreams" message. It is as if they intuitively know they must compensate for the child's lack of belief in anything, which their own social-engineering approach to childrearing has created: the not-trusting in parents nor in themselves, which comes from being insufficiently nurtured; the not-trusting in their own country or government, which comes from an excess of revisionist history; and the not believing in any rational order or justice in the world, which comes from the teaching of moral relativism. As if to free themselves of responsibility for these highly cynical and "alienated" creatures they have created, these adults convince themselves that merely telling children to "believe in themselves" will pull them out of their cynicism long enough for them to "make something" of themselves. The irony is that when self-esteem courses urge teenagers to feel good, they also encourage children to be satisfied with the idea that "I am as I am."

It makes sense that a society which questions the very idea of innate individual goodness would seek financial rather than parental solutions to children's problems. Current generations of parents have placed much more faith in money than previous generations. It is implied that if we give generously to "disadvantaged" children their problems will somehow go away. Giving to the disadvantaged *is* important, but it is not a *sufficient* solution. We cannot discount the sure "advantage" a child receives from limit-setting supervision combined with unconditional love. We must admit that the "social" solution to the problems children face today is all too often a financial solution—one that places faith in the services and industries money can buy.

Today's churches often contribute to this financial definition of caring. Aid to those in need is essential in a thriving economy such as ours and is an essential part of the traditional Christian teaching. But what happens when we so focus on monetary needs that we forget the needs of the heart or, in religious terms, the soul? In repeated sermons in various churches over the last fifteen years, I have heard about the importance of "giving" to the homeless and the needy and to the causes of racial and sexual equality. I have heard about the importance of going beyond the Ten Commandments to achieve divine grace. Only a few times have I heard about the importance of loyalty, responsibility, and fidelity to those we love and who love us, something attention to the Ten Commandments would require. The stories held up for emulation are those of the man who shows kindness to strangers; of the mother who spends her weekends building low-income housing; of the couple who volunteer their time to helping the poor; of the struggling family that gives every spare penny to someone worse off than they are. These indeed are inspiring stories. Generosity and sympathy combined with respect for others is important. But I cannot help viewing it as problematic when churches, reflecting society at large, allow emphasis on the social cause to replace rather than to complement the Old Testament emphasis upon personal responsibility. We are told at church "not to put too much value our own." Taken to extremes, this could mean that everyone is "cared for" by someone they do not "know." Love, then, becomes increasingly abstract, as in love of humanity. This, while important, leaves children in an untenable position. For they need love which is concrete and personal, which is love for them.

Ironically, atheistic Communism has had a big effect upon many of our churches. Communism, of course, is the most materialistic philosophy of all because it asserts that money, i.e., the equal distribution of it, will remedy the worst social ills. In it, matter is what matters. For a capitalist country and a religious people, we put a surprising amount of store on just how much money can do and are surprisingly willing to forget the excesses and the injustices to which this philosophy brought much of the world. In an article entitled "Slime-time TV and Moral Outrage," Thomas Roeser, former fellow of the Kennedy School of Government at Harvard, laments the "erosion of Judeo-Christianity in many churches" and the "post Judeo-Christian" church leaders who are unwilling to speak out against the inundation of society and television with sexual permissiveness and relativism. Admonitions toward chastity and fidelity seem "archaic" by the modern church's standards. "A priest mused that such admonitions are demeaning and would be a lamentable departure from high integrity of purpose, which is to concentrate on alms-giving; on the infinite mercy of God; the condemnation of racism, sexism, and ageism; the deploring of nuclear proliferation; and the supplication of more federal spending for the homeless." [73]

It is not difficult to see what such a philosophy means for the innocence of our children. If we no longer believe in virtue, we no longer believe that anything is corrupting. And if nothing is corrupting, we no longer value our children's innocence. Nor do we see any need to protect it. The evidence that most of us neither value innocence nor see any need to protect it is all around us. From our inability to give children heroes to look up to, to the premature introduction we give them to the ills of their own political system, to our allowing and sometimes facilitating their early exposure to sexual situations and adult themes, to the frenetically busy and stressful lives we create for them, we show that innocence is not, for us, something of value.

What, for many of us, has replaced the valuing of innocence is the valuing of the social cause. Influential Americans have undertaken collectivist experiments in social engineering in the spirit of true Communists. *Determinists have always been forceful in helping history to achieve its inevitable destiny, never mind the contradictions in doing so.* With progress on their side, they are all too often willing to dispense with the question of the justice of the means. Although the United States' political system does not allow for the extremes of injustice to which less democratic societies' social engineering projects have led, it behooves us to beware the more subtle and gradual erosion of our liberties. The unbelievably cruel political extremes of other societies such as Cambodia in the 1970s and North Korea today are a reminder not only of the pitfalls of non-democratic government, but also a warning to free peoples about social-determinism. When the larger cause is an excuse for repressive behavior and the dissemination of false "information," it is a problem, no matter where it is found. Observed Paul Johnson, "Economics, sociology, psychology and other inexact sciences—(had) constructed the juggernaut of social engineering, which (had) crushed beneath it so many lives and so much wealth."

> In a more fundamental sense, the political terrorism of the Seventies was a product of moral relativism. In particular, the unspeakable cruelties it practiced were made possible only by the Marxist habit of thinking in terms of classes instead of individuals. Young radical ideologues who kept their victims, usually diplomats or businessmen chosen solely by occupation, chained in tiny, underground concrete dungeons, blindfolded, their ears sealed with wax, for weeks or months, then dispatched them without pity or hesitation, did not see those they tortured and murdered as human beings but as pieces of political furniture. In the process they dehumanized themselves as well as those they destroyed and became lost souls, like the debased creatures Dostoevsky described in his great anti-terrorist novel, *The Devils*.[74]

Foresaw Horkheimer, "Today, one is too easily induced to evade complexity by surrendering to the illusion that the basic ideas will be clarified by the march of physics and technology."[75]

A society that encourages us to care more about causes than about kind and responsible behavior of individuals is in trouble. A newspaper series I encountered was indicative of the problem. Entitled "Everybody's Children," it encouraged us to view all children as our own. It challenged us to care about children with emotional and behavioral problems and criminal records, and to "rise out of complacency" to help them. Never once did the writers of this series suggest the role parents might play in helping their own children. Never did they consider that the social volunteerism they advocated might be for naught if it were directed toward children neither well-enough brought up nor well-enough loved.

What happens to a society when we see all the children as ours but none as really our own (as in our individual responsibility)? Rather than assuming that community work will somehow trickle down and affect individual relationships, we should realize that active parenting is a tremendous boon for the community. Community work is very important. But it is no *substitute* for parental love and guidance. Day care has been the large social experiment of our times. We have taken the materialism of Marxism and made it fit the individualism of capitalism: Working for money is essential and we define our equality in terms of it. The solution to the world's problems is money, albeit the distribution and expansion of it. The material definition of success is seen in the myth that an end to poverty would *solve* urban problems. Poverty is truly a problem that requires the attention of good minds and good hearts. But the biggest gulf in our society lies not between rich and poor nor, even so much between educated and uneducated, as between those are well-enough brought up and well-enough loved and those who are not. We need only examine the scary depth of the problems our society faces to know that money alone will not solve them and that "progress" has often been more a cause of our problems than a solution to them. Progress has meant liberation from childrearing, but too little attention has been paid to the effect of "progress" upon children.

Moral responsibility begins at home. Innocence is protected at home. Money cannot buy responsibility nor protect innocence. Just now, as I was writing this, I looked out of my office window to witness an older boy, about eleven, push a younger boy, about eight, intentionally down flat in front of a stream of oncoming cars. The older boy ran away as the cars screeched onto their breaks and, thankfully, just missed the younger boy. Money will not solve this eleven-year-old's problems. What this boy lacks is a conscience. He lacks adults in his life who protect his innocence, who could have taught him the dignity of each and every human life instead of instilling in him cynicism, resentment, and hatred. It is safe to bet that this boy has not been well-enough brought up nor well-enough loved. The biggest tragedy in this boy's life is not that his home is too small but that his heart is too small.

When society goes to the extreme of neglecting intimate relationships between husbands and wives, parents and children, it overlooks the most important features in our lives. When it spends money on day care for unwed mothers, for example, but makes no effort to make it less likely that those who have children are prepared for its responsibilities, and that children receive large doses of parental love, it places the impersonal cause over the personal relationship.

A study of Nietzsche helps us to understand our moral-social predicament.[76] This diversion enables us to dig beneath the surface of our modern educational and childrearing practices. The power-seeking behavior of groups, causes, and individuals that has replaced responsibility and love and is so evident in modern America is partly a Nietzschian phenomenon. The themes I have laid out require a brief overview of Nietzsche's philosophy because that philosophy is an undercurrent of our society which, if we are unaware of it, will appropriate us nevertheless. If we would contemplate Nietzsche's criticisms of modern society while rejecting his solutions based on their nihilistic consequences, we would take a large step forward in creating a better world for our children.

Nietzsche understood the threat which modern cynicism, skepticism, scientism, and majoritarianism posed to the "magnanimous" individual. And yet, a trickled-down version of his philosophy has contributed to the leveling relativism he sought to overcome. Nietzsche's solution to modern relativism was not to be found in concepts of virtue—traditional morality was part of the problem of mediocrity in his view. His solution was a relativism more thorough and more complete, a relativism which went beyond the concepts of the objective and the subjective and beyond the concepts of good and evil toward thorough individuality.

In *Beyond Good and Evil,* Nietzsche puts forth the idea that modern philosophers accepted morality as "given" and lacked the courage or conviction to change it. Instead, by finding a rational foundation for it, they confirmed it. By updating it to suit modern times, they validated it. This was partly because they mistook the morality they inherited for *the* morality. They failed to examine and question morality itself. Were they to do that, Nietzsche suggested, they would understand that morality is not an objective truth intelligible to all via "pure reason" but a subjective "value creating process." It was therefore the duty of the proud intellectual "to create new values."

According to Nietzsche, by teaching meek passivity as opposed to energetic liveliness, "slavish morals" passed down from Christianity bred men too timid to overthrow them. "Resentment" motivated the lowly and oppressed to replace noble values which rewarded excellence and achievement with their own values which condoned mediocrity. Out of fear, the "underdog" created a new good via resignation, moderation, and complacence in hopes that the strong would learn these opiate values and spare the weak. Nietzsche was concerned with the degeneration of the "best" in modern society. Intelligent men with the capacity for greatness, Nietzsche warned us, were succumbing to mediocrity—believing they had no right to reject leveling norms with assertive impatience.

Nietzsche believed that the philosophic-scientific belief in an absolute reality only exacerbated the problem. From the epistemological belief in matter to the teleological belief in a universal soul, man postulates a reality which exists beyond man. This belief is augmented by skepticism which, in turn, springs from an admixing of cultures. Once men contrast themselves with their cultural opposites and realize that what they assumed to be true is "only" convention, they assume that they can never know the real nature of a thing and that absolute reality is "out there" and impossible to know. When an absolute reality is conceived, Nietzsche extolled, man's views, being only subjective in comparison, seem futile and insignificant. In fact, the view in a universal soul, asserted Nietzsche, turned the individual into an unfinished and inauthentic being. The belief in objective truth disheartened man still more. Because the only legitimate statements are objective, he modifies his unique ideas to fit universal standards and so compromises himself.

When truths are absolute, Nietzsche believed, man's opinions are "relative" in their mutual inferiority to the truth. Nietzsche believed that relativism combined with absolutism had to be replaced with *complete relativism*. The abandonment of absolutes would recreate a hierarchy among men and their ideas. Once nothing is above and superior to a man, a man's ideas have the potential for dignity. Once general standards beyond man are replaced with the particular relations of one individual to another, the best person is unconditionally the best. Meaning is an assigning of reality. New philosophers "will certainly not be dogmatists. It must offend their pride, also their taste, if their truth is supposed to be a truth for everyman which so far has been the secret wish and hidden meaning of all dogmatic inspirations."

Nietzsche took on modern politics, seeing it too as another facilitator of mediocrity. Politics today, he said, was the "slave morality" legalized. It is a "common war on all that is rare, strange, privileged, the higher man, the higher soul, the higher responsibility." It is characterized by equality of rights which is actually, according to Nietzsche, equality of violating rights; if all are the equal same, all obviously cannot rule, therefore all must follow. Leaders today, Nietzsche warned, are pandering democrats and demagogues, followers of popular sentiment. The people follow leaders who follow them. Equality, Nietzsche believed, means a lack of social distinction for the naturally superior and saps the will of the great individual.

Modern social contract theory, he believed, made possibilities for greatness even worse. According to him, it compels us to modify freedom, for, it sees "fitting" into the social order as requisite for freedom. Modern freedom has a tendency to bring the high down to the low as it makes common law toward the ends of safety, peace, and protected rights so important to freedom that self-law toward the ends of magnanimity, wisdom, and grace are ignored. Freedom, Nietzsche believed, had become so politicized as to not be freedom after all. In order that we understand the absence of greatness in modern society, he asked us to look to the increasing role of the State in "freedom's" parameters.

Nietzsche's solution to modern mediocrity was to be found within his well-known assertion that the world is "will to power." Lively and determined, free from scientism and skepticism, separated from the masses who would bring them down, understanding freedom as a-political and so having the freedom to honor single rather collective virtues, the strong-willed and intelligent had to replace the weak and inferior as leaders of modern society. There are many nihilistic consequences of this assertion of which I will mention a few.

If everything is particular rather than general, we are left without anything "of value." For the essence of a value statement is that it states a relationship. If everything is individual will, even the statement "modern men are mediocre" is invalid. It is general. The uniting of the word men and the word mediocre is an abstraction. The statement itself is a particular having no meaning independent of itself. If things are truly independent, values are only facts among other facts. Every attempt, including Nietzsche's attempt, to elaborate life in order to enhance it becomes a sham.

Because, all things being relative, the act has validity for no one other than the individual, we must ask what meaning the act has of and by itself. For, it is impossible to think of an idea or gesture that has meaning without referring to something outside itself. If the spontaneous act is all, philosophy and the search for meaning are ruined. Life becomes like that art which exists "for its own sake" and unlike philosophy which exceeds itself and has a purpose. Stanley Rosen claims that Nietzsche's nihilism is a logical consequence of the narrow concept of reason he inherited from Descartes. According to Rosen, when reason is associated with the truth, but truth is separated from "the ought statement," there is no "reason" to accept the truth.

The nihilistic implications of Nietzsche's philosophy are mitigated somewhat, however, by his *Gay Science* in which Nietzsche complements his negativism with the concept of joyfully resurrecting the best ideas and virtues of the past:

> Countless things that humanity acquired in earlier stages not so feeble and embryonically that nobody could perceive the acquisition, suddenly emerge into the light much later. Perhaps after centuries; meanwhile they have become strong and ripe. Some ages seem to lack altogether some talent or some individual as certain individuals do too. But just wait for the children and grandchildren—They bring to light what was hidden in their grandfathers and what their grandfathers did not suspect. Often the son betrays the father—and the father understands himself better after he has a son.

This excerpt reveals Nietzsche's belief in the possibility of improvement and growth. Improvement, for Nietzsche, implies that the best individuals can "remember" as well as negate or conform by willing that "what was" to come again. They use the contents of what is and has been as building blocks for the future. Virtues are developed and reinterpreted as well as spontaneously conceived. Originality entails the sapping of potential as well as innovation: "What is originality? To see something that has no name as yet and hence cannot be mentioned although it stares us in the face." The "best," according to Nietzsche, discern potential and discard worn out "actuality." The world is intriguing depth as well as spontaneous change. Self and world were not, then, *simply* reduced to the artist's palette.

But we must ask if this is enough to lead us out of our current predicament—to lead us away from our "herd mentality" and our intellectually debilitating form of relativism. With all of Nietzsche's brilliance, we are still left with no "reasonable" reason why we should accept one moral system over another. And the door is still left open to the political leader or media personality who has the most charm and cleverness, regardless of the goodness of his or her convictions. It seems that Nietzsche, in his struggle against mediocrity, still leaves us with a world where "anything goes" because will predominates over reason. Nietzsche correctly foresaw a weakness inherent in democratic society. He knew that majority politics easily degenerated into the politics of resentment which, in turn, lead to demagoguery and catering to the lowest common denominator. The discarding of the beautiful wording of the old prayer book in most churches is but one manifestation of this phenomenon, and it is testimony to Nietzsche's prediction that modern society would increasingly lower its intellectual and artistic standards. In an act insulting to the intelligence of most people, the old prayers were discarded in favor of new prayers that were "easier to understand" but not nearly so resonant, inspiring, or persuasive. Still, in insisting upon a creative inner self that would allow "the best" to "reconstitute the conditions of their creativity in order to generate values," Nietzsche ultimately contributed to the mediocrity he tried to destroy. Within the cult of the individual lie the seeds of conformism and sameness. For, when individuals do not stand for something other than themselves, they are easily swayed by the crowd. As Allan Bloom understood:

> The active presence of a tradition in a man's soul gives him a resource against the ephemeral, the kind of resource that only the wise can find simply within themselves. The paradoxical result of the liberation of reason is greater reliance on public opinion for guidance, a weakening of independence. . . . Freedom of the mind requires not only, or not even especially, the absence of legal restraints but the presence of alternative thoughts."[77]

As Horkheimer understood, "the absolutely isolated individual" has always been an illusion:

> The most esteemed personal qualities such as independence, will to freedom, sympathy, and the sense of justice, are social as well as individual virtues. The fully developed individual is the consummation of a fully developed society. The emancipation of the individual is not an emancipation from society, but the deliverance of society from atomization, an atomization that may reach its peak in periods of collectivization and mass culture. [78]

The extreme attention to individual expression has left us without anything to uplift us or inspire us. Instead of shooting for the stars, we too often wallow in the here and now. *If we would heed Nietzsche's warnings about the lowering of standards and complacency to which cynicism and scientific skepticism lead us, while rejecting his solutions as ultimately leading to the same problems, I believe we will have taken a great step toward restituting the principled ground in which the American founders intended us to reside.*

A popularized version of the Nietzschian concept of individuality and "will" is all around us. As we seek to express and define our individuality, we expect our children to seek and express theirs. With minimal guidance from their parents and nary a thought given to their education in virtue, good manners, and historical heroes, children are thought to be such strong individual creatures as to be practically capable of bringing up themselves. Many of today's children are "free" from parental oversight and moral strictures, from duties and obligations to family and society. We have set our children afloat in the sea of relativism. At the same time, most "successful" parents give their children strong guidance in one area—personal achievement. Three-year-olds in soccer uniforms and teenagers overcome with the stress of their activities, tutorials, and pre-college coursework are testimony to this trend.

As countless teachers and child therapists are witnessing, children are frightened by their freedom-for-nothing. They long for a moral compass to guide them, parental limits to control them, and adult figures to look up to until they are old enough to direct themselves. They need the parental attention and love, which would give them a sense of place, meaning, and inner worth; an anchor to hold onto within the turbulent waters of modern society.

A confused and inconsistent relativism and a debilitating cynicism are all around us. The alternative to confronting this confusion is to live abstract lives—lives of action but of little meaning. We put down guilt (the tug of the inner) because it might interfere with our pleasures. We keep love under control because it might lead to inefficiency in the workplace. We latch onto media images and intellectual clichés without thinking clearly about the agenda behind them. We rationalize too much and reason tool little, and we rely too much on statistics and too little on common sense. Attention to human nature and to human reason is required if we are to rid ourselves of the numbing abstraction which comes from seeing human nature and human reason as tools for power instead of foundations for understanding.

There are many reasons why we parents who came of age in the sixties, seventies, and eighties should abandon relativism. But the most important one is our children. Children crave shelter from the moral confusion, which has overtaken our country like a tidal wave. Who will provide this shelter if we adults, ourselves, embrace the irresponsibility of childhood? We must, instead, take seriously our roles as teachers and protectors of the young. We must fulfill their inherent request for knowledge regarding right and wrong. It is useful to reflect upon our own childhood, remembering what innocence feels like and recalling the frightening and disturbing sensation, which is the result of that innocence being disregarded.

Human beings naturally incline toward the good and away from the bad. But when human beings are not well-enough brought up nor well-enough loved, the human being has no experience of the good to confirm and sanction that inner desire. The defensive response is to convince oneself that one cares not about love and goodness but, simply, about getting ahead and asserting one's will.

The love between parent and child is in itself proof that relativism cannot account for human nature. If the parent is well-enough adjusted to give into that love, that love is anything but relative. The parent loves the child *more* than anything in the world and recognizes that love as something *good*. The parent knows his or her life is truly better because of it and sees that the obligations that love entails are essential rather than optional. We parents know at heart that life is not just about choices, but about what those choices mean. To stop the search for meaning because the search is difficult is to surrender ourselves and our children to empty lives.

Notes

1.   H. Kent Geiger, *The Family in Soviet Russia*. Cambridge: Harvard University Press, 1968: vii.
2.   *Ibid.*, 51.
3.   *Ibid.*, 45-46.
4.   *Ibid.*, 47.
5.   *Ibid.*, 48.
6.   *Ibid.*, 59, 73.
7.   *Ibid.*, 84.
8.   *Ibid.*, 90-91.
9.   Francine du Plessix Gray, *Soviet Women: Walking the Tightrope*. New York: Doubleday, 1989.
10.   "America's Children in Brief: Key National Indicators of Well- Being, 2006," Federal Interagency Forum on Child and Family Statistics, *National Center for Health Statistics*. (July, 2006).
11.   "Traditional Family Being Replaced by a 'New System,' *American Family Association Journal*. (March, 2000): 6.
12.   Karen Hines, "Role of Motherhood Takes Center Stage," *Duke University News and Communication*. (September 29, 2000): accessed January 30, 2007 <http://www.dukenews.duke.edu/2000/09/mother929.html>.
13.   William Raspberry, "Nonmarriage Trend is Threatening Generations," Washington Post Writers Group.
14.   Andrew Peyton Thomas, "A Dangerous Experiment in Child-Rearing," *The Wall Street Journal*. (January 8, 1998): A8.
15.   Mary Eberstadt, "Revenge of the Rugrats: A New Generation Weighs in on Divorce," *The Weekly Standard*. (October 10, 2005): 20.
16.   Geiger, *The Family in Soviet Russia*. 98.
17.   *Ibid.*, 59.
18.   Media Research Center Report, Media Research Center. Alexandra, Virginia.
19.   *Ibid.*, 74.
20.   Barbara Defoe Whitehead, "Dan Quayle was Right," *The Atlantic* 271. (April, 1993): 47-84.

21. Kathleen Mullan Harris, Frank F. Furstenburg, Jr., and Jeremy K. Marmer, "Paternal Involvement with Adolescents in Intact Families: The Influence of fathers Over the Life Course," *Demography* 35. (May, 1998): 201-216.
22. Hong Mautz, "Fathers are Important in Children's Behavior and Mental Development," CBS Health Watch. (May 18, 2000).
23. David Brodzinsky, Jennifer Clarke Hitt, and Daniel Smith, "Impact of Parental Separation and Divorce on Adopted and Nonadopted Children," *American Journal of Orthopsychiatry* 63. (1993): 451-461.
24. Judith Wallerstein et al., *The Unexpected Legacy of Divorce: The 25 Year Study.* Hyperion: 2001.
25. Elizabeth Marquardt, *Between Two Worlds: The Inner lives of Children of Divorce.* Three Rivers Press: 2006.
26. Mona Charon, "Liberals Discover the Vanishing Father," CIS:CRS-638 (June 12, 1995).
27. William Raspberry, "Black Clergy Warn Families are Failing," Washington Post Writers Group.
28. Bruce J. Ellis Dodge, "Father's Absence Strong Risk Factor for Girl's Early Sexual Activity," *Duke University News and Communication.* (June 5, 2003): January 30, 2007. <http://www.dukenews.duke.edu/2003/06/dodge605.html>.
29. David Blankenhorn, *Fatherless America.* Basic Books: 1995.
30. E.Michael Foster, Damon Jones, and Saul D. Hoffman, "The Economic Impact of Nonmarital Childbearing: How are Older Single Mothers Faring?" *Journal of Marriage and the Family* 60. (1998): 163-174.
31. Patrick Fagan, "Behind the Census Bureau's Good News on Poverty," *Executive Memorandum:The Heritage Foundation.* (October 12, 1995).
32. Arthur B. Elsters, M.D et al., "Judicial Involvement and Conduct Problems of Fathers of Infants Born to Adolescent Mothers," *Pediatrics* 79:2. (1987): 230-234.
33. Patrick Fagan, "The Real Root Causes of Violent Crime: The Breakdown of Marriage, Family, and Community," *Backgrounder: The Heritage Foundation.* (March 17, 1995): 8.
34. *Ibid.,* 11.
35. Geiger, *The Family in Soviet Russia.* 175.
36. Mona Charen, "A White Professor Takes on Black Crime," *CIS: CRS-368.* (June 12, 1995).
37. $35,000
38. Jack Westman, *Day Care: Child Psychology & Adult Economics,* edited by Bryce Christensen. Rockford, IL: Rockford Institute, 1989: 6.
39. David J. Eggebeen and Alan J. Hawkins, "Economic Need and Wives' Employment" *Journal of Family Issues* 11. (1990): 48-66. In "Working for Frills," *New Research.* (February, 1991). See also other issues of *New Research.*
40. Joseph Coyle, M.D., "Preschoolers and Drugs: How Young is Too Young for Ritalin?" <http://familyeducation.com>.
41. Geiger, *The Family in Soviet Russia.* 71.
42. Mark A. Fossett and K. Jill Kiecolt, "Mate Availability and Family Structure Among African Americans in U.S. Metropolitan Areas," *Journal of Marriage and the Family* 55. (1993): 288-302.
43. M. Anne Hill and June O'Neill, "Underclass Behaviors in the United States: Measurement and Analysis of Determinants," New York City: City University of New York, Baruch College, 1993.

44.   C.R.Winegarten, "AFDC and Illegitimacy Ratios: A Vector-Autoregressive Model," *Applied Economics* 20. (1988): 1589-1601.
45.   Mark R.Rosenzweig, "Welfare, Marital Prospects, and Nonmarital Childbearing," meeting of the *National Academy of Sciences.* (December, 1995).
46.   Leon Dash, *When Children Want Children: The Urban Crisis of Teenage Childbearing.* (University of Illinois Press: 2005).
47.   Charen, "Liberals Discover the Vanishing Father."
48.   Geiger, *The Family in Soviet Russia.* 110-111.
49.   *Ibid.,* 114.
50.   Whitehead, *The Divorce Culture.*
51.   Leo Strauss, *Natural Right and History.* Chicago: University of Chicago Press, 1953.
52.   Max Horkheimer, *Eclipse of Reason.* New York: Oxford University Press, 1947: 37.
53.   *Ibid.,* 46.
54.   Sartre, *Being and Nothingness.* Routledge, 2003.
55.   B.F.Skinner, "The Origins of Cognitive Thought," *Recent Issues in the Analysis of Behavior.* Merrill Publishing: 1989.
56.   John B. Watson, *Behavior: An Introduction to Comparative Psychology.* Watson Press: 2007.
57.   Allan Bloom, *The Closing of the American Mind.* New York: Touchstone, 1987: 155.
58.   *Ibid.,* 4.
59.   *Ibid.,* 9.
60.   *Ibid.,* 22.
61.   *Ibid.,* 23.
62.   Lloyd E. Sandelands, *Male and Female in Social Life.* New Brunswick: Transaction Publishers, 2001: 156.
63.   *Ibid.,* 142.
64.   Bloom, *Closing of the American Mind.* 39.
65.   *Ibid.,* 40.
66.   Strauss, *Natural Right and History.*
67.   Joshua L. Liebman, *Peace of Mind.* New York: Citadel Press, 1946: 71.
68.   *Ibid.,* 167-168.
69.   *Ibid.,* 196.
70.   Horkheimer, *Eclipse of Reason.* 30.
71.   Bloom, *Closing of the American Mind.* 247-248.
72.   Strauss, *Natural Right and History.*
73.   Thomas Roeser, "Slime Time TV and Moral Outrage."
74.   Paul Johnson, *Modern Times: The World from the Twenties to the Nineties.* New York: Harper Perennial, 1992: 689.
75.   Horkmeimer, *Eclipse of Reason.* 166.
76.   Anne R. Pierce, "Nietzsche: Possibilities for and Against Nihilism," unpublished paper.
77.   Bloom, *Closing of the American Mind.* 247.
78.   Horkheimer, *Eclipse of Reason.* 135.

4

Education without Moorings:
The Surge Forward that Leaves Innocence
and Introspection Behind

"Father! father! where are you going?
O do not walk so fast.
Speak, father, speak to your little boy,
Or else I shall be lost."

The night was dark, no father was there;
The child was wet with dew;
The mire was deep, & the child did weep,
And away the vapour flew.
—William Blake

Today's educational approach neglects the state of a child's soul on two levels. First, rather than giving the child a set of truths to believe in and standards to live up to, it arms the child with cynicism and "openness." Cynicism toward all ideas and openness toward all ideas go hand in hand, both springing as they do from a relativist philosophy. One way of bringing up children is "as good as" another; "just doing it" is a substitute for doing good; and opining is as good as reasoning as far as moral issues are concerned, the truth about any moral issue being inaccessible.

Second, rather than nurture the child's natural curiosity and desire to play, it imposes upon young children so hectic and goal-oriented an existence as to leave no room for daydreaming and exploration. Children today face this irony: They are taught to believe in nothing higher than the self (the self often being defined in terms of "identity" with the cultural group) and yet they are given no time for self-discovery. They are so laden with activities and spend so much of their time in institutions or in the company of electronic counterparts that they are left with an emptiness if they are left alone. Is it possible that we are bringing up a

191

generation of empty souls—too busy to think deeply about anything, too skeptical to believe deeply in anything, too scarred by unmet needs for nurturing to love with a full heart?

Young children today expend their energy on long days in group situations, on preschool activities and after-school programs, and on team sports and music and athletic lessons. For much-needed relaxation, they collapse in front of the TV, computer, or "play station," the now defining features of "home-life." "Relaxation" no longer signifies quiet and repose. The frenetically hyperactive pace of children's television shows and video games, always accompanied by driving music, exacerbates and surpasses the fast pace of modern life. Children stare at the screen wherein the inanity, violence, and doomsday sociopolitical messages are anything but reassuring. *From doing to staring, from staring to doing.* There is little room in this scenario for idle contentment, playful creativity, and the passionate pursuit of interests. Alternatives to this framework for living are provided neither in thought nor in deed by busy parents who, themselves, end their rushed days with television and escapism.

Love and nurture and, concomitantly, innocence have been demoted as compared to experiencing and exposure. The family is viewed as a closedness to experience, the nurturing role within the family as the most confining of all. Indeed, busyness supplants togetherness in many modern families. The frenetically busy life-style, which American parents give their children, says to the children, "We have only activities to offer you. We can no longer provide you with insight into virtue or with sanctuary from society." The private aspects of life and the search for meaning beneath the surface of life are diminished by the forward-moving drive for societal success.

The busyness of modern childhood and the myopia of the modern outlook reinforce each other. The very idea that beneficial experience is more important than being with the family is a modern one that continually reinforces itself for lack of traditional alternatives. Our busy lives leave insufficient time to question whether all this busyness is necessary and whether the content of our children's education is good.

Drive through our neighborhoods' empty streets and ask yourself not merely where the children have gone but where childhood has gone. It is most unlikely you will see a child sitting under a tree with a book, or friends engaged in collecting bugs, leaves, and sticks. Where are the children? They are in day care centers, now dubbed "learning centers." They are acquiring new skills, attending classes and after-school programs, and participating in organized sports. They are sitting at the computer, in front of the TV, and in front of the "play station." They are not experiencing the comfortable ease of unconditional love or the pleasant feeling of familiarity. They are not enjoying a casual conversation nor are they playing. They are working—at improving their talents, at competing, at "beating" the "enemy" on a computer, at just getting by, at adjusting to the new babysitter or coach, at not missing mom or dad. They are not contemplating. They are not daydreaming. They, like their computers, are "on." Being, for them, is doing, adjusting, and coping. Parenting, for us, is all too often providing things for them to do.

Before nursery school starts, most children who can afford it have participated in organized activities from gymnastics, ballet or piano lessons, to organized sports. There is constant downward pressure upon children of a younger and younger age. When sports for kindergartners first appeared on the scene, soccer, gymnastics, and tennis were preferred. Now, toddlers can be seen on football teams, in fencing lessons, and on the golf course. Indeed, golf clinics for toddlers are an emerging sensation. When my oldest son entered kindergarten, about half of the kindergarteners in his class participated in organized sports; the participation of kindergarteners in organized sports was a new trend. By the time my youngest son entered kindergarten, he was the *only* boy in his class who had not *already* participated in organized sports.

Today, tiny toddlers in uniforms gather on fields and in gymnasiums with frustrated coaches imploring them to "listen" and learn the rules of the game. At the games, parents chide toddlers in the audience for being restless and impatient to get home; toddlers often leave their own practices, only to be brought as spectators to their sibling's games, or to be put in the car to drive siblings to and from their own activities.

Infant "swim lessons," in which an instructor in diving gear repeatedly forces screaming babies underwater so that they are "forced to swim," are an unforgettably sad spectacle that began to appear in the 1990s. Because of the unsafe amounts of pool chemicals that their open screaming mouths ingest, these infants have to be closely monitored for toxicity. They also need mothers or attachment figures close at hand to hold them and comfort them after the trauma of being surrendered to a strange adult who appeared to want to drown them.

When a child enters first grade, rather than being provided with some after school relaxation which might help him adjust to longer school hours, he is provided with more "sports" and "lessons." Increasing numbers of bright young children spend after-school time with tutors or at "learning centers" to attain that ever-elusive "edge." Children in elementary school now "train" and lift weights in preparation for their sports. Football and track are new options for first graders. A recent trend in elementary athletic programs is to recruit professional coaches, due to the supposed competitive disadvantage of amateur coaching done by parents or teachers. It is now common for children to "double up," participating in two team sports at a time. An ever-increasing selection of stimulating activities lures modern families, making downtime elusive. If one attends first grade extracurricular activities, they'll likely find parents eager to discover the activities of other people's children and anxious to sign their children up for—whatever it may be. Many parents appear worried about their child missing out. Some appear jealous of the activities other parents have found. But what is the end goal of all this activity?

Children spend much of their time exhausted by activities, the purposes of which are ill defined. In asking scores of parents why so many activities are important, I rarely received a clear answer. The end, apparently, is unclear other than the idea, often expressed, that if one's child starts activities later than other children, he or she will be "left behind." Some of the more cohesive explanations I received are these: A mother described herself as being "swept along by the inevitable"; she did not want her young daughter to be the only one "missing out." A couple explained their determination to expose their toddler to a wide variety of "opportunities" so that he would know which sports he excelled in "by the time things get competitive." A father said, simply, that he saw his role in terms of "making sure his children were the best at something" and, with all the other kids starting activities at such an early age, this meant that his kids needed to start even earlier. The idea that children need activities in order to have an advantage is something ever important in a society that so values assertion and visible success.

The more families subscribe to this "lifestyle," the more there is another reason for pushing children off to the races. If no children are around to play with then, especially for young children, organized activities become their only opportunity to "play" with other children. Playing is thus thoroughly redefined.

Such priorities and such thinking become even more predominant as children enter their teens. Teenagers are not only expected to juggle academics, sports, and tutorials. They are also expected to "build resumes." Adolescents receive the very loud message that they need to "look good" to colleges. In order to look good, they are told to be "the best" in at least a couple academic areas, to show their compassion through community service, and to demonstrate their well roundedness by excelling at sports and musical instruments. Super-parents are rearing super-kids, supposedly capable of both outstanding performance in individual areas and of effortless versatility. In addition to the advantage all this activity supposedly gives teenagers, there is also the element of convenience. If parents are too busy to supervise their teenagers, it behooves parents to keep them so busy and under the auspices of so many other adults that they are more likely to "stay out of trouble."

We have become unsympathetic to exhaustion, vexation, and demoralization, seeing them as necessary corollaries to high achievement. "Come on, you can do it!" parents shout at teenagers as they "try again" to achieve the perfect pitch of the ball, the perfect ballet pose, the perfect runner's mile, the perfect musical performance. Thus, we are taken by surprise when success strategies backfire; when, instead of gaining momentum, teenagers lose energy, motivation, and enthusiasm.

American society as a whole is finally beginning to acknowledge the increasing toll of stress on our children and teenagers. Adolescent medicine specialist Kenneth Ginsburg authored an American Academy of Pediatrics report warning that more and more teens are burdened by anxiety and depression. Ginsburg was quoted in the press saying that he sees many teenagers whose bodies are showing signs of stress, whether it's headaches or chest pain or belly pain. At the extreme, he noted, he sees signs of self-mutilation. "(It's) a way of taking control of their life when they feel their life is out of control." He also sees eating disorders: "It's kids who just feel like they can't handle everything they're doing."[1]

With statistics on eating disorders, anxiety disorders, cutting, binge drinking, and other self-destructive behavior to back her up, former MIT Admissions Dean Marilee Jones warned in a 2006 interview that the quest for perfection is both "making our children sick" and damaging their creativity. "Because students are so busy all the time, because parents think that's what they need to get into college, and we in college admissions offices reinforce that, they don't get into their imagination enough."[2] She noted that not many students sleep eight hours a night, eat three meals a day, or spend time just staring into space. "Kids aren't supposed to be finished," she said. "They're partial. They're raw."[3] Eating disorders, clinical levels of anxiety and compulsion, binge drinking and other kinds of escapism, depression, and even suicide, are on the rise among teens.

A discussion of stress did not used to be necessary when it came to the average American child. Stress was a common feature of adulthood, not childhood; but, stress is no longer a word that applies primarily to adults. Websites and books on teenagers' physical health or emotional health now typically feature large sections on stress. While being careful to praise the advantages of team sports, and involvement in the community, these sites also warn teenagers not to overdo it. On KidsHealth, a website of the Neumours Foundation, the discussion of childhood stress includes the following:

> Stress can affect anyone—even a child—who feels overwhelmed. A 2 year-old child, for example, may be anxious because the person he or she needs to feel good—a parent—isn't there enough to satisfy him or her. In preschoolers, separation from parents is the greatest cause of anxiety.
>
> As children get older, academic and social pressures (especially the quest to fit in) creates stress. In addition, well-meaning parents sometimes unwittingly add to the stress in their children's lives. For example, high-achieving parents often have great expectations for their children, who may lack their parent's motivation or capabilities. Parents who push their children to excel in sports or who enroll their children in too many activities may also cause unnecessary stress and frustration if their children don't share their goals.
>
> Many professionals feel that a number of children are too busy and do not have time to play creatively or relax after school. Kids who begin to complain about the number of activities they are in or refuse to go to activities may be signaling to their parents that they are too busy.[4]

The writers go on to note other causes of stress such as disturbing images on TV or being caught in the middle of a divorce.

The Neumours Foundation "Teen Health" website advises teens on ways to keep stress under control. Included in the advise is taking a stand against over-scheduling and avoiding the demoralizing trap of perfectionism. Here are the signs of stress overload the website warns teenagers to look out for (signs educators, therapists, and parents are seeing everywhere):

> Anxiety or panic attacks
> A feeling of being constantly pressured, hassled, and hurried
> Irritability and moodiness
> Physical symptoms, such as stomach problems, headaches, or even chest pain
> Allergic reactions, such as eczema or asthma
> Problems sleeping
> Drinking too much, smoking, overeating, or doing drugs
> Sadness or depression[5]

The American Academy of Child & Adolescent Psychiatry, on its website, also advises families on ways to help teenagers with stress, stating, "Some teenagers become overloaded with stress. When it happens, inadequately managed stress can lead to anxiety, withdrawal, aggression, physical illness or poor coping skills such as drug and/or alcohol use."[6] An AACAP book entitled *Your Adolescent* includes the following sad commentary on teen suicide: "That a teenager could be so unbearably unhappy that he would choose to kill himself is something that's almost too painful for a parent to examine. But with the increasing prevalence of teen suicide, no parent can afford to ignore the possibility. Before the mid-1970s, suicide by adolescents appeared to be a rare event; now one out of ten teens contemplates suicide, and nearly a half million teens make a suicide attempt every year. Sadly, suicide has become the third leading cause of death for high-school students. Indeed, the actual rate of death by suicide may be higher, because some of these deaths have been incorrectly labeled accidents."[7]

Also in that book is a discussion of teenage and pre-teenage depression. In addition to genetic factors, depression can be related to too much parental pressure, too much familial conflict, and too little maternal nurturing:

> Depression is a complex and multifaceted condition. Likely rooted in genetic and/or biochemical predisposition, depression also can be linked to unresolved grief, possibility in response to early real or imagined losses of nurturing figures. Depression may also reflect that the adolescent has learned feelings of helplessness rather than feeling empowered to seek solutions for life's problems. Depressed thinking tends to be negative, hopeless, and self-defeating—reinforcing further feelings of depression.
>
> Some seriously depressed adolescents have experienced early life and environmental stresses, including childhood trauma . . . such as the death of a parent or significant other. They may live in families where they regularly witness or are victims of parental aggression, rejection or scapegoating, strict and punitive treatment, and parents abusing each others. Such family pressures may contribute to the development of mood disturbance in teenagers.[8]

The authors note that while, in boys, depression often translates into behavioral disturbances and acting out, girls tend to be preoccupied with their internal feelings, and "as a result, they may be acutely self-conscious about their bodies and their performance."[9]

So often we as a society look for external or abstract causes (poverty or racism) or biological causes (genetically inherited) of teenage depression, failing to look also for *personal* causes. In a peer reviewed report entitled "Exploring Stress and Coping Among Urban African American Adolescents," Anita Chandra of the Rand Corporation and the Center for Adolescent Health in Baltimore notes that, in contrast with other reports that emphasize violence and the neighborhood as the largest contributors to stress, her study of teens in East Baltimore (that used multiple data collection strategies to explore stress) found that teens saw and reported on *relationships with families and friends* within school and home settings as their primary sources of stress. Chandra declares "unmanaged stress" as "critical" for understanding chronic diseases such as depression.[10]

Further supporting the personal component of depression are findings that supportive and secure attachment relationships can contribute positively to emotional health. In 1992, S. J. Blatt and E. Homann published their findings on a connection between insecure attachment and depression and a wide range of externalizing behavior.[11] In 1999, Richard Thompson and David C. Zuroff published an article entitled "Development of self-criticism in adolescent girls: dissatisfaction, maternal coldness and insecure attachment." Describing self-criticism as a "destructive personality tendency that has wide-ranging ramifications," they found that parents who are cold, dissatisfied, and perfectionist—who "do not accept children, but urge them to do better,"—contribute significantly to adolescent self-criticism. Another contributor, they found, is earlier insecure attachment, which prevents children from ever forming a working internal model of themselves as competent and worthy. Self-criticism and perfectionism, in turn, the authors find, contribute to depression and to self-destructive tendencies such as eating disorders.[12] (Steiger et al. found strong association between self-criticism and eating disorders.[13]) Also worth exploring is a recent article in the *Journal of Genetic Psychology* called "Loneliness and Depression in Middle and Late Childhood: The Relationship to Attachment and Parenting Styles."[14]

The signs of emptiness and feeling overwhelmed are everywhere, one of the surest signs being the very visible one of "cutting." A 2006 study by the American Psychological Association reported that *nearly 20 percent* of American teens engage in self-mutilation. Said psychologist Sylvia Gearing in an interview with CBS News, "This disorder refers to various self injurious behaviors such as cutting, carving, hitting, biting, scratching and burning. It is a deliberate behavior intended to inflict pain on the body to relieve a painful or uncomfortable feeling. This is a coping mechanism and it is used to escape a painful feeling and to focus on physical pain instead. This type of self-abuse seems to serve several purposes—to relieve severe anxiety, extreme anger, and frustration or to cry for help. Whatever the motivation, the self punishment aspect of this behavior is profound." Cutting is a fast growing and "contagious" trend in high-achiever colleges. Added Dr. Gearing, "I believe self mutilation is a symptom of a high performance generation of kids who emphasized performance over psychological resiliency. When placed in a competitive

academic environment, they turn to self-mutilation as a method of soothing their overwhelming anxiety. They are simply not coping."[15] Indeed,
modern America emphasizes performance over resiliency. Another way
of saying this is that we ignore the "being" of the child for the sake of
their "becoming."

The legacy of Freud, Piaget, and Pavlov and the behaviorists, neo-
developmentalists, and social scientists who followed them has been the
decreasing respect for the child's being and the increasing emphasis upon
his "becoming." The child is seen as "socializable"; the child is studied
as a clinical object whose observable response to this and that "environmental stimulus" becomes more important than the child's deeper,
more complicated features. With the clinical interpretation of childhood,
social engineering projects gained ever-increasing currency. Schemes to
mold, shape, and construe our children into highly competitive, highly
competent achievers sprang forth, along with institutional mechanisms
for reinforcing those schemes. Recent findings regarding the "plasticity"
of the brain fed further into American society's social engineering frenzy.
Luckily, brain and anthropological research have also led to the conclusion that genes and human nature matter, that we can only do so much
to reshape human society. Our children will be better off if we refuse to
indulge the claims of those who say it is all inborn or of those who say
it is all conditioning. Then, we can acknowledge our essential role as
nurturers and educators while also acknowledging children's own role in
discovering the world and, cliché as it sounds, "finding themselves."

It should be noted that mothers will also be better off. The "it's all
genetics" argument not only ties women and girls to their biology in too
monochrome a way; it also leads mothers to underestimate their power to
do good in their children's lives. The "it's all the environment" argument
leads to the belief that parents have to plan and orchestrate every little
aspect of their child's experience and existence in order for their child to
reach their "potential." Children and adults alike deserve liberation from
these extremes. One leads to the neglect of children. The other leads to
an unhealthy obsession with children. It helps to remember that we do
not "own" our children, even though they are "our own."

It is the being of the child which, I believe, cries out for new attention
and respect, both in our homes and in our educational institutions. What
makes a young human "being" thrive rather than just surviving in today's
world? The answer is, first of all, love—the being-there kind of love which
gives a child the ability to explore by providing a firm base to fall back
upon and which provides limits to that exploration—physical, moral,

and social. The answer, second of all, is a good education—one which provides children with a firm base from which to explore, that challenges children without exhausting their emotional resources, that allows young children to believe in something while also teaching older children to search hard for the truth, and that respects each child's uniqueness but also emphasizes kindness, responsibility, and civility.

We have adopted a view of growth and education as struggle, adaptation, improvement, and expansion. Education and growth certainly include these, but they also invariably depend on what Erik Erikson calls the epigenetic principle. "Somewhat generalized, this principle states that anything that grows has a ground plan, and that out of this *ground plan* the parts arise, each part having its *time* of special ascendancy, until all parts have arisen to form a *functioning whole*."[16] This is a way of saying that human beings are inherently ready for different kinds of growth at different times in the life cycle. "Personality can be said to develop according to steps predetermined in the human organism's readiness to be driven toward, to be aware of, and to interact with, a widening social radius, beginning with the dim image of mother and ending with mankind, or at any rate that segment of mankind which 'counts' in the particular individual's life."[17] Healthy growth, Erikson insisted, happens in its own good time.

This is not to say that children should guide their own education, but it is to say that the adults educating them should take into account age-appropriate parameters. Erikson notes that grammar school education swings back and forth between "the extreme of making early school life an extension of grim adulthood by emphasizing self-restraint and a strict sense of duty in doing what one is *told* to do, and the other extreme of making it an extension of the natural tendency in childhood to find out by playing, to learn what one must do by doing steps which one *likes* to do."[18] Allowing children to avoid work and teaching children to avoid play are extremes to which there is no need to succumb. Work and play in childhood are naturally entwined.

As important as a "good education" is, we must remember that some of the best learning experiences in early childhood happen not in an institution but at home, not with a teacher but while playing freely alone or with close friends. In short, some of the best learning experiences happen in a child's independent "research" of the world at hand. As the child interprets the world around him, creates new things with the materials available to him, and extracts new ideas from the recesses of his own mind, he is learning to be an active, contributing participant in the world. He occupies the physical, temporal, and intellectual space in which he resides in a positive, resourceful way. Conversely, if he is constantly stuffed with edifying material and "beneficial" experience, resentment and or lack of autonomy are the likely result.

In an age when institutionalization and "socialization" into society's ideals is accepted, even for babies and toddlers, we should remember that institutionalization even for older children is a relatively new phenomenon. Mass education was a post-industrial revolution invention, one which served the dual purposes of preparing children for the industrial work structure and freeing parents to contribute fully to that structure. With the public schooling of children came the separation of work and family. No longer was work something which families did together as a unit. The separation of children from the family's work paved the way for schools and social reformers to assume the task of "preparing children for life." This is a lofty role. *As parents, we need to inform ourselves as to what our children are being prepared for and how they are being prepared.*

Adolescent years, in the past, often included helping parents with chores, getting an unskilled job, and gradually taking on more responsibility both at home and at school. Those years also included discovering one's own taste in literature and music, learning how to dance and chat with the opposite sex, going to parties, occasionally "slacking off" for the sake of social life, and moving gradually toward independence through close attachments with friends and falling in love. Teens still go to dances, listen to music, and fall in love, but, for many, the adolescent years are a time of already lost innocence and intense pressure. Their extracurricular camps, jobs, and experiences and their academic pursuits are often so predetermined by societal and familial expectations that they miss the opportunity to take gradual steps toward adulthood. Winnicott counseled and warned, "There exists one real cure for adolescence, and only one, and this cannot be of interest to the boy or girl who is in the throes. The cure for adolescence belongs to the passage of time and to the gradual maturational processes; these together do in the end result in the emergence of the adult person. This process cannot be hurried or slowed up, though indeed it can be broken into and destroyed, or it can wither up from within, in psychiatric illness."[19]

At the same time as they are missing opportunities for independence, they are longing for adults they can depend upon and look up to. Children learn how to be maturely independent through the predominant influence of adult role models. Ideally, those adults educate and guide them, love them and place limits upon them while also allowing them to stretch and grow. Peter Blos sees adolescence as the second phase of "individuation," the first one having been completed toward the third year of life, "with the attainment of self and object constancy." "Individuation implies that the growing person takes increasing responsibility for what he does and what he is rather than depositing this responsibility on the shoulders of those under whose influence and tutelage he had grown."[20] Blos sees the "reengagement of infantile drive and ego positions" as "an essential component of the adolescent disengagement process." Blos explains that in order to move away from someone, you have to define yourself *in relation to them*. As the teenager moves away from his mother, he uses his early close relationship with her as the base from which he grows. "Paradoxically, only through drive and ego regression can the adolescent task be fulfilled."[21] If the parental ego has "made itself available to the child" and "lent structure and organization to the ego as a functional entity," the regression will be a healthy one. According to Blos, "ego regression lays bare the intactness or defectiveness of the earlier ego organization, which derived decisive positive or negative qualities from the passage through the first separation-individuation phase in the second and third year of life. Adolescent ego regression within a defective ego structure engulfs the regressed ego in its early abnormal condition."[22] If the parental ego has not been reliably available, the regressive adolescent period can lead to a "developmental impasse," and resentment, anger, and even psychosis can ensue. If the relationship with parents was never secure and comfortable in the first place, adolescent growth can be conflicted and distorted. Blos sees infancy and adolescence as critical times of vulnerability. If the adolescent was not cared for properly as an infant, that vulnerability is acute.

As children mature, consistent parental presence, although not as "critical," is still essential. Social scientist Jean Richardson and her colleagues did a study of eighth grade students and found that those who took care of themselves for eleven or more hours a week were twice as likely to be abusers of controlled substances as those who were actively cared for by adults.[23] Extensive research by Steven Cemkovich and Peggy Giordano reveals that "maternal employment affects behavior indirectly through such factors as lack of supervision, loss of direct control and attenuation of close relationships."[24] Travis Hirschi found lack of supervision strongly correlated with delinquency.[25] A study published in the *Journal of Drug Education* in early 1997 compiled the results of interviews with 636 fifth through seventh graders in both urban and rural communities. "Latchkey kids," the study found, were three times more likely than their peers to report that they had ever been drunk.[26] As we have seen, substantial bodies of research also indicate a connection between delinquency and uninvolved or absent fathers.

Being a parent is not easy—it is full of infinite potential for fulfillment, growth, and joy—yes—but it is not easy. For, children need from their parents *both* firm limits and clear guidance (the protection of innocence) and opportunities to forge their own destiny and make their own mistakes (age-appropriate steps toward independence.). Bowlby put it beautifully in *Attachment and Loss*: "Among the characteristics of the over-controlled person are constrained and inhibited responses, reduced expression of emotion, and narrow restriction of the information processed. Among characteristics of the under-controlled person are impulsiveness, distractability, open expression of emotion, and too little restriction on the information processed."[27]

Children and teenagers long for knowledge of what is true and what is right and wrong. When their parents are incapable of providing answers or too busy to attempt answers, when "family life" allows no time for pursuit of those answers—whether through casual conversation at the dinner table or through opportunities for solitude or through books—children, especially teenagers, are more likely to turn to their peers. They are more likely to fall for faddish panaceas to the human predicament. Observed Allan Bloom:

> The family requires the most delicate mixture of nature and convention, of human and divine, to subsist and perform its function. Its base is merely bodily reproduction, but its purpose is the formation of civilized human beings. In teaching a language providing names for things, it transmits an interpretation of the order of the whole of things. It feeds on books, in which the family believes, which tell about right and wrong, good and bad and explain why they are so. The family requires a certain authority and wisdom about the ways of the heavens and of men. The parents must have knowledge of what has happened in the past, and prescriptions for what ought to be, in order to resist the philistinism or the wickedness of the present.[28]

The dinner table, infrequently inhabited due to late work schedules, sports practices, and tutorials, provides an invaluable platform for the transference of morals and manners and for intellectual discussion. A recent study, so widely announced that the results apparently came as a surprise, found that family time around the table is good for teen's development. Based on a survey of twelve to seventeen-year-olds by Columbia University's National Center on Addiction and Substance Abuse, it found a link between family meals and lowered risk of smoking, alcohol abuse, and drug abuse. The center's founder and director, Joseph

Califano, stated, "Our research has shown that if you get a child through age 21 without smoking, without using illegal drugs, and without abusing alcohol—most will drink something—that child is virtually certain to be home-free for the rest of his or her life."[29]

A good upbringing teaches children and teenagers how to relate, not just how to behave and how to succeed. It provides clear but reasonable limits, not just demanding expectations. In this kind of upbringing, the family relationship is primary. Another study released by the Center for Alcohol and Substance Abuse documents the dramatically positive effects of "hands-on parenting" by parents who see themselves as "parents not pals." These are parents "who have established a household culture of rules and expectations for their teen's behavior and monitor what their teens do: such as the TV shows they watch, the CD's they buy, what they access on the internet, and where they are evenings and weekends." Finding that children who live with "hands off" parents are at four times the risk of substance abuse as teens with "hands on parents," the CASA report emphasizes this sad statistic: "Only one in four teens in America (27 percent, about 6.5 million) live with "hands-on" parents.[30]

How we define the self in relation to the group has a lot to do with how we raise children and how we define the family's role. If we define the self as a blank slate, a tabula rasa, we will work very hard to control and program them. If we define the self as a hard shell, as a container that houses the "essence" of a person, we will push children to be assertive, expressive, and independent. One view often leads to behaviorism, the other to individualism. Combined, they lead to the idea that adults should make sure that each child "becomes" successful—however that success might be defined. These definitions are insufficient even when they are combined, for, human beings are neither automatons nor autonomous, nor are they only interested in themselves. In *Family Group Conferencing*, Catherine Love argues that the problem with the notion of the self as an independent container already full or in need of filling is that it does not take into account the part of being human that is in-between people, which occurs as a result of the *relationship* between them. Referring to Landrine (1992), Love posits, "Within this conception of self and other, self is seen as primary, with relationships being derivative (that is, the self is seen as preexisting relationships) and relationships may be rejected if they do not meet the needs of the self." "Boundary maintenance and boundary defense" become essential features of being a healthy person.[31]

Our human concerns and our language indicate that we are not so self-contained, that much of what we are lies in our relating. Someone "hurts our feelings" or "makes us feel good." We are "attracted to" or "appalled by" someone. We observe "tension in the air" and appreciate a "good work climate" or a "good home environment." There is no question that modern society needs more "individual responsibility," but what is responsibility? Responsibility exists in our own work and creativity, but it is also exists in our conduct and approach toward others.

Love discusses the saga of New Zealand social workers who were determined to help the Maoris by placing them under the auspices of social welfare. With the blank slate idea merging with the container idea, the state assumed the role of "helping" the Maoris become independent and successful members of modern society. Many Maori children were removed from their "whanau" and placed in foster care homes. It became popular to adopt Maori children, giving them a chance for success. What the well meaning social workers and adopting families did not take into account, according to Love, was how harmful it was to disrupt family relationships even if the families were poor and under stress. The Maori welfare kids of the 60s, 70s, and 80s "grew up to be the social problems' of today."[32] Delinquency and psychological problems became commonplace. Now the New Zealand social work system, along with many others, has been redesigned to be community and family based—the idea being to draw on the family's own relationships, creativity, and strengths.

Like the New Zealand scheme for the Maoris, many of our modern-American educational practices hinge upon schemes for success which push out the family and push traditions aside. The very idea that education is a race and that preschool age children's participation in "activities" is more important than playing or spending time with parents is a modern one, which continually reinforces itself for lack of traditional alternatives. Do we exhibit an extreme case of unexamined means to unexamined ends? Are we energetically working toward ends the majority has embraced with such authority that they are simply assumed? Because the ends are apparently given, are we grabbing onto whatever means are available to achieve them, so that the means are assumed as well?

Our busy lives do not allow time to question whether all this busyness is necessary or good. The possibility that children might find these activities less rather than more desirable when they are older because these activities were forced upon them at an inappropriately young age is not addressed. The possibility that they will never find their own passionate interests because they spent so much time pursuing interests their parents chose for them does not enter in. *The possibility that having a competitive edge might not be as important as leading a virtuous, intel-*

ligently thought out life is not addressed nor is the fact that one needs time to be a thinker, freedom to be creative. The suggestion that longer school years and school days and shorter recesses create more time for "information absorption" only at the expense of time for creativity and independent thought is shoved aside. The end of all this activity is vague and inadequately justified, even though the means are everywhere all around us. *There is a definite sense that, if everyone else is increasing their step, we had better increase our step too, never mind the why.* All year school and after school programs certainly fulfill a societal need. But need and preference are too often muddied, and we too often rationalize our decision to keep children in institutions all day and all year rather than thinking it through. Such is the basis of many modern choices. Children spend much of their lives exhausted by activities the meaning of which is ill defined.

Conformism and convenience are contributing factors in the hectic existence and the premature introduction to academics, which we prescribe for our children. For example, before the 1960s, it was generally accepted and believed that placing very young children in out-of-home learning programs was harmful to the child. This concern for the harmfulness of such experiences was abandoned when it became convenient and popular to abandon it. Headstart used to start at six or seven, not at infancy. Nursery schools were the exception and never lasted all day. Even all-day kindergarten was highly unusual and was originally introduced in only a small percentage of schools as a "pilot program." What started as a pilot program suddenly, and without the majority of parents preferring it, became the only program available. Dr. Jack Westman writes of the "hot-housing" movement for infants and toddlers that advocates institutional learning at a younger and younger age:

> The rapid expansion of day-care, preschool, and extended kindergarten programs has been accompanied by a widespread tendency to move the elementary school curriculum downward to younger children. In addition, many parents feel obligated to expose their children earlier to educational experiences. The result is what is now referred to as the 'hot housing' movement for infants and toddlers devoted to expediting their development. (Gallagher & Coche, 1987) This is occurring in spite of the evidence that the long-term outcomes of early didactic, authoritarian approaches with younger children relate negatively to intellectual achievement. (Sigel, 1986 a & b)[33]

The facts have been conveniently distorted to bolster modern lifestyles. In *Miseducation: Preschoolers at Risk*, David Elkind notes that those advocating early instruction in skills and early out-of-home education rely upon youngsters who are very disadvantaged at home to taut early education's advantages. "Accordingly, the image of the competent child introduced to remedy the understimulation of low-income children now serves as a rationale for the overstimulation of middle-class children." Elkind expresses dismay at the fact that age-inappropriate approaches to childhood education have gained such momentum in spite of the undeniable evidence that pushing children into academics and activities before they are ready does more harm than good:

> What is happening in the United States today is truly astonishing. In a society that prides itself on its preference for facts over hearsay, on its openness to research, and on its respect for "expert" opinion, parents, educators, administrators, and legislators are ignoring the facts, the research, and the expert opinion about how young children learn and how best to teach them. . . . When we instruct children in academic subjects, or in swimming, gymnastics, or ballet, at too early an age, we miseducate them; we put them at risk for short-term stress and long-term personality damage for no useful purpose. There is no evidence that such early instruction has lasting benefits, and considerable evidence that it can do lasting harm. . . . We can change the level of the content and the methods we use to instruct children, but we cannot change the ways in which children learn. To say that a child can learn anything at any age ignores all that we know about the growth and development of children.[34]

Elkind points to the consistent result of reputable studies such as that conducted by Benjamin Bloom showing that a love of learning and not the premature inculcation of skills is the key to the kind of "early childhood development" that can lead to great things. These findings, says Elkind, point to the fallacy of early instruction as a way of producing children who will attain eminence. He notes that, with gifted and talented individuals as with children in general, the most important thing is an excitement about and an enthusiasm for learning: "Skills are easily learned when the motivation is there. Miseducation, by focusing on skills to the detriment of motivation, pays an enormous price for teaching infants and young children what amounts to a few tricks."[35]

The last twenty years have been characterized by the exploration of "alternatives" to the age-appropriate tiering of nurturing and to education underlain by the idea that children are only ready for certain kinds of experiences and learning at certain ages. We have forgotten that childhood evolves through stages, each stage being suitable for more advanced learning than the previous one. There are "critical periods" for learning certain things. If children are forced to "learn" certain skills before the appropriate age for learning them has been reached, they may forever reveal the lack of the more fundamental skills that would allow the more advanced skills to be done well. For example, the preschool age is not the appropriate age for reading and writing, but for listening and talking, discussing, and playing. If children are taught to read too early, their reading may forever suffer from the lack of the previous freedom to explore the language through play and conversation. My first son's kindergarten teacher put it well. On parents' night, she reminded us parents, "Reading is so much more than the technical comprehension of words, sentences, and paragraphs. It is also the ideas and the understanding that go with it." She asked, "Which kindergartner is reading? The one who can read all the words but has little understanding of the story or the one who cannot decipher the words but interprets and comprehends the story well?"

At a minimum, we must heed the recent brain research which connects a young child's ability to learn with her reception of love and her feeling of security. Jane Healy states the case for allowing young children to play before requiring them to learn academic and athletic skills. She intones, "Driving the cold spikes of inappropriate pressure into the malleable heart of a child's learning may seriously distort the unfolding of both intellect and motivation. This self-serving intellectual assault; increasingly condemned by teachers who see its warped products, reflects a more general ignorance of the growing brain."[36] She goes so far as to describe the damaging effect of the "functional organization" of the brain in pushing too hard too soon:

> The same mentality that attempts to engineer stimulation for baby brains also tries to push learning into schoolchildren much like stuffing sausages. For example, some parents now wonder if their schools are any good if they don't start formal reading instruction, complete with worksheets, in preschool. Likewise, many schools have reading lists or advanced math courses for older children that look impressive but, being out of the reach of most of the students, convince them that reading or math are difficult and boring activities. I call this the "cosmetic curriculum" because it sounds impressive, but the learning is often, unfortunately, only skin deep.
> Before brain regions are myelinated, they do not operate efficiently. For this reason, trying to "make" children master academic skills for which they do not have the requisite maturation may result in mixed-up patterns of learning. As we have seen, the essence of functional plasticity is that any kind of learning - reading, math, spelling, hand-writing, etc.—may be accomplished by any of several systems. Naturally, we want children to plug each piece of learning into the best system for that particular job. If the right one isn't yet available or working smoothly, however, forcing may create a functional organization in which less adaptive, "lower" systems are trained to do the work.[37]

As child psychiatrist Dr. Stanley Greenspan insists, young children suffer greatly if there is inadequate "emotional learning" in their daily lives. The child's emotional development is, he explains, not only requisite for their ability to relate well with others; is also the foundation of cognitive learning. Warned Greenspan in an interview for *Parent and Child* magazine:

Emotional development and interactions form the foundation for all children's learning—especially in the first five years of life. During these years, children abstract from their emotional experiences constantly to learn even the most basic concepts. Take, for example, something like saying hello or learning when you can be aggressive and when you have to be nice—and all of these are cues by emotions. Your child doesn't learn to say hello because there are rules like "I say hello only to people who live near me." He learns to say hello to people who invoke a warm feeling. Even skills we ordinarily think of as purely cognitive are emotionally based. Understanding how to group things, a skill essential for later math learning, is derived from sorting out how members of the family go together—who's a sibling, who's a parent. It doesn't begin with how to sort and group squares and circles or apples and oranges.[38]

Peter Blos argued that, even in adolescence, intellectual growth could not happen simply free of emotional growth. "Without doubt, during adolescence, unique and new ego capacities or faculties appear, such as, for instance, the spectacular advances in the cognitive sphere (Inhelder and Paiget, 1958). However, observation has left us wondering about their primary autonomy and, furthermore, their independence from drive maturation. Experience teaches us that, whenever drive development lags critically behind adolescent ego differentiation, the newly acquired ego functions are, without fail, drawn into defensive employment and lose their autonomous nature."[39]

Play in childhood is important both for intellectual growth and for psychological growth. Play is both a way for children to relish the experience of childhood and a way for them to prepare for adulthood. As Simon Grolnick explains, Winnicott understood this and warned us not to underestimate the importance of play:

Winnicott's *playing*, an action concept, is *developmental play*. Play in childhood and throughout the life cycle helps to relieve the tension of living, helps to prepare for the serious, and sometimes the deadly (e.g. war games), helps define and redefine the boundaries between ourselves and other, helps give us a fuller sense of our own personal and bodily being. Playing provides a trying out ground for proceeding onward, and it enhances drive satisfaction. . . . Winnicott repeatedly stressed that when playing becomes too drive-infested and excited, it loses its creative growth-building capability and begins to move toward loss of control or a fetishistic rigidity. At normative levels, the free play of the nursery during latency gives way to the more rule-oriented play of games. Civilization's demand for controlled, socialized behavior gradually, and sometimes insidiously, supersedes the psychosomatic and aesthetic pleasures of open system play. Hopefully, the basic core of more innovative spontaneous play can still persist in the social, territorial, and even recreational games in which, by definition, we all become involved. Then the progressive capacity to regress can sometimes allow even highly social and traditional adaptors to return to the playful delights of nursery experience.[40]

It is sad to think of young children with little time for play. They are missing the multifarious opportunities that play provides for relaxing,

imagining, exploring, creating, interacting, relating, role-playing, learning, and just having fun.

In *The Erosion of Childhood*, Valerie Polakow insists upon the child's
ability to "make history" as opposed to simply receiving it. Lamenting
the over-institutionalization of children both in day care centers and in
schools, she warns, "Children as young as a year old now enter childhood
institutions to be formally schooled in the ways of the social system and
emerge eighteen years later to enter the world of adulthood having been
deprived of their own history-making power, their ability to act upon
the world in significant and meaningful ways." She adds, "The world in
which children live—the institutional world that babies, toddlers, and the
very young have increasingly come to inhabit and confront—is a world in
which they have become the objects, not the subjects of history, a world
in which history is being made of them."[41]

The minimal amount of quiet and family time children and teenagers
are permitted means that thinking and introspection are demoted as well.
For, thought requires being and not always doing. Children who are not
allowed to retreat within themselves are not allowed to find out what
is there within. Our busy lives are a wonderful way of hiding from the
recesses of the mind. Teaching children to be tough and prepared for the
world, achieving doers instead of capable thinkers, has its consequences.
Children's innate curiosity is intense. When that curiosity has no room
to fulfill itself, it burns out like a smothered flame.

It is impossible to retreat within ourselves, to think, daydream, or
invent when we are imbibing media content and imagery. And, we are
imbibing in unbelievable quantities. A 2006 Washington University study
found that "next year, Americans will spend 65 days watching TV, 41 days
listening to the radio and about a week each surfing the Internet, reading
a newspaper and listening to recorded music. —Next year's estimated
total of 3,518 hours per person spent with the media is an increase of
nearly 300 hours—more than eight days—over the average of 3,333 hours
each American spent on these activities in 2000. But it's 37 hours—a day
and a half—less than they are projected to spend in 2009."[42] Any teacher
will attest that the amount of time on TV and the computer has a direct
negative correlation to the amount of effort and thought bright students
put into their work. Teachers report on the ill effects on behavior and
learning of being computer or television "obsessed."

*The world of television and video games saps our energy away from
each other and away from our own brainpower.* A 2005 Kaiser Foundation paper entitled "The Effects of Electronic Media on Children

Ages Zero to Six" confirms this. Noting that "stimuli that optimize the development of brain architecture include interaction with parents and other humans, manipulation of environmental elements like blocks or sand, and creative, problem-solving activities," the writers also note that screen media "does not perform any of these functions."[43] They point to wide research that links media exposure to "a variety of health risks," from obesity to violent behavior and anxiety, and to research showing that young children who watch even small quantities of violent programming are more aggressive. They also note that children exposed to more violence became "desensitized," needing greater levels of violence to become "aroused."[44]

"Desensitization" is one more societal indicator of the loss of innocence. We have forgotten the age-old understanding that childhood is *not only a manifestation of but also a request for innocence.* Children who are exposed to adult situations and adult dilemmas before they are ready often spend much of their lives longing for that innocence lost.

Again, television is particularly damaging. The Kaiser document also highlights multiple studies showing that media exposure leads to poorer achievement in school and to shorter attention spans. One states that "children who watched more television at ages three, four and five (according to parental estimates) had lower grades and were rated as less sociable by their peers at age six."[45] Even "educational programming" is overrated; "the ability for children to learn from televised images lags behind the ability to learn from live, observed events."[46] In spite of all this, the authors note, studies also show that the vast majority of American parents "continue to allow and even encourage their very young children to use screen media." We simply must see regular television viewing by the young and vulnerable for what it is: a harmful way of educating them that interferes with beneficial ways of educating them and has a negative effect on how well they will perform in educational institutions. "Media influences on young children are not only strong and pervasive, but also potentially controllable—especially in the early years when parents determine the majority of their children's media exposure."[47]

Parents today face an uphill battle in monitoring the time their children and teenagers spend on the TV and the computer, but it is a battle well worth fighting. In the first study with a nationally representative sample, Dr. Douglas Gentile of the National Institute on Media and the Family, in collaboration with Harris Interactive, found that nine in ten youths reported that they play video games and that 8.5 percent (ages eight to eighteen) displayed pathological patterns of play, "exhibiting at least six out of eleven symptoms of damage to family, social, school or psychological functioning."[48] Noting that playing a lot does not in itself necessarily indicate addiction, Dr. Gentile advises parents to be alert to addiction's signs.

Television ruins family life if we allow it. I have argued that concepts of the self should not be separate from concepts of relationships. Teenagers are particularly concerned with and interested in relationships, and yet, they are often too busy to really work on relationships with family, friends, and the opposite sex. (No wonder "hooking up" is popular; there is little time in modern American life for leisurely time spent getting to know each other, and modern American culture has done away with the expectation that getting to know each is required.) Too often, they receive their ideas about relationships from television. The more exposure children and adolescents have to the ideas and morals of TV characters, and the less exposure to the ideas and morals of their parents, the less room for the growth of their own intellect and character. Parents are disparaged on television. So are teachers. Most television parents and teachers have little control over their children, little regard for them, and no exemplary or didactic behavior to offer them. On television, children are incidental to more dramatic adult happenings and, when the focus is on them, it is definitely not on their need for good parents and a good education. Teenagers are "taught" to place a premium upon a sexy, jaded, opposite-of-innocent look and outlook.

Looking through the lens of the last three decades of television, we see the ever-accelerating locomotive of debasement. In the 1980s, The American Family Association found the four major networks had an average of forty-seven incidents of sex, violence, and profanity in each hour of prime-time television in their combined broadcasts. Television actively promoted premarital and casual sex and saturated us with violence to the point of numbness. Dr. George Gerbner, Dean of the Annenberg School of Communications at University of Pennsylvania, authorized a study titled "Violence Profile 1967-1989: Enduring Hours" which found that 90 percent of programs during children's viewing hours were violent. The AFA also found that almost all prime-time families with teenagers dealt with the theme of teen sex and found that in only one episode of one show did the word marriage occur.[49] The Media Research Center found that sexual material formerly limited to the nine to eleven time slot had migrated to the "Family Hour," where premarital sex outnumbered portrayals of sex within marriage by an eight to one ratio—and was almost always condoned. As early as 1983, on "Family Ties," parents taught their seventeen-year-old son favorably about sex without marriage. His seduction by an older woman was seen as "maturing" by his father. His mother worried only that he had not called to say he would be late. Dad congratulated him, cautioned him to separate sex from love, and urged him to continue the affair.

In the 1990s, the trend of debasement—the de-personalization of sex, the dehumanizing of the individual, and the disparagement of family—accelerated. The Media Research Center found that the use of obscenities during the "Family Hour" had risen dramatically, to the point that it was "now constant in the 8 p.m. hour." In television's own rewriting of history, for example, the 1996 prime-time mini-series "Buffalo Girls" filled the screen with the illicit sex, profanity, and hard-as-nails behavior of the female characters. Swearing and sexual jokes were usually treated as funny and commonplace, never as distasteful and surprising. As another example, on the October 9, 1995 showing of "The Nanny," the title character referred to a female cousin who had "ground her teeth down to the gums," adding that her husband had "never been happier." As another example, in a September 1996 airing of "Bless This House," a man told his wife, "On the way home, we'll stop by your mother's (house) and I'll tell her what a small ass she's got."

In 2000, Brent Bozel wrote, "What was on television in 1989 is 'The Sound of Music' compared to the sewage that has taken over the airwaves today." He referred to a 1999 Parents Television Council study showing that sexual material had increased three-fold. "As with language, it's not the numerical increase but the content—what Hollywood considers is now acceptable programming for the family that alarms. Nothing, but nothing is considered off-bounds any longer. During the four-week reviews of 1989 there are no references found to oral sex. Ten years later—they found no fewer than 20 examples. In '89 there were seven references to pornography; by '99 the number was 28, an increase of 300 percent. References to different forms of kinky sex increased by 357 percent; references to genitalia were 650 percent higher; references to masturbation increased by—ready?—700 percent."[50]

In the new millennium, television's cheap depiction of human relationships continued apace. In 2003, the Kaiser Foundation released a study finding that, now, two-thirds of all shows from *seven a.m. to 11 p.m.* had some sexual content, ranging from talking about sex to explicit sexual behavior. One out of seven shows now featured sexual intercourse, up from four years earlier, when the number was one out of fourteen.[51] In addition, taboos against displaying certain kinds of sexual behavior were steadily breaking down; for example, girls kissing each other erotically were now commonplace on television. Said Jane D. Brown, a professor of communications at the University of North Carolina at Chapel Hill, "The most important message kids are getting from television is that sex should be a very important part of their lives." [52] In a BBC article entitled "Sexualization Harms Young Girls," that refers to an American Psychological Association study, sexualization is defined "as occurring when a person's value comes only from her or his sexual appeal or behaviour, to the exclusion of other characteristics, and when a person is portrayed as a sex object." [53] The study pointed out that in teen magazines, shows, and video games targeted at girls, it is now all about sex and how to look and act "sexy."

In 2007, Timothy F. Winter of the Parents Television Council testified before Congress that, between 1998 and 2006, violence had increased in every time slot and was increasingly associated with graphic sexual perversion. "In addition to the marked increase in the quantity of violence, we are seeing several disturbing trends. First, the depictions of violence have become far more graphic than ever before, thanks in part to enhanced computer graphics and special effects in television production today. Second, there is an alarming trend for violent scenes to contain a sexual element. Rapists, sexual predators and fetishists appear with increasing frequency on prime time programs. Third, we are now seeing the protagonist—the person the audience is supposed to identify with—as the perpetrator of the most violent acts. And, lastly we see more children being depicted as the victims of violence." [54] (See Chapter 1 for discussion of the way mothers and children are depicted on television.)

Television just cannot get enough of the crazed degenerate. Television shows just cannot stoop low enough to satisfy what producers conveniently perceive to be the public's ever-increasing craving for degeneracy. According to this rationalization, the "American public" has reached the point of satiety and cannot be shocked or stimulated unless the violent and sexual content is ever expanded. Premarital sex and sexual jokes are nothing compared to the scary parade of homicidal and perverted rapists, murderers, child abusers, and child molesters who march across our prime time screen. Warned Senator Robert Byrd in September 1990, "With each dose of vulgarity, profanity, pornography, promiscuity, assault, murder, and other violence, we become less and less uncomfortable with those crimes and vices, until at last our consciences lose the ability to object to them." [55]

As I was finishing this book, I decided to do a little "channel surfing" between 7:15 and 7:45 p.m. Within that short time span, a time span when children are watching television, I came across this specter: a husband and wife were sitting by the kitchen table discussing her excitement over having tickets to the "Oprah" show. The accompanying friend walks in, to whom the husband remarks, "You're finally going to get to experience the "big O." The friend responds, "Yeah, and, for all these years all she [the wife] got to experience is the 'Oh that's it?'" On another show, two women, about twenty, sit on a couch discussing how unsatisfactory their sex life is with their most recent lovers. On another show, a pregnant woman is on the table in a gynecologist's office. Her husband walks back into the room and remarks to the doctor, "It only took you two seconds to get in there. —It took me two whole days." Other shows I came across included a hard-edged crime drama and a reality show featuring models whose bodily features were being analyzed and criticized by a judge who apparently was to choose the "best one."

We are diving in a free fall toward more and more desensitizing material, and we had better tear ourselves away from the material long enough to assess it. The anti-characters with anti-morals, the desperate criminals, sex-offenders, and suicidal perverts depicted on these shows, if one stops to think about it, probably were not well-enough brought up nor well-enough loved. The same medium which focuses upon and exaggerates the byproducts of a society with twisted priorities also demeans and diminishes the very idea of "bringing up" children thoughtfully.

Of great concern is the combination of degeneracy and inanity to which any sweep through the channels exposes children. One of the defining features of our society is that, year by year, children watch more and more television and spend more and more time staring at some screen or another. Virtually all reputable studies that have been done on the subject indicate that saturation time on television and the computer affects children's behavior and moral judgment. For, the least behaviorally or morally limited behavior is presented to children who watch TV as the most appealing. As but one example, a University of Alabama study conducted by researchers Jennings Bryant and Steven Carl Rockwell shows that teenagers exposed to large doses of casual sex on TV are more likely to treat sex casually.[56]

Perhaps even more damaging is the relentless media emphasis on "sexiness," which encourages girls to focus obsessively on their looks and to put attraction above substance in human relationships. Who would have ever expected the generation that went braless and without makeup to be the generation that would absolutely inundate the young with the fake—in media images and advertising and in the whole range of media content. Even the supposedly intellectual stars and newscasters have had extreme plastic surgery. Just watch them in a movie or show from several years ago and you will see that virtually every one of today's actresses and female reporters has been remolded to bionic standards. The quest for perfection is the mantra of conformists who think everyone's body and face, especially their own, should mimic Hollywood's ideal. The more girls are exposed to the monotonous conformity of media images and idols, the less they are able to resist its insidious pressure. Already burdened by their own unreasonable expectations of themselves, imagine what it does to young women in the prime of their youth to be surrounded by older women trying to outdo them and setting an unrealistic, nay impossible by any natural measure, standard of beauty.

Sadly, brain research and MRI scans are being used to track ways to stimulate the female brain with sexy advertising images and to stimulate the male brain with violent gaming images. In *Born to Buy: The Commercialized Child and the New Consumer Culture,* Juliet Schor documents ways the development of neuro-marketing is being used to market a myriad of products and to draw in our children.[57] Studies that follow the behavior of children show that the more involved a child is in the consumer culture, the more likely the child is to be depressed or anxious or to have physical ailments such as frequent stomachaches and headaches.

Television's influence is dramatic, as it desensitizes children to violence and makes them leery of the very concept of morality, prodding them to instead focus on sexiness, success, and power. In a New York Times article entitled "What TV Drama Is Teaching Our Children," Herbert London found that, for children who watch television regularly, who are therefore repeatedly exposed to the idea that "the end justifies the means," (that successful people do what is necessary to get ahead) the end does indeed justify the means. These students readily admitted that they would engage in immoral practices as a last resort to succeeding in business. Children Now, a national children's advocacy group, conducted a nationwide poll asking 750 children between 10 to 16 years of age how television shapes them. More than two-thirds said they are influenced by television. More than two-thirds said that shows such as "The Simpsons" and "Married . . . with Children" encourage disrespect for parents. At least these two shows have a redeeming quality compared to most shows targeted at adolescents; they are sometimes clever as opposed to incessantly inane. (The effect of sheer stupidity upon children whose cognitive "advancement" we care so much about it should not be underestimated.) "An overwhelming majority of young people polled also said that television should help teach them values, but instead often showed people getting away with—and sometimes triumphing by—deceitful behavior or physical aggression." According to the National Institute of Mental Health, there is "overwhelming" evidence that television violence leads to aggressive behavior in children and teens. Recent research by Thomas L. Jipping confirms this. Jipping found that "more that 1,000 studies going back almost forty five years have established a connection between media violence and aggressive behavior in society."[58]

The fact that many of us allow media figures to manipulate and distort our children's thought processes and moral sense in these ways points to the larger problem. Our dismissal of innocence as practically irrelevant allows us to excuse all kinds of actions which would otherwise be inexcusable. It allows us to put down the guilt we would otherwise feel when our choices turn out to be disadvantageous to the child. A TV show ends up giving our child nightmares, or hardens a child to behavior which should be repugnant, or inspires the trying-out of crude, brutish behavior. Excessive, relentless exposure to computer games and hand-held electronics impairs a child's ability to think clearly, to relate well, or to concentrate. I have heard parents rationalize their decision to allow very young children to see popular movies with explicit sex scenes and graphic, titillating violence with the hypothesis that "those scenes go right over their head." (These children must have unusually impervious heads.) Hours upon end at video games, I hear, "improves hand-eye coordination." (Never mind the child's ability to coordinate his thought processes with the real world!) Educated parents who allowed their toddler to watch "Are You Afraid of the Dark?" explained in unison that their child "likes the show and swears it doesn't upset him." (Since when does a terrifying show not scare four year olds? Have we forgotten our own youthful reactions to much more innocuous material?)

Not only does television cater to the base and the low. It also takes full advantage of its tremendous propaganda potential. Children's television is a glaring and unforgivable example of hidden adult purposes. "Quality" television is as guilty as any other in this respect. For example, of the four "Sesame Street" shows I watched when my children were young, three had a clear underlying agenda. One of the shows depicted a girl singing about girls who like trucks and boys who like dolls—part of the never-ending attempt of my generation to de-masculinize boys and defeminize girls. (The only "Sesame Street" show I came across showing a girl with a doll showed her using it as a football.) Another "Sesame Street" show demonstrated the devastating effects of the logging profession. Loggers were contrasted with concerned puppets singing about the worthiness of trees. Another show included a song apparently entitled, "We're a family." This song contained the didactic message that no type of family is preferable to another, and it implicitly warned children against feeling sorry for themselves if their family unit was not intact. All different types of family situations were described: living with just mom, just dad, just grandparents, with mom and her friend, etc. The "Barney" show, although generally uplifting and sweet, occasionally featured a similar song about all the different family situations which are just as good as any other. The song implicitly reprimanded children who think having a mom and a dad around is the best situation of all! The show was released for video.

I only mention "Barney" and "Sesame Street" because they are evidence of how early these messages are disseminated, and on "quality" shows. These messages have been continually transmitted in innumerable other televised mediums, and in much more explicit and harmful ways. As but one example, a 1993 *after school special* entitled "Other Mothers" focused upon the injustice of a boy being ostracized because his "parents" were lesbians. Apparently, the lesson provided by this show was thought to be so important that it overrode any considerations about whether the very young children who would be watching television at such an hour were ready for such a subject. On "Friends," watched by sizable numbers of preadolescent children, casual sex and the unraveling of "traditional" relationships were continual themes that provided a source for sarcastic jokes and audience laughter. In a typical episode on March 3, 1997, there was a lengthy conversation about sexual arousal and women's breast sizes. Ross's wife planned a romantic dinner with her lesbian "wife" to celebrate their anniversary. In another episode, Joey finally learns to accept his sister's (sensible) decision to give birth to her baby without marrying its father. Joey is shown to accept with ease his friend's decision to have *her* child with marrying the father; it was his inability to see his sister's situation objectively that made him slow to come around.

Although such shows might be useful in helping children to accept their own and others' family situations, whatever they are, the danger is that it discourages them from striving toward an intact and committed relationship when they are older. If relationships are defined in terms of sexual preferences, if just about any situation constitutes family life, and if the very idea of getting married for the sake of children is disparaged, then what incentive do children have to be good and faithful husbands, wives, and parents? Lest children aspire to some sort of "traditional" family situation, educational programming "teaches" them not to be so narrowly focused. On non-educational television, the sexual options are displayed appealingly to them, like so many candies beneath a glass counter. Also shown as optional are commitment, love, responsibility, and kindness. Given all the emotional and intellectual advantages of being brought up in a loving, considerate, intact family and of having both mom and dad around, one has to question whether the casual discarding of the age-old definitions of parents, mothers, and fathers is really done out of compassion and concerns for diversity. It is not that we should be closed to alternative family situations but, if we are to extend our compassion and concern to children, we must be open to the benefits that come from two-parent families. *To be closed to the very idea of the traditional family is to focus too much on adult preferences and not enough on children's needs.*

The "options" presented to older children on prime time television show no limits. As Randall Murphree, editor of the American Family Association Journal, puts it, "prime time (gives) us every conceivable form of unconventional domestic arrangement and (calls) each a family."[59] As early as 1986, Newsweek reported that of the networks' *sixty eight* weekly series that season, *only three* focused on a traditional family: mother, father and blood-related children. CBS's Kate and Allie once defined a family as any group of people who care about each other and want to live together. As examples of this theory: In a 1992 episode of "Civil Wars," the protagonist, dealing with a lesbian divorce case, supported the non-biological "mother's" right to sue for custody of a child she helped raise. In 1993, a Herman's Head protagonist contemplated obliging a lesbian friend's request to "father" her child. Put together, these uses of the words mother and father imply (a) that whoever "looks after" a child is a "parent" and (b) that being a (biological) parent need not imply taking care of a child and being part of a child's life. As Newsweek put it, "Mom and Dad are being shoved out of the picture."

Again, the mountains of evidence documenting the negative effects of divorce and "single parenting" and the positive effects of a secure, stable childhood base and of "attachment" should be enough to stop us in our tracks no matter how ardent our fervor. As Netherlands researchers note in an article entitled "Adolescents' Attachment Representations and

Moral Reasoning," substantial bodies of recent research have confirmed "attachment theory" not only as it relates to later socio-emotional and cognitive functioning, but also as it relates to moral development.[60] Ohio State University sociologists Sharon K. Houseknecht and Jaya Sastry put it succinctly: "Children are better off when they live in a society in which traditional family patterns are strong."[61] In an examination of data collected from four industrialized nations, the U.S., Sweden, Italy, and West Germany, they discovered a correlation between family structure and six measures of children's well-being: academic achievement, child poverty, infant mortality due to abuse, juvenile delinquency, drug abuse, and suicide. When family decline was greatest, the well-being of children in all of these respects was most jeopardized.

While children watching TV are exposed to a multitude of "options," the one option they are not permitted is innocence. Innocence—either sexual or political—is close to impossible for television watchers. On vacation at Christmas time, I agreed to allow my young children to watch "Cartoon Christmas Hour." We "settled into" the show anticipating an uplifting experience. The first show alluded to the fact that Santa Claus is imaginary by showing the cartoon children in bed while their father, dressed as Santa, placed presents under the tree. The second show did even less for our Christmas spirit. It revolved around a group of young chipmunks and their grandfather. One of the chipmunks had discovered a hard to identify item while wandering in the forest. It turned out, as grandfather explained, that this item had once belonged to "humans" who, he explained, were now extinct. He told the frightening story of how the humans' failure to realize the danger of nuclear weapons had resulted in their annihilation. Flashbacks of people in gas masks, bombs aflame and cities exploding, marched across the screen. The cartoon ended with Grandfather Chipmunk imploring the little Chipmunks to learn the lessons of peace that "the humans" had ignored—so much for innocent Yuletide pleasures.

Appalled by this "Christmas hour," I began to watch cartoons in the morning, a time I would assume, devoted to preschool age children. Approximately half of the new shows I encountered contained some sort of socio-political message. These messages were so ridden with resentment and anxiety they were sure to impair the innocent spirit of the young. On one day, every single show I came across had either an environmental, a feminist, or a political message. (I took notes.) The first show depicted a flower come to life. The flower befriended a cute little lamb which, it turned out, was destined to die at the hands of humans

who would slaughter him for food. The show ended with the flower singing a song of lament for her lost friend. The next show began with a girl
running carefree through a field of strawberries. She made the mistake
of eating one. Suddenly, the carefree and pretty girl became deathly ill.
Her parents, frightened out of their minds, discovered that her illness
was caused by the pesticides in the strawberry field. The show revolved
around the search for a cure, finally found in a magical antidote provided
by a wizard. The third show provided the animated depiction of a knight
who learned his lesson. He underestimated the princess to whom he was
betrothed and had failed to realize that she was a better warrior than
even the strongest of men. He vowed never again to view women as less
capable fighters than men.

This was the most recurring didactic theme I encountered in children's
programming. Boys were put in their place as they learned that the girl
they had underestimated was stronger than them, smarter than them, a
better athlete than them, and a better fighter than them. As one more
example, a modern video rendering of "Encyclopedia Brown" edited a
girl into the story. This girl was the tough replacement of Encyclopedia's
intellect. Whereas, in the book, Encyclopedia defeats a bully through
humiliation, proving he was lying about the authenticity of a Civil War
Sword, in the video rendering the humiliation comes in the form of a
knock out punch from the girl. Of all the characters in the video (almost
all male), she is the only one who resorts to physical violence. She gives
a bully twice her size and a man five times her size daunting blows.

Advertising executives reinforced the girl-power mystique. I am reminded of the Nike add showing a girls' basketball team and boasting of
them: "They are not sisters, they are not classmates, they are not friends:
they are not even the girls team. They are a pack of wolves."

In order to assure the victory of their image of reality and to ensure that
no other image has a chance, many feminists have attempted to monitor
the books children read and to ban certain classics from the classroom.
Children's books and history books are sanitized and robbed of their
original meaning and content. In an article entitled, "Mother Knows
Best," Bruce Frohnen provides examples of educational tools and books
that are so formulated as to be more indoctrinational than educational.
(All American parents have encountered many such "books and tools.")
When androgyny and, in particular, the teaching that girls are as tough
as boys is not the goal, proving the superiority of female to male is.
Typical, says Frohnen, is the introduction to a guide to "nonsexist books
about girls for young readers" entitled "Little Miss Muffet Fights Back."

It shows "Little Miss Muffet, with curds and whey on her lap, her rosy cheeks and cherubic smile rendered macabre by the spoon raised in her hand, set to smash the hapless spider dangling in front of her." This guide provides an annotation for a story entitled Petronella: "A smart and plucky princess rescues a prince from an enchanter by passing three dangerous tests with wit and bravery. Unfortunately, the prince is a fool and the princess goes off with the enchanter instead—a wise choice, though so clever a princess might have questioned marriage itself."[62]

Frohnen, who lives in Portland, Oregon, describes the Portland library system's "Guide to Role Free: Non-Sexist Readings for Children:"

> "Role-free" is a veritable goldmine for the seeker of androgyny. (On) the cover . . . one girl apparently is about to knee one boy in the groin, while the other girl holds his friend at bay, wrestling his arm out of the way. Inside is a listing of "good" books that emphasize nontraditional roles along with a listing of other bibliographies such as *Little Miss Muffet Fights Back* and, of course, *Girls Are People, Too!* . . . And Little Miss Muffet would make our children so by recommending books that, for instance, depict female bullies. After all, kids "might as well know early" that bullying knows no gender. Praise be.[63]

Such "guides," says Frohnen, recommend for the young reader such books as these:

> Judging from books such as *My Mom Travels a Lot, The case of the Scaredy Cats, Mitch and Amy,* and *Anastasia Krupnik,* there has been some success in this endeavor. Father "caringly" plays with his daughter while Mother is away on business; young girls oust girl-hating boys from their fort through physical violence because they are insulted by the boys' bigotry in not letting them join their club; a young girl learns from her friend's hippie mother (complete with Volkswagen bus, knapsack, and a filthy house) that there are more important things in life than cleanliness, an ordered family life, and personal responsibility; a ten-year old girl discusses poetry with her academic father and sexual encounters with her artist mother while planning to name her soon-to-be born brother something I cannot bring myself to cite in a family journal, but which tougher ten-tear-olds are invited to read and laugh at, along with other less anatomical four-letter words which "children hear all the time."[64]

We are all familiar with such books, difficult to miss, wherein the message is "that once women overcome the handicaps imposed on them by Western society's history of male oppression—the traditional refusal to allow the female to compete—the female is superior to the male, even at his own games." Modern American families have been bombarded with books that, as Frohnen puts it, "reflect reality" in a way that promotes the break-down of the traditional family while denigrating those who aspire to it. We must stop and think, however, if we are ready for the consequences of the obsolescence of the feminine and the disparagement of manhood.

We must stop and think if we are ready for the consequences of holding up for emulation girls who are "tougher" than boys. Of course, we need to give girls the same opportunities we give boys and we need boys to respect girls who partake of those opportunities. Given the tremendous propaganda potential of television, we must be sure that girls with talents and strengths are favorably depicted. But we needn't depict girls as uniformly "aggressive" to do so. Nor do we need to depict boys as stupid and arrogant to do so. Wouldn't true respect for girls include respect for girls who are less interested in "action-games" and physical aggressiveness than boys, but who have their own invaluable intellectual or athletic strengths? *Do we really want the world to become more uniformly masculine?* The world suffers from an excess of violence and a deficiency in reason. Why, then, do we downplay girls' ability to discuss their way out of difficulties and instead hold up for admiration girls who can fight their way out of difficulties? It is but another form of sexism to insist that there is only one path to female assertion.

Reformers depict femininity as highly uncool. In popular culture, raw sex appeal is advocated while femininity is proscribed as a harmful idea perpetuated by males. Girls are taught to subsume feminine, nurturing tendencies into harder, aggressive ones and to sublimate the longing for the love of a man into the bodily desire for sex and sexiness. What a strange inversion of the Freudian idea of sublimation!

There is the documented need to build up girls' confidence in the early adolescent years, years when girls have been known to downplay their academic strengths for the sake of popularity and appealing to boys. Many tremendously successful books such as *Reviving Ophelia* have been written on the subject. Some of those books were misleading. An article by Jeanne C. Bleur and Garry R. Walz argues that a hugely influential report of the U.S. Department of Education in 2000 entitled "How Schools Shortchange Girls" "was just completely wrong" and that "what was so bizarre is that it came out right at the time that girls had just overtaken boys in almost every area."[65] "Based on an extensive analysis of data from the National Longitudinal Study (NLS), the high School & Beyond (HSB), and the National Education Longitudinal Study (NELS), Riordan (1998) concluded there is no evidence for a one-way gender gap favoring males beyond 1992 in public secondary schools. As of 1992, females possess a significant advantage on most central educational outcome indicators. Boys, rather than girls, are now on the short end of the gender gap in many secondary outcomes." In spite of this, throughout the 1990s, the media mantra remained firmly in the camp of schools shortchanging girls.[66]

Now, the fact that just the opposite is true has become so obviously apparent that even the media and popular books are asking, Why are boys falling behind girls in every conceivable educational category? School administrators are wringing their hands over unmotivated, uninspired, under-achieving boys. Colleges have gone so far as to lower admissions standards for males, the relative quality of the male applicant pool has so declined. As Tom Chiarella put it in an article in *Esquire*, "If you're a boy in this country right now: "You're twice as likely as a girl to be diagnosed with an attention-deficit or learning disorder. You're more likely to score worse on standardized reading and writing tests. You're more likely to be held back in school. You're more likely to drop out of school. If you do graduate, you're less likely to go to college. If you do go to college, you will get lower grades and, once again, you will be less likely to graduate. You'll be twice as likely to abuse alcohol, and until you are twenty four, you are five times as likely to kill yourself. You are more than sixteen times as likely to go to prison."[67] *All signs indicate that we went too far in putting boys in their place.*

In empowering girls, we degraded boys, depicting them as relatively superficial and incompetent. Now, the boys who grew up under the watchful eye of our Orwellian scheme to make the sexes the same are in high schools and colleges, some of them living up to the image we gave them of themselves. We should have been careful that we were not indoctrinating girls and that we were not demoralizing boys. We need to be sure that we are not so "correct" that we are false—that we are not so extreme in casting our brave new world that we leave no room for human nature. We need to show girls and boys both that we will work hard to bring out the best in human nature—but not that we will take it upon ourselves, as did Hitler, to reinvent the human race. Our role as parents and educators should not be that of propagandists. Again, in encouraging girls to achieve great things, we do not have to hold up a masculine model as to how those things might best be achieved. Nor must we encourage boys to do things in a feminine way.

In an article in *News And Views,* Jeffrey Leving and Glenn Sacks argue that the "boy crisis" in our schools has something to do with the trend toward "lessons in which there are no right or wrong answers, and from which solid conclusions cannot be drawn." Such lessons, say Leving and Sacks, tend to frustrate boys who see them as pointless. They also point out that the emphasis on women writers and women's issues has gone so far as to push aside "the action and adventure literature which boys have treasured for generations." Some of the "subtle and reflective works" hold "little interest" for preadolescent boys.[68] Let me stipulate that I would not take this line of thinking so far as to support the "boys will be boys" cliché. Too often this is used, simply, as an excuse for reckless or narrow-minded behavior. The best educators find a balance between teaching boys and girls in ways that are comfortable to them and uplifting them by intellectually stretching them beyond their comfort zones.

We need not enforce the idea that femininity precludes brains, accomplishments, and vigor. Nor do we need to deprecate the accomplishments and unique attributes of males. Why should there be only one kind of intelligence, one kind of assertiveness to which we all surrender? Do we really desire such a dull and uniform world? The answer to a more equal society surely cannot be to insist that girls and boys deny their natures altogether. I cannot imagine anything more "oppressive." The answer might instead include affirming that femininity, and—yes—desirability, are perfectly compatible with a strong, active mind. The answer might include a reminder that "popularity" is fleeting and insignificant compared to intellectual growth, moral integrity, and independence of thought. The answer might also include expectations that both boys and girls act civilized, that they demonstrate respect toward each other, and earn respect from each other.

Boys and girls are taught to deny rather than to ennobolize their natural tendencies. Boys are taught that all boys are insensitive, that society is inherently chauvinistic, and that they are inevitable byproducts of that society. At the same time, they are exposed to video games and media displays wherein girls are nothing more than titillating "images." Boys today receive these conflicting messages: They should apologize for their masculinity; they should tame it; they should understand that masculinity does not "really" exist. Girls are taught that they are victims of a false feminine, maternal ideal, that the femininity and masculinity which they feel to be real is actually "socialization." At the same time, they are exposed to the brutish and violent images of men upon which box-office hits often depend, to actresses who emphasize sexiness over substance, to glamorized images of superficial girls, and to articles and advertisements that show them how to lure men or boys into bed and suggest new ways to enjoy sexual encounters. Neither these stereotypes nor these hypocritical images will do much to help boys and girls respect each other or themselves. *What is sadly lacking in both feminist propaganda and in society's sexist images is any suggestion as to how boys and girls might behave kindly and gently toward each other.* Girls and boys have as their model for behavior the modern indicators of resentment and aggression.

Contributing to aggressiveness in our society, boys are not permitted to acknowledge the influence of masculine hormones, everything being a product of "socialization." Some are therefore unequipped to deal with the sensations those hormones inevitably create and to tame those sensations when necessary. Unable to acknowledge their innate masculinity, they are less likely to control those masculine impulses which are sometimes detrimental to girls. They lack the age-old resources used to curb the male's aggressive instincts. Today's male is less likely to seek an understanding of feminine and masculine differences. He is also more likely to hit his wife, to sexually molest his daughter, to abandon his pregnant girlfriend, and to have sex without obligation, commitment, or love. The concept of the gentleman, which arose in part from the desire to control the violence and irresponsibility of medieval men toward medieval women, has been cast off with abandon by my generation. But wishing men were not masculine does not make it true. We cannot wish away the male tendency toward more aggressiveness than women. We can, however, by understanding that tendency, aim to civilize young men. But in order to do this we must reinvent the concept of the civilized.

Instead of abandoning the concept of the gentleman, we should have improved upon it so that it included respect for a woman's mind and her capabilities. The idea of respect, which was inherent in the idea of the gentleman, should have been used against the paternalism which was also inherent in the idea. The concept of the gentleman was not without fault but neither was it without worth. Again, before we destroy traditions, we should ask whether it would be better to improve upon them, perhaps updating them to suit modern society.

For most of us, the mere living with boys and men has made it impossible to buy into the androgynous ideals held up for emulation, however hard many of us have tried. Anyone with respect for the truth finds it difficult to deny the innate differences between the sexes. (For those for whom living with a husband, a father, a brother, or a son is not enough proof that boys are different, the biological and behavioral sciences have now provided us with proof, mentioned above.) Mothers of young boys tend to be astonished by the extent to which their offspring live up to "male stereotypes." Today's woman shakes her head at her young boys' obsession with gadgets and mechanical objects, with cars and trucks, with weapons and swords, with building things and wanting to know how things work. They are appalled when the child to whom they have forbidden toy guns, manages to turn carrots, building blocks, and even dolls into weapons. They find it cute, but surprising, when their boys seem to need to know everything there is to know about such things as light bulbs, fans, and motors.

Girls often seem more attuned to nuances and less attuned to "things." They are generally more interested in the role-playing of social situations. They are likely to find backhoes and garage door openers relatively uninteresting. As a general rule, boys tend to be more wildly physical than girls are. My son's six-year birthday party was typical. The boys repeatedly ended up on a heap on the floor and actually seemed to enjoy being there! I was constantly worried that the bottom one in the pile would be smothered. The girls looked at the boys aghast and were much more interested in verbal interaction.

I was in a playgroup with other mothers which started when our babies were only six months old. Right from the beginning, the boys preferred each other; the girls preferred each other. Right from the beginning, they showed different interests and different ways of interacting. While the girls as toddlers frequently showed an interest in what the mothers were saying to each other, the boys never did. Their focus was more on what they were building, banging, or taking apart. As much as parents try to socialize these tendencies out of boys and girls, the tendencies tend to be there.

Science writer Deborah Blum was similarly impressed with the innate masculinity of her two boys. She ended up writing a book entitled *Sex on the Brain,* which documents biological differences between male and female brains and explores the inevitable influence of emotions and hormones on our thought processes. Such differences, she demonstrates, go much deeper than "culture" and cannot be explained away by it. (See Chapter 1 for the neuro-biological evidence of differences.)[69]

In our attempt to liberate adults, we have shackled children, depriving them of the earnestness of youth. We do this not only by exposing them to adult situations and adult stresses, but also by burdening them with our grudges and our causes. The popular culture some of us have embraced and many of us have tolerated presents the very confusing message that masculinity and femininity are both wrong, while simultaneously urging girls to be more masculine and boys to be more feminine. Making the message even more confusing, as if allowing the repressed to rear its head in distorted forms, the entertainment industry ballyhoos exaggerated, fake sexiness in females and exaggerated, fake physical strength in males. The educational approach some of us have embraced and many of us have tolerated marks our children with cynicism, apathy, and a disrespect for past ideas. Gone is the idea of giving children something to believe in before we arm them with the tool of "critical analysis." Gone is the idea of starting with the basics, whether the basics be defined as playing with blocks before learning to read or learning to respect and understand the Western tradition in which we are all situated before going on to criticize it.

In an age where we place so much emphasis upon input as opposed to output, when we fill children up with experiences and experience while allowing them little opportunity to fill their own days, we seem remarkably unattuned as to just what we are filling our children' days with. Recent years have been characterized by the reformulation of many American schools and universities according to a relativist, left-leaning ideology rent with contradictions. This ideology leaves students with little moral-intellectual ground to stand upon as they are taught disrespect not only for past ideas and literary works but also for the American political system and Judeo-Christian ethics. Modern American education has failed and is failing to give American children a sense of common belonging to and mutual pride in an American tradition and to give them a set of moral-intellectual standards. Most children are, for example, neither appreciative of their "right" to liberty and justice nor mindful of the diligence required to preserve those rights because the backdrop to the events of 1787 is never explained to them.

Not only the American tradition but also traditions in general have been disparaged by many modern educators. Teaching children about the great thinkers, writers, and statesmen of the past is too often neglected, as the very ideas of greatness and heroism are disputed. No old work or historical fact can withstand the onslaught of the trend of judging people, works, and deeds of the past according to their adherence or lack thereof to feminism, "openness," and multi-cultural sensitivity. Thus, the respect for greatness, which might have caused children to glance their eyes upward toward something nobler than their present TV show, and the stories about their country's founding ideas and traditions which might have given them respect for a time when computer games did not exist, are not a large factor in their lives. The word *preoccupied* acquires new significance, for children's minds are stuffed with the here and now.

American schools have been given the job of providing students with a "social conscience." For the sake of this cause, school curriculums have been routinely reformulated. *Before* many American children know who the founding fathers are, they are taught that the American move westward was based upon an injustice to the American Indians. *Before* they are taught about George Washington, they are taught about Martin Luther

King's assassination. Therefore, they fail to understand that King wanted our country to live up to the principles inherent in the founding. It is not unusual for children to learn about the Vietnam War before they learn about the Revolutionary War. They, therefore, fail to understand that the ideas used to criticize the Vietnamese War were the very revolutionary *American* ideas of liberty, equality, and self-determination. They are more likely to have a negative opinion of Richard Nixon and Lyndon Johnson than they are to have a positive opinion of Thomas Jefferson and John Adams, let alone any knowledge of them.

"Environmental concerns" are taught in a backwards and age-inappropriate way as well. Before children learn how a tree grows or, simply, to appreciate a tree's beauty, they are taught to despise the loggers who have chopped so many trees down. Before they have had a chance to revel in nature's magnitude (perhaps by taking a happy first grade walk through the woods), they are taught to worry about the rainforests. Before children know the first thing about the animal kingdom, before they can define the word "mammal," they are taught to despise the hunters who have caused certain species to be endangered. Told over and over again about the need to "Save the Planet," they are frightened at a very young age regarding impending environmental doom.

In short, before children are taught to believe in anything, they are taught not to believe in anything— that is, except self-expression and cultural identity—nebulous and difficult concepts for children whose lives are spent in group activities and for whom "culture" is defined in terms of distant customs on distant shores. Rather than being asked to think about the American culture in which they reside and to find common ground therein, they are asked to identify their "cultural roots," the implication being that any "roots" worth talking about are non-American ones. The shore they are actually standing on is, seemingly, irrelevant.

The modern concept of cultural identity has thus, ironically, contributed to children's sense of uprootedness. This concept takes the ground out from under children *by implying that the ground they are standing on is not theirs*. It belongs to some other—i.e. the affluent white male. It encourages them to identify with the culture of their ancestors (who lived elsewhere). They are urged to "appreciate" other cultures (located elsewhere). Children are taught to seek their identity as a distinct caste—resisting and even despising the American "norm." They are taught that American culture has been too ethnocentric to understand each person's calling to cultural identity. That this teaching is the teaching of alienation and dissatisfaction is rarely addressed. But it is precisely that.

This demotivating teaching contributes to the phenomenal numbers of teenagers who are apathetic and alienated. If the culture they are taught to identify with is other than the one which surrounds them—both physically and intellectually—then to be a member of American society signifies not freedom but, instead, imprisonment. Underprivileged children are taught not, "This is my country and I will improve upon it," but rather, "This is *their* country and I will resent it." Thus, are students who need inspiration most in order to move out of less fortunate circumstances taught that hard work and good character do not pay.

The unspeakable truth is that multiculturalism, as it has been defined so far, has often been deeply damaging to the groups it "represents." For the multiculturalist's "representation" of certain groups is underlain by the demoralizing idea that American society is not representative. If the affluent white male is the only segment "empowered" by society and government, why even try to compete in such a society and government? Competing in such a society, logically, would require rebellion. This is not to deny that there have been injustices in our society toward which alienation and defiance were *well justified*. The Civil Rights Movement is a proud and fine example. The Women's Movement before it was distorted by propaganda is another. But when alienation and defiance become goals unto themselves, overshadowing the goals of integrity and truthfulness, we fall prey to stereotypes and slogans. *Such slogans and stereotypes are valued because they mobilize people, not because they reflect reality.* The politics of resentment which has won so many votes for so many politicians succeeds because children are taught at an early age to resent that which they are not required to understand.

Multiculturalism is a very good thing if it means that we enjoy and strive to understand different cultures, that schools teach about other cultures, that we are proud of our ancestry, and that we beware the complacent, jaded eye of self-satisfied Americanism. It is, for example, a good thing for children to try to understand the Native American perspective during the frontier days. If, however, the old textbooks that evaded that perspective are replaced with new textbooks which evade the perspective of the frontier-person, then we have replaced one imbalance with another.

As adults have taken sides in the culture wars, children have become guinea pigs in educational schemes designed to defeat "the other side." If we value diversity, why can't we pull from the best in both the traditional and the progressive methods? There is no need to abandon tradition in order to make progress. At the same time, there is no need to lump all progressive educational ideas into one negative category. Why not acknowledge that conservatives are merely pointing out the truth when they say that classical education has been deconstructed? Why not also acknowledge that the progressive move toward "child centered" education emerged in response to a rigidity that sometimes stifled creativity? I believe that the best schools are those that allow young children to be playful, while also having clear expectations about what children need to learn; that encourage teenagers to question and think for themselves, while also instilling the lessons of history and the moral-philosophical foundations of political liberty.

Unfortunately, multiculturalism has been twisted by the agendas and, yes, the biases that hide behind it. It is often a code word for anti-Americanism. And it is often riddled with distortions. In the 1960s, schools, starting with the universities, were told by students and by social reformers to change their lists of required courses and to change the content of courses toward the cause of eliminating racism, sexism, elitism, and any American or Western "bias." With great misgivings on the part of many professors as to what this would mean for academic freedom and excellence, schools, typically, caved in. Better to give in to interest groups than be branded reactionary. Allan Bloom, who experienced the overhauling of the Cornell University curriculum which was mimicked in countless other universities, described the process:

> The social sciences were of interest to everyone who had a program, who might care about prosperity, peace or war, equality, racial or sexual discrimination. This interest could be to get the facts—or to make the facts fit their agenda and influence the public. The temptations to alter the facts in these disciplines are enormous. Reward, punishment, money, praise, blame, sense of guilt and desire to do good, all swirl around them, dizzying their practitioners. Everyone wants the story told by social science to fit their wishes and needs. . . . Thus, it was in social science that the radicals first struck. . . . Historians were being asked to rewrite the history of the world, and of the United States in particular, to show that nations were always conspiratorial systems of domination and exploitation. Psychologists were being pestered to prove the psychological damage done by inequality and the existence of nuclear weapons, and to show that American statesmen were paranoid about the Soviet Union. Political scientists were urged to interpret the North Vietnamese as nationalists and to remove the stigma of totalitarianism from the Soviet Union. Every conceivable radical view concerning domestic or foreign policy demanded support from the social sciences. In particular, the crimes of elitism, sexism and racism were to be exorcised from social science, which was to be used to fight them and the fourth cardinal sin, anticommunism.[70]

As Bloom noted and as many others confirmed, it became impossible to question the radical orthodoxy without "risking vilification, classroom disruption, loss of confidence and respect necessary for teaching, and the hostility of colleagues."

A friend of mine who is a professor of American History at a prominent liberal arts college has been repeatedly chided by the chairman of the department for using the Declaration of Independence, The Federalist Papers, and the Constitution in her early American history course! Such documents are considered too Western-elitist for consideration. When applying for her position, she had been very careful to mask her respect for the American founders. Other colleges had rejected her outright when she had admitted her respect. In September 2004, the John William Pope Center for Higher Education Policy released a study of the eleven universities of the UNC system. The study shows that students can earn their degrees without ever taking courses that used to be considered fundamental. Students can graduate without taking a single course on American history or Western civilization, although most of the schools have a "cultural diversity" requirement. Great literature, too, is optional.[71] At least, in the UNC system, such courses are *available*. In perusing college websites, I was sad to see that, in many highly respected colleges and universities, courses in American history, the American political system, Western civilization, and classical literature are not even an option.

For the sake of avoiding an American or Western or elitist or male orientation, many schools adopted what Bloom called a "cafeteria-style" approach to education, wherein requirements were all but eliminated and students partook in a little bit of this culture and a little bit of that—a little bit of this country's literature and a little bit of that. Most schools no longer required that students read great works, for the very idea of great works was "elitist" rather than egalitarian and too many of those "so-called" great works were written and achieved by white, Western males. If historical facts had to be distorted and literary standards lowered in order to produce a more "representative" education, then so be it.

Often, rather that being taught about the history and the literary roots they have in common, students are required to look for their roots in ways which pull them apart. Their hodgepodge curriculum fails to give them the opportunity to understand the society in which they are all ineluctably "rooted." *It is not that understanding other cultures is unimportant nor that Western students should focus exclusively on Western ideas or literature—that certainly would be narrow-minded. But we must provide students with an understanding of the moral and intellectual ground in which they reside.* Like it or not, that American ground has its imprint on us all. Like it or not, it is our greatest recourse against our degeneration into "interest groups" with nothing in common and nowhere to go but apart.

College students often learn about *their own sub-culture* and associate mainly with those who will confirm rather than expand their horizons. Indeed, it is now possible to go to college to, in effect, *study oneself* and to choose an entire curriculum that reinforces oneself. If one is woman, one can study women; if one is a feminist, one can focus on courses that confirm that viewpoint from every angle imaginable. African Americans can live in all black housing and study black culture. Once again, it is balance between the new and the old that is absent. It was good to add feminist and black history courses into the college curriculum, just as it was good to offer more courses in non-Western culture and ideas. It was not wise to throw out the old curriculum. In an article entitled "The Mushing of America," Thomas Sowell argued that there was an anti-intellectual consequence of the rush to multiculturalism:

> To challenge the buzzword of the hour by demanding evidence is to betray your age—and your recalcitrance in the face of attempts to raise your consciousness. When the buzzword "diversity" is used, all brain cells are supposed to stop functioning, so that a rosy glow of feeling can take other. Nothing is more rigidly conformist than "diversity." Use the generic "he" and it proves that you despise women. Fail to keep up with the ever-changing names for various racial and ethnic groups, and it proves you are a racist. In an age when four-letter words come easily to people's lips, you cannot use the four-letter word "work" without offending the hopeless or a word like "quota" without betraying depths of malign intentions to all sorts of groups. Neither logic nor evidence is considered an acceptable excuse for violating the taboos against questioning sacred buzzwords. . . . Issues are presented in terms of how you "feel" about this or that situation, not what structures of logic or what reservoirs of information are necessary for dealing with it responsibly. . . . Mush is self-reinforcing. As fewer and fewer people are trained to analyze, those who do can be considered mere oddballs, and both our personal and our national decisions can increasingly be made on the basis of mush.[72]

We have robbed American children of a common thread, of common traditions wrought in the founding of the American political system and in the incorporation into that system of important philosophical ideas. Moreover, we have deprived them of the goal of the "melting-pot," which, even though imperfectly achieved, had until recently been steadily advancing throughout our nation's history. The melting pot idea served the larger idea that all cultures—Western and non-Western—had a place in American society so long as they assimilated to the basic American principles of liberty, equality, and justice. Of course, the melting pot idea should never require the self-effacement of "ethnic groups" nor should it require their "forgetfulness" of their ancestry. (It is true that the ideal of assimilation can go too far.) We must remember, however, that most immigrant groups were drawn to this country because of the promise of assimilation into a free society, not in spite of it. Agreeing on the foundations of liberty means agreeing to respect fellow citizens' rights and to live in peace with those with whom we disagree or are very different from us—and expecting that respect in return. It is a force of liberation, not oppression.

Anyone born into this country is born into its traditions and ideas. Only those who are educated about those traditions and ideas have the capacity to understand American society or to improve upon American society in a thoughtful way. A knowledge of those traditions helps us to acknowledge our debt to those ideas while at the same time preventing us from being unknowingly appropriated by them. In encouraging each student to search for their own authentic course, we have deprived them of an understanding of their history and, hence, rendered that self-aware-ness superficial. At the same time, we have deprived them of alternatives to current ways of thinking, thus rendering their search for self even more narrow. Warned Bloom, "Freedom had been restricted in the most effective way—by the impoverishment of alternatives."[73] We have fallen prey to the parochialization of knowledge. In *The Leveling Wind*, George Will describes the consequences well:

> It has taken humanity eons to rise—the portion that has risen—above the fallacy that all knowledge is parochial and is the property of particular groups. Today we must be vigilant against people who would retribalize knowledge. They say there must be a black theory of this and a woman's perspective of that and so on. Schweder says, "The authority of a voice has a lot to do with what is said and very little to do with who says it."[74]

At the same time as children are taught that "culture" is a particular group phenomenon, they are taught that "values" are individual rather than universal. In other words, part of seeking identity—whether for a person or for a group—is to define one's own "values." Values are opinion rather than truth, bearing no significance broader than the individual. Oddly, then, the call for cultural identity can contribute to the demeaning of group assertion. For, any assertion by any cultural group is said to be (merely) indicative of their group perspective and bears no significance beyond the group itself. This is but one of the inherent contradictions of relativism. The underlying message of the teaching that we must free ourselves of our American bias is that *all* opinions are biased in their ethnocentricity, i.e., tainted by the environment from which they spring! As Bloom argued, if all cultures are valid but none are superior, then nothing really is to be learned from other cultures other than an open-ness to their "life-style;" the study of history and philosophy are debased because they no longer provide us with insights into truth but, rather, merely into the opinions of other peoples in other places and times. To be really open to everything is to be closed to reason's possibilities, to be closed to understanding cultures as they truly are. Openness is not openness after all if it requires us to shut down reason in favor of opinion. Of the Greeks, Bloom noted that, to them, a culture was "a cave." Plato "did not suggest going around to other cultures as a solution to the limitations of the cave."[75] Nature, he taught, should be the standard by which we judge our own lives and the lives of other people.

Given the modern outlook wherein everything is a bi-product of "culture," searching for a nature beyond the "bias" of culture is useless. Still, the extreme advocates of this viewpoint are usually willing to "appreciate" any culture so long as it not "Americanized." They often base this appreciation upon an untruthful exaggeration of our nation's shortcomings and a glorification of other cultures, which ignores their faults. By celebration of surface aspects of other cultures, such as costume and dress, schools are able to ignore the political and social oppression which often lies beneath the surface. Moreover, they can ignore the fact that these cultures are not, themselves, "open" to other cultures, but instead view their own as superior.

It is by now apparent that those same people who insist upon seeing the world as chaotic and indeterminate, who refuse to set intellectual standards for our young, also insist upon seeing individuals as "determined" by their political-economic-cultural-racial environment. It is upon this basis that they see every action of the American government as underlain by selfish economic motives, every action of American corporations by the social-economic agenda of the white male, etc. As I have argued, determinism and relativism grow from the same soil. For, both are based upon the assumption that every truth is "particular," in that no truth has universal validity. Each person's agenda is his or her own and, in the eyes of the determinist, stems from the environment to which she is affiliated. No wonder many educators regard the U.S. with such cynicism. To them, the universal principles of life, liberty, and the pursuit of happiness are not universal but, rather, are rooted in the particular "interests" of the American founders. They view the highly principled Farewell Address and Gettysburg Address as explained away by the economic motives of Washington's and Lincoln's particular "class." Thus is the American child taught not to believe in the validity of American principles, to see the American experiment as *important* for human freedom, or even to consider that there are crucial lessons in our history.

As in the case of day care centers, many of today's schools lie in the thralls of a grand social experiment wherein we accept and teach something not because human nature, history and reason tell us it is true, but because our social conscience dictates that it *should* be so. In *The Devaluing of America*, William Bennett observed that, starting in the 1960s, rather than being taught to live up to certain standards and to refer back to certain historical examples of greatness, many American children from kindergarten to college were being taught to "change the culture." The idea was that in order to change society, we have to change the way children think; the task of changing society could then be passed to the next generation. At the same time, many children were being led into "values clarification programs" which urged them to find and define their own "standards" apart from the American norm. But, intoned Bennett, the "values clarification" movement "didn't clarify values; it clarified wants and desires. This form of moral relativism said, in effect, that no set of values was right or wrong; everybody had an equal right to his own values; and all values were subjective, relative, personal."[76] This philosophy, which undermined the example-setting role of both parents and teachers, too often left children without "values" to refer to other than their own whims. Bennett questioned the insistence upon defining individual identity in terms of the socio-economic group and individual preferences, believing that the more important indicator of a child's identity is their education (or lack thereof) into virtue. He wanted educators to "empower" children by teaching that they are not determined by cultural group, economic status, or race. He urged children to set their sights high toward standards of academic performance and good character, which go beyond the satisfaction of wants. "What determines a young person's academic, sexual and social life are his deeply held convictions and beliefs. They determine behavior far more than race, class, economic background or ethnicity. Nature abhors a vacuum. So does a child's soul." He added, "and if the world can't decide what the best things are, at least to some degree, then it follows that progress, and character are in trouble."[77]

Both the seeking of self in the cultural group and the search for one's own "values" contribute to the atomization of American society. If there is no common political-social ground and if there is no truth beyond the individual definition of it, it behooves each of us to seek power for *our* opinions and for *our* group. This is the opposite of civic-mindedness. George Will described this "postmodernist" approach:

Postmodernism is all about the wielding of power, because it is not—it cannot be—about anything other than power. It has no content other than the assertion of any proposition, any book or any mind is arbitrary, or the result of race of ethnicity or sex or class, and deserves no more respect than any other content of any proposition, book of mind. . . . The ideas are profoundly dangerous. They subvert our civilization by denying that truth is found by conscientious attempts accurately to portray a reality that exists independently of our perceptions or attitudes or other attributes such as race, ethnicity, sex or class. Once that foundation of realism is decried, the foundation of a society based on persuasion crumbles. It crumbles because all arguments necessarily become ad homonym. They become arguments about the characteristics of the person presenting a thought, not about the thought.[78]

Thus are American children taught to discover their own roots and their own "values" at the same time as they are taught that foundations and values are essentially meaningless. Thus does the modern approach to education, in spite of its lip service to self-esteem, undermine a child's confidence. For, it reminds him or her that his or her opinion is only that—one opinion among many, all meaningless in the end. The hypocrisy of those who teach that all opinions are relative while inflicting upon children their own causes is, of course, unapparent to the children themselves. They, by nature, want to believe the messages they receive and are vulnerable to adults who push their particular agendas in the guise of "openness."

At the same time as the self-esteem movement encourages children to "feel good" about themselves, it fails to provide them with the opportunities for accomplishment upon which real rather than phony self-worth is based. Children are often taught that they are "victims" of an elitist-sexist-capitalist society; then, they're told to feel good about themselves. But people do not feel good about themselves merely because they are told to. Rather, they tend to feel good about themselves if they *are* good, if they *are* productive, and if their parents have given them the love, the limits, and the encouragement they need to move forward. Recently, the self-esteem movement has fallen into disfavor. Its failures were too obvious to ignore. Observed columnist Georgie Anne Geyer:

The whole self-esteem movement . . . is nearly as removed from any genuine reading of human nature as is bilingual education. It believes that young people will develop self-confidence by being told endlessly that they are good and worthy. No one has to do or perform or prove anything: They just need to "be." This, not unexpectedly, has led to the next step,. which is the dumbing down of our school curricula so no students can feel bad about themselves, even while the country itself is declining, but genuine self-esteem comes from early, rational parental discipline, which gives children a sense of protective and moral love, from schooling in the traditional arts and sciences, and from having to prove oneself in a society that knows what is important and nurtures it. It seems to me that America is only now beginning to realize what our busy-busy social engineers in the education establishment, academia and much of government have really wrought.[79]

Some schools have set up character development goals to repair some of the damage done by an over-emphasis upon self-esteem. We must beware, however, of those who use character as a front for the instillation of *their* hidden agendas. So too, we must beware of those who would usurp the role of the parent. Non-religious schools should not have to "teach virtue" per se if the lessons of history and literature to which they expose children foster a love of learning and give examples of good character and if the schools have clear rules as to acceptable and unacceptable behavior. Schools should be able to require civil behavior of children and to demonstrate a belief in "right and wrong" and in basic kindness without going so far as to usurp the parents' role of "bringing up" the child. Schools clearly need to emphasize virtue more than they have in the last twenty years, but not to the point of replacing one form of social conditioning with another. We can heed Bennett's call to take the education of virtue more seriously, while at the same time being careful that knowledge, not ideology, is the overriding parameter of education.

Children today are floundering in a sea of hidden adult purposes. In the meantime, the age-old intention of early education—to teach children the "basics," (so that they may, if they wish when they are older, pursue advanced studies from solid foundations, so that those who do not pursue such an avenue will nevertheless have the same advantageous beginning); to teach them the self-discipline and good study habits which will enable them to work hard at something; to instill in them respect for others and respect for self which are a basis of civilized society; and finally, to teach them to appreciate "great works" and "great ideas" (so that those who are so inclined may someday strive for greatness and so that all can benefit from exposure to the best thinkers and artists)—is gone.

It should be admitted that there are ways in which the unraveling of the "basics" has paved the way for creative ideas. Some schools today do a wonderful job of encouraging the love of learning and the process of learning as opposed to the "by rote" assimilation of set material. In some schools, the developmental approach includes the idea that even young children should be able to take an idea and "run with it." In my child's second grade class, children had the opportunity to do "research" on topics of fervent interest to them. Each student then became an "expert" about something and shared his or her knowledge with the other students. As controversial as "inventive spelling" is, I have witnessed the way in which it frees up very young children to become "writers," as they express ideas without the fear that the worthiness of an idea is less if the spelling is wrong. Of course, children need to learn how to spell correctly, and "inventive spelling" should not preclude spelling requirements. It should not be taken to extremes. But the creativity and curiosity of young children is so intense that we should do what we can to fan the flame. As we begin to admit that a "back to basics" approach is requisite, we must be careful not to define the basics in dry, burdensome terms. Reducing recess is one of the saddest proposals along these lines. The "spirit" of inquiry must be the propeller of education.

Wouldn't it be wonderful if we could take some of the recent innovations in education which encourage children to think deeply and independently and combine them with academic requirements which would allow that thinking to be rational and *informed*? Without knowledge of early American history, for example, children will either fail to appreciate and understand the source of our liberty or they will be appropriated by the American tradition (or reactions against it) without awareness of it. The perils of throwing academic standards and the inspiring story of our history out the window should have been obvious. More and more parents and teachers see the pattern: the curriculum is watered down and made deadly dull by political correctness. Test scores plummet. The tests are changed. The curriculum is geared toward the tests. "Outcome-based" reforms legitimize the pattern.

Let us look at third graders being educated with today's popular approach. They know next to nothing about George Washington. They know nothing of the Constitution or the Declaration of Independence. Their school has, however, had a multicultural celebration. Each child's family was to bring to school something to do with their cultural heritage. Walking through this festival, children experience vibrant, exciting examples of other cultures—colorful costumes, lovely music, pleasing aromas, and posters of beautiful places suited, it seems, to an idyllic vacation. Nothing is said about any of the injustices which occur in any of these places. Nothing is learned, for example, about the oppression of women in many Muslim countries, the prevalence of dire poverty in India, political chaos in Indonesia, the lack of freedoms we take for granted in China, or the horrible evils inflicted upon certain groups by the past regimes of Germany, the Soviet Union, and Japan and currently in North Korea and the Sudan.

By the time of fifth grade, these students are learning a lot about American history and "culture" and, quite contrary to the upbeat feeling created by the international festival, the mood is downbeat and discouraged. These young students are taught to view any action and words of the American government as suspect, to look at it "critically." The American founding, they are told, was based upon an injustice to minorities and economic expansionism. Thus, when and if they do read the Constitution and the Federalist Papers, they read them with the jaded eye of worldly college students. The words of the founders are treated as mere "fronts" for selfish intentions.

If they come across Washington's Farewell Address, they will fail to hear its message about America's peaceable mission and fail to take seriously its warning about the dangers to our unity of viewing politics as an interest-group phenomenon. When they come across the Gettysburg Address, they will fail to appreciate the insistence upon traditional American principles as a way out of slavery. Lest they grasp onto the hope that America stood for something noble in World War II, their hopes are quickly dashed by the false teaching that the post-war U.S. committed "economic imperialism" which was just as unjust as Soviet imperialism.

In an article entitled *Hiroshima Mon Petit*, Charles Krauthammer laments the "deliberate disturbing" of the "cozy, rosy view of the world" of elementary school children. Lest they would tend toward some sort of faith in their country, that tendency is squashed. If American institutions or American government has committed the wrong, the wrong is divulged to them in graphic detail with no perspective provided as to reasons and events behind the said injustice. On the other hand, if someone or some country has committed a wrong against American institutions or government, the injustice tends to be treated in a "value-neutral" way. Krauthammer's dissection of three "historical" books targeted toward seven-year-olds—yes, seven-year-olds—is worth our attention:

> When America is the cause of suffering punches tend not to be pulled. Consider three picture books—all designed to reduce children to tears about the American bombing of Japan in World War II. The most notorious of these, the one that in 1980 helped launch the whole trend toward social realism for kids, is Hiroshima No Pika, a shockingly graphic picture book about the dropping of the atom bomb and the horrible deaths that ensued. The book is not coy about who caused the suffering. It identifies the offending country, the military service, the plane, even the bomb . . . It notes additionally that among the dead at Nagasaki "were people from many other countries, such as Korea, China , Russia, Indonesia and the United States." These are about the only historical facts in a story otherwise devoted to burning flesh and dying babies as seen through the eyes of a seven year old. Faithful Elephants: A true Story of Animals, People and War is more subtle. It describes how the animals in Tokyo's Ueno Zoo were put to death by their keepers for fear that the bombing of Tokyo might set them free in the city. The Japanese protagonists, the zoo keepers, are portrayed most tenderly. There is not a hint, not a word about the motivation—let alone the humanity—of those manning the "enemy planes." Might our children be told amid their sobs how this war began? My Hiroshima, another searing picture-book memoir, is typical. It has

this single sentence of historical context: "In the winter of my fourth year at school, a big war started." Again, no one is asking for a picture book on the Bataan death march. But if we must—which I deny—introduce our seven-year-olds to the agony of the a Pacific war, might we not start with a bit of historical honesty? These books go beyond the robbing of innocence. They are a perversion of innocence. They don't just forcibly bring the young to face with evil. They lie about it.[80]

It is not that children should remain indefinitely ignorant of their country's faults. There is, however, an age too young for such learning. It is important, moreover, that children are taught to understand their country's institutions and principles before they are taught to disregard them. And with understanding, with the truth about those institutions and principles (with the truth about, for example, the Second World War) would come respect. For, there is *truthfully* much that is noble and noteworthy in our history. When children take for granted their own belief in equality and justice for all, accusing their own country of failing to live up to those principles, it is often because of a failure in their education. These children have never learned that their principles stem partly from their Americanism. Propaganda must never take the place of truth.

Our democratic-liberal tradition has been criticized to the point that, for many of us, to be an American is to be a cynic about the possibilities for goodness in government. Many of those who went through school in the sixties, seventies, eighties, and nineties were bombarded with the trend, perpetuated by left-leaning interpreters of American politics, which sees any moral arguments in support of American policies or, for that matter, any non-economic arguments as "mere rationalizations for economic motives." Clearly, we should not blindly believe everything that is said in support of American policies, but neither should we blindly ignore it. We can misrepresent ideas (and American history) as much by being overly skeptical as we can by being overly believing. Should we, for example, ignore Abraham Lincoln's principled and ideological arguments against slavery simply because he also had economic reasons to oppose it? This requires not only disregarding the principled speeches he and his secretary of state, William Henry Seward, made but also ignoring the very history of the Republican Party. And yet such a narrow interpretation of the Civil War is perfectly standard fare for many high school students. The truth is that the Republican Party was able to form a political consensus against slavery by insisting that the Northern way of life was superior in *both* an economic and a moral sense. We see in Lincoln and Seward the tight intertwining of moral and practical concerns in that "free labor" was seen as both more dignified and as more productive. As Eric Foner demonstrates in *Free Soil, Free Labor, Free Men,* the fundamental achievement of the Republican Party before the Civil War was "the creation and articulation of an ideology which blended sectional interest with morality so perfectly that it became the most potent political force in the nation." Lincoln and his party reinvigorated the principles of the founding, finding those principles totally incompatible with the institution of slavery:

> Through their examination of history, ironically, they were rediscovering the antehistorical state of nature Locke had described. Lincoln explained that the new territories of the West were still in a 'state of nature' and that it would therefore be criminal to introduce slavery into them as the British had once introduced it into the colonies. . . . The Republicans saw their anti-slavery program as one part of a world-wide movement from absolution to democracy, aristocracy to equality, backwardness to modernity, and their conviction that the struggle in the United Sates had international implications did much to spread their resolve. They accepted the characteristic vision of the United States as an example to the world of the social and political benefits of democracy, yet believed that so long as slavery existed, the national purpose of promoting liberty in other lands could not be fulfilled.[81]

For both Lincoln and Seward an irrepressible divergence existed not merely between the Northern and Southern way of life but also between democratic principles and slavery. They rightly saw that slavery was a gargantuan, horrific violation of American ideals.

Should we, as another example, ignore the fact that Harry Truman, in spite of being the architect of America's entrance into European geopolitics vis-à-vis the Cold War, admonished against a self-aggrandizing approach not only to foreign policy but to life in general? In an interview with biographer Merle Miller, Truman voiced a sentiment he alluded to many times as president, "Nowadays in politics and just about everywhere else all anybody seems to be interested in is how much he can get away with. And I don't like it. I don't know what's going to become of us if everyone starts thinking and acting that way." As I discuss in an earlier work, traditional American principles of generosity and fair play, of equal rights for all nations and all men, of self-determination, and of freedom and justice for all, according to Truman, sustained us as individuals within a community and as a community in relationship with the rest of the world.[82] They were the reasons we fought the war and they were part of the reason we won it. They were the basis of our postwar plans for others and for us as well. Without these principles, Truman counseled, we were but one power among others. With them, we were a nation and people with a particular vision and purpose which could demonstrate for all the world to see the advantages of its way of life and its peculiar dreams.

In order to have lasting influence over the hearts and minds of mankind, Truman believed, we had to do good and be good. Truman, like Washington and Lincoln, articulated the practical advantages to both individuals and nations of leading a virtuous (democratic) life. Truman warned, however, against treating our democratic ways as "mere" means to an advantage. He taught that democratic principles should guide democratic interests and not the other way around. He continually focused upon the spiritual-philosophical underpinnings of democracy. Both religion and democracy were, he said, "founded on one basic principle, the worth and dignity of the individual man and woman."

We must ask whether we are doing our children a service or a disservice when we teach children about Truman's skillful construction of "containment" of the Soviet Union through the forging of alliances and the building up of "the national security state" while leaving out as "mere rationalizations" all the principled pronouncements he gave in support of these measures. Who are we to discount every speech he made, every homage to principle? In interpreting American history from the perspective of economic selfishness and geopolitical strategizing we run the risk of rearing children who are themselves selfish and who themselves know how to strategize to their advantage—but do not how to discern right from wrong. We do students an injustice if we refuse to allow them to view the principled waters in which the American regime, even if imperfectly and inconsistently, has been bathed. In removing traditional American concerns from their view, we detach them from complexity and pave the way for the simplistic political analysis of today, which prefers labels and slogans to careful analysis.

American students have been bombarded with the single-theme view of American politics which denies discontinuity and depth in American political life. For example, various historians and politicians, most notably, the "consensus historians," have viewed American "exceptionalism" as a deterrent to a sensible foreign policy. Richard Hofstadter, Louis Hartz, George Kennan, and others have suggested that isolationism and internationalism are two sides of the same coin. One chooses to ignore the outside non-liberal world. The other chooses to deal with it but only insofar as it is molded to become liberal like us. Although I agree that the tendency to see the world through the guise of our own liberal values has at times caused us to ignore the unique aspirations of other peoples and at other times to neglect the exigencies of power, I disagree that the American "mission" is one unchanging idea that we passive Americans have been appropriated by ever since its inception. Can Hartz be sure that Americans are simply appropriated by the liberal ethos or is it possible that they propagate it and adapt it to the present because it works for them and because there is truth in its principles?

> Consensus writers seem to be appropriated by their own preconceptions. For example, Sakvan Bercovitch's idea that the American Revolution, the Civil War, the imperialism of the 1890s and the women's movement are all minor variations of a 'singular middle class scheme' is underlain by his assumption that the only change which can truly be *called* change is one of class struggle. The fact that Americans agree over a middle class way of life can only be seen as a consensus regarding America as such if class is the only way by which we account for our identity. If other factors are viewed as equally important, the changes in our past can be recognized *as* changes... A failure to recognize change would allow politicians to hide behind the rhetorical guise of upholding America's "mission" without defining what *they* mean by it. The acknowledgment of change both prevents us from clinging to an idyllic past and prevents us from rejecting the past altogether under the pretext that in order to improve, we must destroy.[83]

Throughout their history, Americans have found ways to improve upon American life without destroying the American dream. From the time of Washington to the present, American ideals have had political punch and have been essential both to defending and criticizing American policies. They have been used both to steady and to change the American course. Would the American experiment with imperialism in the 1890s have been abandoned with such distaste and haste and would the Vietnamese War have seemed such an outrageous extreme to so many Americans if Americans had not been taught that self-determination, the peaceful settlement of disputes, and the universal concern for individual rights were an essential part of the American tradition? The difference between the American rejection of imperialism in the 1890s and the American rejection of the Vietnamese War in the 1960s was that the former was rejected on the basis that is was alien to American principles, whereas the later was rejected without a realization that the very principles we were using to reject American policies were traditional ones.

By the 1960s, our forgetting was starting to overshadow our remembering. We were beginning to forget our foundations. Marxist leanings on the part of many educators allowed us to believe that the country which, more than any other nation in history had stood for universal freedom (albeit imperfectly and with deviations from that path), was itself "imperialistic." Rather than viewing transgressions from principle as transgressions from our American/Western roots, many viewed such transgressions as endemic to democratic-capitalism. While focusing obsessively on Western mistakes, many of us appeared to stop caring about the incredible, horrific suffering then being endured by citizens of Communist regimes.

It would do us well and would do our children well to think hard about what it means to be an educated American. The diluting of standards in American schools is symptomatic of a rejection of standards in general. It is symptomatic of the conviction that standards are nothing more than opinions, all opinions (and all regimes) being relative. As parents, we must ask that our schools put the pursuit of truth above the pursuit of political ideology and social plans. As teachers, we must be careful to balance the spirit of inquiry with that which makes inquiry worthwhile in the first place—the quest for truth. In asking students to pursue truth, we reveal that we believe in such a thing and that academic pursuits are meaningful. We must respect both the curiosity and the innocence of young minds. We must either demand the same from television or insist that our children turn the television off. We must draw a fine line between encouraging adolescents to be skeptical enough to "see through" dogma and weak arguments, and going so far as to encourage cynicism itself.

The early surrendering of our children to adult agendas; the early surrendering of our children to institutions; the inordinate amount of time young children spend with adults hired to take care of them; their premature introduction to sports, academics, and activities of all sorts; the ruination of the very concepts of nurture and nature; the distortion of historical facts and the subjection of literature to modern formula; the influence of "value-free" teachers appropriated by left-leaning ideas; the ever-increasing power of the media and the ever-declining position of the family are but some of the trends which leave our children without a home base as it were. Why do we fail to provide our children with a foundation upon which and from which to grow? Warned Anthony Harrigan, in *The Acceleration of Modern History*:

> Our minds are conditioned by what is strictly contemporary, as though every human being were compelled to adopt a single way of life and mode of thought. We should realize that this is a fundamental goal of totalitarian societies which are a distinctly modern phenomena. One suspects that moderns are over-specialized, over-concentrated on the knowledge derived from a small band of time. . . . And with the over-specialization and concentration I have referred to has come a diminishment of a sense of awe about life, which surely is dangerous inasmuch as the story of human life is the story of the unpredictable occurring—the happening that can't be calculated. [84]
>
> One of the most disturbing of modern phenomena is the inability of many people to take seriously previous eras and the people who lived in them. There has been the fear in modern times—in connection with totalitarian societies—that children born into an Orwellian world would have a consciousness and a conscience completely sundered from the consciousness and conscience associated with the pre-totalitarian

world. And one must also wonder—and, yes, fear—that the children of today and tomorrow will lose all contact with the values and time sense of the past and not miss at all what they haven't known personally—and this in a democratic society. If this fear proves to have been justified, the future will be a cemetery of values.[85]

We must resuscitate our memory of that time in childhood when all social and political knowledge was new knowledge. We mistakenly assume that little ones know the basics, so we proceed on to the minutiae of information which pleases the information-oriented society in which we reside. We proceed on to history's and our own country's low points, *forgetting that children do not yet know history's high points.* We provide children with lectures about "openness," forgetting that a child's mind is not closed in the first place. On the contrary, wonder, awe, and eagerness to learn are part of a young child's make-up.

We expose young children to complicated, sophisticated political, social, and environmental messages, forgetting that the child does not yet understand what politics, society, and the environment are. Our forgetting of what a child knows and does not know leads us to raise "forgetful" children, who know little of any mental framework other than the current. For, the "basics" of history, the fundamentals of education, the fundament of family, and the guiding concept of virtue are too often missing from their lives.

As we have seen, the insistence upon early academic instruction for toddlers and group "activities" for young children and the grooming of children toward "correct" social and political viewpoints are connected. In both cases, human nature and its limitations are overlooked for the sake of the larger cause. That it is children's nature to learn and play as children and not as adults is ignored for the sake of giving children the edge over the competition. That children need their parents on a steady and continual basis is ignored for the sake of "women's liberation." That boys and girls are, by nature, different is denied for the sake of "gender equality." Admirable principles and traditions of the American regime are downplayed *to the point of being lied about* for the sake of instilling in young minds an "openness" to other cultures. But are our children free if they are only exposed to that "truth" that fits our *projected* vision of reality? Reality has to include the perspective of time.

We have convinced ourselves that children "can take it" whether "it" refers to early academic instruction, long days in institutions, a frequent change in care givers, inanity and perversion on TV, early knowledge of adult shortcomings, or early awareness of the cruel misdeeds of history, especially those of the U.S. We tell ourselves that children will become more "tolerant" (rather than more jaded) if "critical thinking" replaces "understanding," and pursuit of preferences replaces the pursuit of knowledge. *We have forgotten that innocence is connected to the possibility that goodness is real.* If the adults in a child's life are not good to him and do not value his childhood; if the adults in his life inform him about the bad and teach him to be skeptical of the good, the child will not be innocent for long.

As I have argued, the devaluing of innocence stems in part from the devaluing of virtue. If there is no virtue, there is no *reason* to protect innocence. If virtue were acknowledged as vital to individuals, relationships, and communities, as it should be, then we parents would take more seriously our roles as protectors of the innocent. We would shield our children from the insidious television. We would build for them a strong inner foundation, knowledge of right and wrong, and belief in the goodness and sincerity of those who love them—a foundation which will become their sanctuary and repose from the corrupting influences of life.

A startling example of the dismissal of innocence came from an acquaintance of mine. She decided to go to law school in another town and to leave her four-year-old behind to live with her parents. She explained to me that the "child would never remember this time" when he was older. This was the true disregarding of innocence, for it showed not only that she viewed her child's experiences through her own adult perspective but also that she viewed her child's adulthood as more significant than his childhood. What mattered was what he would "remember" as an adult, not what he was feeling as a child—as if the child would not live on in the adult.

Innocence is vital. Innocence allows children a freshness, vitality, and creativity which artists since there was art have tried to recapture. When we let children into a hardened adult world, we risk putting out their flame. Once a child's need for trust in their world and in their parents is threatened, the child's fresh approach to life is jeopardized. The child is required to adopt a defensive posture. She holds her innocence at bay for fear that it might allow the world to get the best of her.

We "baby boom" parents, who so rejected the impersonal quality of corporate life when we were young, have surrendered our children to institutions as mediums of raising them and "activities" as ways of keeping them busy. The buzzing, technological powerhouse of a society we helped forge delivers a second by second onslaught of depraved media images and inane media content to our young. We, who claimed to have entered a level of thoughtfulness and creativity our parents could not have hoped for, give our children such structured, organized lives as to leave little room for creative thought. We, who were such a playful generation, who indeed saw the world as a canvas upon which we would paint, who saw traditional strictures regarding right and wrong as choices to be embraced or abandoned at our discretion, have left our children little freedom to explore their way through their days. We have bequeathed to them a harried, preordained, stressful way of life. We who saw love as the answer give, perhaps, less importance to the love between parent and child than any generation before. Parental love, intensely personal, is belittled as we tell ourselves that our children are "just fine" spending most of their days, most of their time, without the direct experience of it. We, who embraced compassion as a social/political ideal, reveal our lack of compassion when we place adult burdens on our young.

I do not buy into the theory that children can take all that we have dished out to them. Infants are expected to handle the return of their mother to full-time work and their mourning the loss of her (which truly is experienced to them as a loss) is denied. They are expected to adjust to the highly turbulent and loud world of day care before they have had a chance to attach to their mothers. Toddlers are expected to succeed in many "activities" and not to mind constant busyness, continual time in the car, and frequent separation from the home. Children are educated at a very young age regarding the horrors of war, dangers to the environment and the "mistakes" of our own government. Adolescents are supposed to suppress their feminine and masculine instincts and at the same time live up to absurd, fake ideals of beauty and strength. They are pressured to build resumes and taught to prepare feverishly for the future. Children of all ages are allowed to inhale, in excess, a confusing barrage of media images and ideas: exciting and entertaining shows that are also lurid and violent; glamorous and gorgeous characters that are also unintelligent and crude; potent and sophisticated messages that are also misleading and misinformed. Television, movie, and video game producers are playing a huge part in bringing up America's young.

We must set our children free from our adult agendas and our frenetic, goal-oriented pace. The path that we have accepted for ourselves is the wrong path for children. Children do need a foundation upon which to grow and children do need their parents. They need to belong to a community, not an interest group. They long to know right from wrong and long for adults in history and in their lives to look up to. They need time to play and to forge meaningful relationships with family and friends. They need the opportunity to retreat within themselves—to find out what is there. As they grow older, take on gradually larger responsibilities, live up to gradually greater expectations, and learn how to "think for themselves" (making their own mistakes and forging their own triumphs), they still need clear limits and unconditional love. Within this secure space, the possibilities are endless. With this stable base to fall back upon, children and teenagers will dare to dream, think, and explore. They will compete, learn, and socialize as the blossoming individuals that they are, not as automatons engineered for results.

Children living in the new millennium need a refuge from the impersonal, the mechanical, and the programmed. We must provide them with more than opportunities for skill learning, socialization, and competition. Otherwise, something will be missing in their humanness. For, to be human is to have the capacity for intimate attachments based upon love (which can grow more intimate because of the closeness that family life provides); it is to reason and to have a moral sense of things; it is to be capable of spontaneity that stems from original thought or from some passion within.

Today's children suffer from a pace and caliber of life that impedes familial intimacy, deters introspection, and ruins innocence. We can provide them with some relief by allowing them the luxuries we do not allow ourselves: the luxury of daydreaming and playing, the luxury of believing in goodness and justice, the luxury of soaking up love in a dependent and vulnerable way. We can help them if we stop in our tracks and acknowledge what we *know at heart*: children are not ready for the fast world we have given them. Their unrequited childhood cries for our attention.

> When the voices of children are heard on the green
> And laughing is heard on the hill,
> My heart is at rest within my breast
> And everything else is still.
> —William Blake, "Songs of Innocence"

Notes

1.   Michelle Trudeau, "School, Study, SATs: No Wonder Teens are Stressed," *National Public Radio.* (May 16, 2007): accessed May 16, 2007, <http://www.npr. org/templates/story/story.php?storyId=6221872>,
2.   *Ibid.*
3.   Justin Pope, "MIT Admissions Dean Warns about College Entrance Stress," *WTIC News Talk.* (September 11, 2006): accessed September 19, 2006, <http://wtic. com/pages/81338.php?contentType+4&contentId+203332>.
4.   David V. Sheslow, Ph.D. and Meredith Lutz Stehl, MS, "Childhood Stress," *Kids Health for Parents,* Nemours Foundation. (June, 2005): accessed May 16, 2007, <http://kidshealth.org/parent/emotions/feelings/stress.html>.
5.   D'Arcy Lyness, Ph.D., "Stress," *Teens Health,* Nemours Foundation. (August, 2004): accessed May 16, 2007 <http://kidshealth.org/teen/your_mind/emotions/ stress.html>.
6.   "Helping Teenagers with Stress," *American Academy of Child and Adolescent Psychiatry.* (May, 2005): accessed May 16, 2007 <http://www.aacap.org/page. ww?section=Facts+for+Families&name=Helping+Teenagers=...>.
7.   David B. Pruitt, ed. *Your Adolescent: Emotional, Behavioral, and Cognitive Development from Early Adolescence through the Teen Years.* New York: Harper-Resource, 2000: 213.
8.   *Ibid.,* 210.
9.   *Ibid.,* 210.
10.   Anita Chandra, "Exploring Stress and Coping Among Urban African American Adolescents," *Preventing Chronic Disease: Public Health Research, Practice, and Policy.* (March 15, 2006): accessed May 16, 2007, <http://www.pubmedcentral. nih.gov/articlerender.fcgi?artid=1563979>.
11.   S. J. Blatt and E. Homan, "Parent and Child Interaction in the Etiology of Dependent and Self-Critical Depression."
12.   Richard Thompson and David C. Zuroff, "Development of Self-criticism in Adolescent Girls: Roles of Maternal Dissactisfaction, Maternal Coldness, and Insecure Attachment," *Journal of Youth and Adolescence* 28:2. (1999).
13.   Steiger et al. "Personality and Family Factors of Adolescent Girls with ...in a Non-clinical Population," *Addiction Behavior* 16. (1991): 303-314.
14.   Maria Cristina Richaud deMinzi, "Loneliness and Depression in Middle and Late Childhood: The Relationship to Attachment and Parental Styles," *Journal of Genetic Psychology.* (June 1, 2006).
15.   "Cutting Teens," CBS 11 News. (June 11, 2006). *Gearing Up!* Accessed May 16, 2007, <http://gearing up.com/html/SpeakingAndMedia.htm?article_id=100>.
16.   Erik H. Erikson, *Identity and the Life Cycle.* New York: W.W. Norton, 1980: 53.
17.   *Ibid,* 54.
18.   *Ibid.,* 88.
19.   D. W. Winnicott, *The Family and Individual Development.* London: Tavistok, 1965: 40-41.
20.   Peter Blos, *The Adolescent Passage: Developmental Issues.* New York: International Universities Press, 1979: 148.
21.   *Ibid.,* 152-153.
22.   *Ibid.,* 157.
23.   "Latchkey Kids Risk Substance Abuse," *Science News.* (September 16, 1989): FindArticles.com, July 28, 2007. <http://findarticles.com/p/articles/mi_m1200/ is_V136/ai_7951377>.

24. Rankin and Wells, "The Effects of Parental Attachments and Direct Control of Delinquency," *Journal of Research in Crime and Delinquency* 27. (1990): 140-165.

25. Travis Hirschi, *Causes of Delinquency.* New Brunswick: Transaction Publishers, 2006.

26. "More Latchkey Kids Drink," *Gannett News Service.*

27. John Bowlby, *Attachment and Loss* vol. 1. New York: Basic Books, 1973: 363.

28. Allan Bloom, *The Closing of the American Mind.* New York: Touchstone Books, 1987: 57.

29. Ed Thomas, "Family Time Around the Table Good for Teens' Development," *Agape Press.* (September 26, 2006).

30. "Hands–On Parents Affect Teens Positively," CASA News Release, *About: Alcoholism and Substance Abuse.* (July 11, 2006): May 16, 2007, < http://alcoholism. about.com/libray/blcasa010223.html>.

31. Catherine Love, "Family Group Conferencing: Cultural Origins, Sharing, and Appropriation-A Maori Reflection," *Family Group Conferencing,* edited by Gale Burford and Joe Hudson. New Brunswick: Aldine Transaction Publishers, 2005: 22.

32. *Ibid.,* 25.

33. Jack Westman, "The Risks of Day Care for Children, Parents, and Society," *Day Care: Child Psychology & Adult Economics,* edited by Bryce Christensen. Rockford: Rockford Institute, 1989: 18.

34. David Elkind, *Miseducation: Preschoolers at Risk.* New York: Knopf, 1993: 3-4.

35. *Ibid.,*22.

36. Jane Healy, *Endangered Minds: Why Children Don't Think and What We Can Do About It.* New York: Touchstone, 1990: 242.

37. *Ibid,* 67.

38. Stanley Greenspan, M.D., "On How Emotion Affect Learning," interview in *Parent and Child.* Scholastic Press, September/ October 1996: 33.

39. Blos, *The Adolescent Passage.* 145.

40. Simon Grolnick, "The Work and Play of Winnicott," *Theory.* (February 3, 2006): 35-36.

41. Valerie Polakow, *The Erosion of Childhood.* Chicago: University of Chicago Press, 1992: 188.

42. Bob Dart, "A U.S Picture, by the Numbers," *The Atlantic Journal-Constitution.* (December 15, 2006).

43. Marie Evans Schmidt, Ph.D. et al., "The Effects of Electronic Media on Children Ages Zero to Six: A History of Research," Kaiser Family Foundation *Center on Media and Child Health,* Children's Hospital Boston. (January, 2005): 1.

44. *Ibid.,* 3.

45. *Ibid.,* 4.

46. *Ibid.* 7.

47. *Ibid.,* 11.

48. Douglas Gentile, Ph.D., "Three News Studies Offer More Concrete Evidence of Violent Video Games Effects on Kids," *National Institute on Media and the Family.* (June 4, 2007): <http://www.mediafamily.org/research/3_new_studies.shtml>

49. Randall Murphree, "Experts Say TV has Devastating Effects," *AFA Journal.* (August, 1991): 5.

50. Brent Bozell, "Has Television Gone Too Far?" (April 12, 2000): <http://www. townhall.com/columnists/brentbozell/bb000412.shtml>.

51.   Alessandra Stanley, "Prime Time Shows are getting Sexier," *MMC*, listserv for the Mass Media & Communication Ph.D Program, Temple University. (February 5, 2003): June 28, 2007, <https://listserv.temple.edu/cgi-bin/wa?A2=ind0302a& L=mmc&P=1434>.
52.   *Ibid.*
53.   "Sexualization Harms Young Girls," *BBC News*. (February 20, 2007): <http://news. bbc.co.uk/2/hi/health/6376421.stm>.
54.   Timothy F. Winter, "Testimony Before the United States Senate Committee on Commerce, Science and Transportation," Parents Television Council. (June 26, 2007): <http://www.parentstv.org/ptc/publications/news/testimonyviolenttv-clip. asp>.
55.   Senator Robert Byrd, *Congressional Record*, September 18, 1990, reprinted in *AFA Journal*. (October, 1992): 5.
56.   "New Study Links Sexually Oriented Prime-Time Television to Adolescents' Moral Judgement," *AFA Journal*. (April, 1994).
57.   Juliet B. Schor, *Born to Buy: The Commercialized Child and the New Consumer Culture*. New York: Scribner, 2004.
58.   Thomas L. Jipping, "Report Details Media's Influence on Violence," *American Family Journal* 23: 10. (October, 1999).
59.   Randall Murphree, "Experts Say TV has Devastating Effects,"
60.   Ijendoorn and Hylda A. Zwart-Woudstra, "Adolescents' Attachment Representations and Moral Reasoning," *The Journal of Genetic Psychology* 15: 3. (1995): 359-372.
61.   Sharon Houseknect , "It's Not Just Family: Government Policies Affect Child Wellbeing." houseknecht1@osu.edu, July 29, 2007 <http://researchnews.osu. edu/archive/famdec2.htm>
62.   Bruce Frohnen, "Mother Knows Best," *Chronicles*. (November, 1989): 50-51.
63.   *Ibid.*, 51.
64.   *Ibid.*, 51.
65.   Jeanne C. Bleur and Garry R.Walz,"Are Boys Falling Behind in Academics?" *ERIC Digest*. (July 3, 2007): <http://www.ericdigests.org/2003-4/boys1.html>.
66.   *Ibid.*
67.   Tom Chiarella, "The Problem with Boys," *Esquire*. (July 1, 2006).
68.   Deborah Lambert, "Squeaky Chalk: Can Boys Survive in a Feminist World?" *Campus Report*, Accuracy in Academia, 21:7. (July, 2006): 3.
69.   Deborah Blum, *Sex on the Brain: The Biological Differences Between Men and Women*. New York: Penguin Books, 1997.
70.   Allan Bloom, *The Closing of the American Mind*. 354-355.
71.   George C. Leef, "What Do Students Have to Learn to Graduate from College?" *Clarion Call* 6: 4. (September 23, 2004).
72.   Thomas Sowell, "The Mushing of America," *Forbes*. (July 18, 1994): 69.
73.   Bloom, *The Closing of the American Mind*. 319.
74.   George Will, *The Leveling Wind: Politics, The Culture & Other News 1990-1994*. New York: Penguin Books, 1994: 34.
75.   Bloom, *The Closing of the American Mind*. 38-40.
76.   William Bennett, *The De-Valuing of America: The Fight for Our Culture and Our Children*. New York; Touchstone Books, 1992: 56.
77.   *Ibid.*, 35.
78.   George F. Will, *The Leveling Wind*. 135.
79.   Georgie Anne Geyer, "Bilingual Education, Self-Esteem Movement Died, Thank Goodness," *Universal Press Syndicate*.

80. Charles Krauthammer, "Hiroshima, Mon Petit," *Time.* (March 27, 1995): 80.

81. Eric Foner, *Politics and Ideology in the Age of the Civil War.* New York: Oxford University Press, 1980.

82. Anne R. Pierce, *Woodrow Wilson and Harry Truman: Mission and Power in American Foreign Policy.* New Brunswick: Transaction Publishers, 2007.

83. *Ibid.*, x-xii.

84. Anthony Harrigan, "The Acceleration of Modern History," *Modern Age* 31:3-4, (Summer/Fall 1987): 285.

85. *Ibid,* 287.

Selected Bibliography

Adelson, Joseph. *Inventing Adolescence*. New Brunswick, NJ: Transaction Publishers, 1986.

Ainsworth, M., Blehar, M. C., Waters, E., and Wall, S. *Patterns of Attachment: A Psychological Study of the Strange Situation*. Hillsdale, NJ: Erlbaum, 1978.

Bennett, William J. *The De-Valuing of America: The Fight for Our Culture and Our Children*. New York: Touchstone, 1992.

Blankenhorn, David. *Fatherless America*. New York: Basic Books, 1995.

Bloom, Allan. *The Closing of the American Mind*. New York: Touchstone, 1987.

Blos, Peter. *The Adolescent Passage: Developmental Issues*. New York: International Universities Press, Inc., 1979.

Blum, Deborah. *Sex on the Brain: The biological differences between men and women*. New York: Penguin Books, 1997.

Borkowski, John G., Ramey, Sharon Landesman, and Bristol-Power, Marie, eds. *Parenting and the Child's World*. Mahwah, New Jersey: Lawrence Erlbaum Associates, 2002.

Bornstein, Mark. *Handbook of Parenting*. Mahwah, New Jersey: Lawrence Erlbaum Associates, 1995.

Borysenko, Joan. *A Woman's Book of Life*. New York: Riverhead Books, 1996.

_____. *A Woman's Journey to God*. New York: Riverhead Books, 1999.

Bowlby, John. *Attachment and Loss*. New York: Basic Books, 1973.

_____. *Separation: Anxiety and Anger*. New York: Basic Books, 1973.

Bozell, Brent L. III and Baker, Brent H., eds. *And That's the Way it Isn't*. Alexandria, VA: Media Research Center, 1990.

Brizendine, Louann. *The Female Brain*. New York: Broadway Books, 2006.

Bronfenbrenner, Urie, ed. *Making Human Beings Human*. Thousand Oaks, CA: Sage Publications, 2005.

Bruner, J. *Child's Talk: Learning to Use Language*. New York: W. W. Norton, 1982.

Burford, Gale, and Hudson, Joe, eds. *Family Group Conferencing*. New Brunswick, NJ: Aldine Transaction, 2005.

Caldwell, John Thornton. *Televisuality*. New Brunswick, NJ: Rutgers University Press, 1995.

Cardozo, Arlene Rossen. *Sequencing*. Brooklyn, NY: Brownstone Books,

Note: See chapter endnotes for journal articles and internet sources.

2000.

Christensen, Bryce, ed. *Day Care: Child Psychology and Adult Economics.* Rockford, IL: The Rockford Institute, 1989.

Dash, Leon. *When Children Want Children: The Urban Crisis of Teenage Child-bearing.* University of Illinois Press, 2005.

Davidson, Christine. *Staying Home Instead.* New York: Lexington Books, 1993.

Davis, Madeleine and Wallbridge, David. *Boundary and Space: An Introduction to the Work of D. W, Winnicott.* New York: Brunner/Mazel Publishers, 1990.

Diamond, Marian and Hopson, Janet, eds. *Magic Trees of the Mind.* New York: Plume, 1999.

Demos, John. *Past, Present and Personal: The Family and the Life Course in American History.* New York: Oxford University Press, 1988.

Du Plessix Gray, Francine. *Soviet Women: Walking the Tightrope.* New York: Doubleday, 1989.

Elkind, David. *Miseducation: Preschoolers at Risk.* New York: Alfred A. Knopf, 1993.

Erikson, Erik H. *Childhood and Society.* New York: Norton, 1963.

_____. *Identity and the Life Cycle.* New York: Norton, 1980.

Faludi, Susan. *Backlash.* New York: Anchor, 1992.

Firestone, Shulamit. *The Dialectic of Sex: The Case for Feminist Revolution.* New York: Morrow, 1970.

Fleming, Thomas. *The Politics of Human Nature.* New Brunswick, NJ: Transaction Publishers, 1993.

Foner, Eric. *Politics and Ideology in the Age of the Civil War.* New York: Oxford University Press, 1980.

Fraiberg, Louis, ed. *Selected Writings of Selma Fraiberg.* Columbus: Ohio State University Press, 1987.

Geiger, H. Kent. *The Family in Soviet Russia.* Cambridge, MA: Harvard University Press, 1970.

Greenspan, Stanley I. *The Growth of the Mind.* Cambridge, MA: Da Capo Press, 1997.

Grolnick, Simon A. *The Work and Play of Winnicott.* Norvak, NJ: Jason Aronson, Inc., 1990.

Handel, Gerald, ed. *Childhood Socialization.* New Brunswick, NJ: Aldine Transaction, 2006.

Healy, Jane M. *Endangered Minds.* New York: Touchstone, 1990.

_____. *Your Child's Growing Mind.* New York: Doubleday, 1994.

Hirschi, Travis. *Causes of Delinquency.* New Brunswick, NJ: Transaction Publishers, 2006.

Horkheimer, Max. *Eclipse of Reason.* New York: Oxford University Press, 1947.

Howard, Pierce J. *The Owner's Manual for the Brain.* Austin, TX: Leornian Press, 1994.

Hoyles, Martin, ed. *Changing Childhood.* London: Writers and Readers Publishing Cooperative, 1979.

Johnson, Paul. *Modern Times: The World from the Twenties to the Nineties*. New York: Harper Perennial, 1992.

Kuhn, Reinhard. *Corruption in Paradise: the Child in Western Literature*. Hanover, NH: Brown University Press, 1982.

Leach, Penelope. *Children First*. New York: Alfred A. Knopf, 1994.

Lerner, Gerda. *The Creation of Patriarchy*. New York: Oxford University Press, 1986.

Lichter, S. Robert, Lichter, Linds S., and Rothman, Stanley. *Watching America*. New York: Prentice Hall, 1991.

Liebman, Joshua L. *Peace of Mind*. New York: Citadel Press, 1994.

MacKinnon, Catherine. *Toward a Feminist Theory of the State*. Cambridge: Harvard University Press, 1991.

Magid, Ken and Kelvey, Carole. *High Risk: Children Without a Conscience*. New York: Bantam Books, 1989.

Marquardt, Elizabeth. *Between Two Worlds: The Inner Lives of Children of Divorce*. New York: Three Rivers Press, 2006.

Miller, Alice. *The Drama of the Gifted Child*. New York: Basic Books, 1981.

National Institute of Child Health and Human Development. *NICHD Study of Early Child Care and Youth Development: Findings for Children up to Age 4 ½ years*. Rockville, MD: National Institute of Child Health and Human Development, January 2006.

Pierce, Anne R. *Woodrow Wilson & Harry Truman: Mission and Power in American Foreign Policy*. New Brunswick, NJ: Transaction Publishers, 2007.

Pinker, Steven. *The Blank Slate*. New York: Penguin, 2002.

Polakow, Valerie. *The Erosion of Childhood*. Chicago: The University of Chicago Press, 1992.

Pruitt, David B., ed. *Your Adolescent*. New York: HarperCollins, 2000.

Pufall, Peter B. and Unsworth, Richard P., eds. *Rethinking Childhood*. New Brunswick, NJ: Rutgers University Press, 2004.

Randall, John Herman Jr. *The Making of the Modern Mind*. New York: Columbia University Press, 1976.

Revel, Jean-Francois. *The Totalitarian Temptation*. New York: Penguin Books, 1978.

Sacks, Karen. *Sisters and Wives: The Past and Future of Sexual Equality*. Westport, CT: Greenwood Press, 1979.

Sandelands, Lloyd E. *Male & Female in Social Life*. New Brunswick, NJ: Transaction Publishers, 2001.

Sartre. *Being and Nothingness*. London: Routledge, 2003.

Schor, Juliet B. *Born to Buy: The Commercialized Child and the New Consumer Culture*. New York: Scribner, 2004.

Schulz, Mona Lisa. *Awakening Intuition*. New York: Harmony Books, 1998.

Schwartz, Tony. *The Responsive Chord*. New York: Doubleday, 1974.

Stern, Daniel N. *The Interpersonal World of the Infant: A View from Psychoanalysis and Developmental Psychology*. New York: Basic Books, 1985.

Straus, Leo. *Natural Right and History*. Chicago: University of Chicago Press,

1953.

Thistle, Susan. *From Marriage to the Market*. Berkeley: University of California Press, 2006.

Wallerstein, Judith et al. *The Unexpected Legacy of Divorce: The 25 Year Study*. New York: Hyperion, 2001.

Watson, John B. *Behavior: An Introduction to Comparative Psychology*. New York: Henry Holt, 1914.

Whitehead, Barbara Defoe. *The Divorce Culture: Rethinking our Commitments to Marriage and Family*. New York: Vintage, 1998.

Will, George F. *The Leveling Wind*. New York: Viking 1994.

Wilson, James. Q. *Crime and Public Policy*. San Francisco: Institute for Contemporary Studies Press, 1983.

Winnicott, D. W. *The Family and Individual Development*. London: Tavistok, 1965.

Yeats, W. B. *Selected Poems*. Avanel, NJ: Gramercy, 1992.

Index